To Matt,

thanks for your
encouragement in
getting this published.

Andy

STRUGGLING FOR A SOCIAL EUROPE

Struggling for a Social Europe

Neoliberal Globalization and the Birth of a
European Social Movement

ANDY MATHERS
University of the West of England, UK

ASHGATE

Published by
Ashgate Publishing Limited
Gower House
Croft Road
Aldershot
Hampshire GU11 3HR
England

Ashgate Publishing Company
Suite 420
101 Cherry Street
Burlington, VT 05401-4405
USA

Ashgate website: http://www.ashgate.com

British Library Cataloguing in Publication Data
Mathers, Andy
    Struggling for a social Europe: neoliberal globalization
    and the birth of a European social movement
    1. European Union 2. Anti-globalization movement – European
    Union countries 3. Social justice – European Union
    countries 4. Social legislation – European Union countries
    I. Title
    303.4'84'094

Library of Congress Cataloging-in-Publication Data
Mathers, Andy, 1964–
    Struggling for a social Europe: neoliberal globalization and the birth of a
European social movement / by Andy Mathers.
        p. cm.
    Includes index.
    ISBN 978-0-7546-4580-1
1. Anti-globalization movement--Europe. 2. Social movements--Europe. I. Title.
    HN373.5.M374 2007
    303.48'4094--dc22

                                                                    2006100190

ISBN: 978-0-7546-4580-1

Printed and bound in Great Britain by MPG Books Ltd, Bodmin, Cornwall.

Contents

Acknowledgements

I would not have been able to write this book without a great deal of assistance from both activists and academics for which I would like to express my thanks. In particular, I would like to acknowledge the academic advice and encouragement I received from Dr. Graham Taylor, Professor Colywn Jones, Colin Barker, and Professor Paul Stewart as well as from two anonymous reviewers.

I would also like to acknowledge the people at Ashgate Publishing who encouraged me with the production of the book. In particular, I thank Caroline Wintersgill and Mary Savigar who commissioned the book and Maureen Mansell-Ward who was very patient even when I made numerous alterations to the text.

Chapter 1

Introduction:
Struggling for a Social Europe

15 June 1997 may prove to be a significant date in the development of the labour movement in Europe. Fifty thousand people from across the continent of Europe demonstrated in the streets of Amsterdam on the occasion of the EU summit. The demonstration was led by a cortege of several hundred 'Euromarchers' who had taken part in a series of international marches that had snaked their way across the continent during the preceding two months. Although mainly unemployed, the marchers made common cause with groups of homeless, workers and migrants to demand that the EU and its member states take concerted action to tackle the problems of rising unemployment, job insecurity and social exclusion.

As they proceeded from as far afield as Tuzla and Tangiers towards Amsterdam the marchers engaged in numerous high profile actions such as occupying the *Château de Versailles* to highlight their demand for universal social rights. The marchers were supported by local and national networks of grass roots activists drawn from a diversity of unions, associations and political organizations that were co-ordinated at the European level. These networks played an important part in organizing more than a thousand public meetings at which the immediate social issues and the broader question of European integration were debated. These networks also proved vitally important to the success of the initiative as the marches received an unsympathetic response from the ETUC: the official representative of the interests of European workers within the EU.

Amongst the militants engaged in the marches there was a widespread concern to go beyond the strategy of social partnership being employed by the ETUC and its national affiliates as a way of addressing the problems of unemployment, job insecurity and social exclusion. Their aim was to pursue a strategy of social protest thereby attempting to mobilize a movement around a radical agenda. The desired outcome was to deliver a solution to the immediate and pressing social problems through instituting a social and democratic Europe as part of a different world order and this aim has been epitomized by the development of the slogan of 'For Another Europe In Another World'.

Leading commentators on social movement activity noted the growing debate around the issue of 'social Europe' and suggested that the European Marches would be an interesting test of whether the protests against austerity measures seen in France would converge with other struggles in the remainder of Europe.[1] It was argued at the time by militants involved in them that the European marches marked a

---

1 Tarrow, S. (1997) 'Protest in France: La crise à la française', *French Politics & Society,* 15 (2) pp. 30–33.

challenge to the neoliberal course of European integration. They also 'made credible the idea of pan-European political mobilisation' and also advanced 'the struggle for "a different Europe"'.[2] This was an expression of a new enthusiasm that, after years of struggle within nation states to defend existing social rights, this was the beginning of the construction of a transnational social force that could deliver the aspiration of a Social Europe. This expression encapsulated the desire for the institution at the transnational level of a new set of social rights which would counter the 'race to the bottom' between nation states in the face of neoliberal globalization.

This hope and aspiration for a Social Europe was shared and given intellectual credibility by leading academics the most prominent of whom was Pierre Bourdieu who had already allied himself with the wave of resistance to neoliberal reforms in France.[3] Bourdieu argued that far from the EU offering a new level of social protection in the face of neoliberal globalization, '*European construction currently amounts to social destruction*' (p. 54).[4] This was the product of a 'policy of depoliticization' (p. 38) that took policymaking out of the democratic arena and placed it in the hands of remote institutions such as the European Commission that enforced economic and social deregulation upon nation states. The answer, for Bourdieu, was to 'restore politics', (p. 38) but at the transnational level through mobilization to install a social and democratic Europe. History, he asserted, taught that such a goal could only be achieved through the mobilization of a social movement and therefore he called 'For a European social movement' (p. 53). Bourdieu identified the European Marches in particular as an exemplary case of the necessary 'internationalization of modes of thinking and forms of action' (p. 63) that were required to bring such a transnational social movement into existence.

Ten years have passed since the first set of European Marches and the mobilization in Amsterdam, yet the formation of an effective European social movement desired by Bourdieu still seems a somewhat distant prospect. Moreover, the EU has increasingly become a mechanism for advancing neoliberal economic and social reforms and thereby for creating an 'Unsocial Europe',[5] albeit in the name of the modernization of the so called 'European Social Model'. Nevertheless, the European Marches Network, through which the European Marches were co-ordinated, is now but one small component of the much larger and broader set of organizations that are engaging in the European Social Forum (ESF) process through which the project for a Social Europe is being pursued.

A decade into this period of mobilizations against neoliberal globalization seems an opportune time to document the birth and infancy of this nascent transnational social movement. This documentation covers the period from its inception prior to the Summit in Amsterdam in June 1997 to its emergence as an identifiable part of

---

2   Aguiton, C. & Cremieux, R. (1997) 'Euromarch against Unemployment Reach Amsterdam', Politique: La Revue 5 photocopied version in English – no page numbers available, German version available at <*www-pluto.informatik.uni-oldenburg.de/~also/eusep136.htm*> accessed on 01/07/2001.

3   Bourdieu, P. (1998) *Acts of Resistance*, (Cambridge: Polity Press).

4   Bourdieu, P. (2003) *Firing Back* (Cambridge: Polity Press).

5   Gray, A. (2004) *Unsocial Europe* (London: Pluto Press).

the 'global justice movement' (GJM)[6] at the EU Summit in Nice in December 2000. The GJM has provoked huge interest amongst both social movement activists and academics which is underlined by the welter of publications which have focused on it.[7] However, the European dimension of this phenomenon has not received due attention. This book attempts to address this deficit not only by the aforementioned process of documentation, but also by focusing on the idea of a Social Europe which has been the main point of convergence for the individuals and organizations engaged in the mobilizations at EU summits.

A decade on from the initial mobilizations against neoliberal Europe also seems like a propitious moment to reflect upon the project to form an alternative Social Europe. This is not least because not only has there been a struggle for a Social Europe which has pitted the Left against the Right which has been advancing its project for a neoliberal Europe, but also because Social Europe has been a field of struggle within the Left.

This process of reflection has led me to engage critically with a highly influential set of writers in European sociology.[8] Their work has laid the basis for the emergence of what I have characterized as a 'New social democratic Left' which has increasingly identified the EU as an institutional space in which an alternative to neoliberal globalization can be developed. In chapter two, I outline the earlier work of these writers from the period of the early 1980s, which saw the initial electoral successes of the neoliberal New Right, to the mid-1990s: a turning point which saw a renewed concern with 'the social question' (p. 33) and the return of 'movements of the poor' (p. 35) alongside 'the transformation of labor action' (p. 46).[9]

This latter point is particularly significant as these writers were influential in the formation of what amounted to a dominant paradigm in the sociology of social movements that rendered labour an anachronistic social actor and promoted its replacement by the New Social Movement (NSMs) as the new progressive social force. This was due to a purported shift in socio-structural conditions which I characterize as, firstly, a move from an industrial to a post-industrial society, or, secondly, a crisis and reformation of modernity. The corollary of this analysis was that for these writers from the 'New social democratic Left', a 'new' social subject is required as the agent of a 'new' social settlement needed to civilize the 'new' social order.

---

6   The movement which has emerged to contest neoliberal globalization has been named as the anti-globalization movement as well as the anti-capitalist movement. For the purposes of this book, I have adopted the term global justice movement which encompasses the diversity of ideological positions within the movement as well as highlighting its international scope and its internationalist outlook.

7   These publications have become simply too numerous to list.

8   I have chosen to concentrate my attention on eight of these writers whose earlier work is set out in chapter two and whose later work is the main focus of chapter seven. These writers in no particular order of significance are Alain Touraine, Alberto Melucci, André Gorz, Manuel Castells, Ulrich Beck, Anthony Giddens, Jürgen Habermas and Claus Offe.

9   Della Porta, D. & Diani, M. (2006) *Social Movements: An Introduction* (Second Edition) (Oxford: Blackwell).

In the latter part of chapter two, I develop a critique of this analysis based initially on its misconception of class as an economic category rather than a social relation. This gave rise to a classification of social movements as either class or non-class based to which I would oppose a conception of social movements as manifestations of, and moments in, the process of class formation. I also challenge the primacy of the NSMs based on the radical disjuncture in socio-structural conditions. I argue that changing conditions are understood more accurately in terms of the ongoing crisis and restructuring of the capital relation which produces specific conjunctures. This alternative analysis not only draws attention to the possibility of renewing labour as the focal point of an anti-capitalist social movement, but also opens up the terrain for the development of more radical projects of social transformation.

The advance of the NSMs and the retreat of the labour movement are then related to the developing conjuncture of the crisis of Keynesianism and the emergence of neoliberal restructuring. This is considered in such a way as to highlight how the argument advanced by the dominant paradigm was not a necessary response to new realities, but an ideological intervention which not only described the demobilization of the organized working class, but also served to reinforce it.

I conclude chapter two by highlighting the significance of the strikes over welfare reform in France in 1995 which marked a breakthrough for those critical currents inside and outside of mainstream labour organizations which had been challenging the dominant strategy of social partnership. These currents were also at the forefront of promoting cross-national and transnational initiatives such as the European Marches to which I turn in chapter four.

However, before so doing, in chapter three, I provide the reader with an outline of the methodological approach adopted for my investigation of the European Marches as part of the broader social movement which emerged to contest neoliberal globalization in Europe and promoted an alternative Social Europe. This begins with a discussion of the role of intellectuals in relation to social movements opposed to neoliberal globalization. This discussion is structured around Touraine's model of four ideal types of intellectuals.[10]

The 'accuser' (p. 106) provides a critique of neoliberal ideology and makes the suffering it engenders visible. The 'ideologue' (p. 107) declares solidarity with the victims of neoliberalism and bears witness to their suffering. The 'interpreter' (p. 110) analyses the protests and demands of social actors so as to assist them in forming an independent social movement. The 'utopian' (p. 109) focuses on developments in personal and cultural life out of which such a social movement may emerge. I argue that in relation to the opposition to neoliberal globalization, writers from the 'New social democratic Left' such as Gorz and Touraine have played the role of the utopian and interpreter. However, Bourdieu went beyond the role of accuser to adopt the utopian role which led him to engage in initiatives alongside social movement activists which focused on developing alternatives to neoliberalism. I highlight how some intellectuals have rooted themselves within the resistance to neoliberal globalization in such a way as to defy their labelling as ideologues and to suggest a renewal of the role of 'organic intellectual'. While wishing to shy away

---

10   Touraine, A. (2001) *Beyond Neoliberalism* (Cambridge: Polity Press).

a little from this somewhat grandiose title, I suggest that I adopted a similar role of 'activist researcher'. This described the way that not only did I participate in the struggle for a Social Europe that I was investigating, but I also attempted to intervene into it so as to have a minor influence over its course of development.

In the remainder of chapter three, I set out initially the theoretical ideas which underpinned my methodological approach which I describe as 'critical ethnography'. I then say how I adopted the 'extended case method' developed by Burawoy[11] to investigate the European Marches as a critical case study of transnational resistance to neoliberal globalization. I then move on to describe the process of the actual investigation focusing on such issues and dimensions as gaining access, the extent of my participation, how I participated in the role of 'activist-researcher', how I selected respondents and conducted interviews, and the use of documentary sources of information.

In chapters four, five and six, I provide an account of the European Marches in relation to the broader social movement of which it formed a part. In chapter four, I describe the actual events that mobilized citizens in 'protesting Europe'. This means setting out in as much detail as possible the mobilization of transnational protests which is based on materials produced by those individuals and organizations involved in the mobilizations as well as drawing on extracts from interviews with prominent activists and on my own eye witness accounts of events. This chapter not only focuses on the mobilization of the European Marches and the demonstrations at the EU summits at which they culminated, but also provides some background on the constituent social struggles occurring within nation states and how they related to the transnational protests. The chapter is structured around the three phases of mobilization which spanned the EU summits in Amsterdam, Cologne and Nice.

Despite the emphasis on providing as detailed a description as possible of the phenomenon of transnational mobilization, this empirical material is also related at the start of chapter four to some of the existing literature (mainly from the discipline of political science) on transnational social movement mobilization. This serves to alert the reader to the possible significance of the European Marches for understanding how the structure of political opportunity in the EU is affecting the mobilization of social movements. It also helps to explain how actors operated in a difficult set of circumstances to produce largely unlikely and somewhat unexpectedly successful transnational mobilizations. To this end, I highlight the elements of 'brokerage'[12] (p. 248) in the European Marches Network and the way that its flexible organizational form assisted in overcoming the obstacles to transnational mobilization.

In chapter five, I delve behind and beneath the visible protests against neoliberal globalization to examine the hidden bonds of solidarity that developed in and through these events which I characterize as the emergence of a 'Europe of Citizens'. Once again the emphasis is on utilizing the experiences and words of those engaged in the protests. This was not only to produce as detailed an account as possible, but also

---

11   Burawoy, M. (1998) 'The extended case method' *Sociological Theory* 16 (1) pp. 4–33.

12   Tarrow, S. (2001) 'Contentious Politics in a Composite Polity' in D. Imig & S. Tarrow (eds) *Contentious Europeans* (Lanham, Maryland: Rowman & Littlefield).

to assist in providing a voice for those who have been made voiceless by neoliberal globalization.

I begin by developing Bourdieu's idea that the formation of the unemployed movement in France was a 'social miracle' (p. 89),[13] to state that its formation at the transnational level was yet more remarkable. This development was due, in no small part, to the deployment and generation of such non-material resources as a sense of dignity, social standing and moral authority along with the bonds of camaraderie and a revitalized internationalism. These resources were constituted in part by the discursive framing of issues. From this perspective, I argue that the European Marches was engaged in a clash between two interpretative frames of unemployment: the competitiveness frame advanced by the European Commission and a counter-frame of solidarity promoted by the European Marches. I then describe this effort to form a Europe of solidarity between citizens in terms of a series of struggles against individualization and insecurity, against inequality and indignity and against invisibility that were the everyday outcomes of lives subject to the neoliberal Europe of competitiveness. I also attempt to present how this series of struggles was also a process of production. This was in the sense of the formation of new personal and collective identities amongst the unemployed and their allies as well as of new collective representations such as that of an international and internationalist movement engaged in a struggle to produce a 'different Europe'.

In chapter six, I examine how the European Marches developed a set of common demands for social rights which formed its concrete proposals for a 'different Europe' from the neoliberal version being promoted by the European Commission. This agenda for a Social Europe was developed in relation to the policy contexts which surrounded the summit meetings in Amsterdam, Cologne and Nice. The focus in Amsterdam was on the austerity measures associated with European Monetary Union (EMU) along with the lack of a social dimension to European integration. This gave rise to demands for social rights centred on the call for full employment policies. This shifted subsequently as the EU developed an Employment Strategy adopted as a result of the inclusion of an Employment Chapter in the Treaty of Amsterdam. This generated disagreement and division especially in relation to the goal of full employment which was agreed as the central plank of the Lisbon Strategy. This goal was rejected by the European Marches as it was to be achieved through the proliferation of low paid, insecure jobs in the service sector in which the unemployed would be compelled to work due to increasingly restrictive eligibility criteria for benefit and the extension of training programmes which resembled 'workfare' schemes. It outlined a different policy course which included demands for the creation of socially useful and ecologically sustainable jobs, a guaranteed income, a shorter working week without loss of pay and free access to a range of public services. These demands formed the content of an 'Alternative Charter' to the 'Charter of Fundamental Rights' which was being promoted as the forerunner of the European Constitutional Treaty.

---

13   Bourdieu (1998) *op cit*

These demands were debated and adopted at 'coalition forums'[14] (pp. 243–4) such as the *Assises* meetings at which the European Marches were launched and which assembled hundreds of social movement activists from across the continent. There were also smaller meetings such as the 'European Parliament of the Unemployed and Insecure Workers in the Struggle' (the Parliament) held in 1999 and its equivalent 'European Assembly' (the Assembly) held in 2000. These events epitomized the principle of citizen participation and provided a demonstration of the 'democratic Europe' which social movement activists were counterpoising to the remote and bureaucratic decision-making structures of the EU.

In the concluding part of chapter six, I discuss the existence of two main strategies in the European Marches.[15] These strategies focused, firstly, on mobilizing pressure to achieve the common demands so as to produce immediate improvements in material living standards and, secondly, on utilizing these demands as a basis for forming a broad social movement aiming at longer-term social transformation. I focus more on the latter strategy to show how this produced an expansion of the issues addressed from the social questions of unemployment, job insecurity and social exclusion to link these matters with the issues of racism, war and environmental protection. However, rather than juxtapose the idea of seeking immediate material improvements through social reforms and that of seeking longer-term social change, I present how the European Marches linked the solutions to pressing social questions with the utopian goal of social transformation and, in particular, how this was expressed through the demand for a guaranteed income.

In chapter seven, I return to the writers from the 'New social democratic Left' and provide an outline and critical assessment of their most recent work which includes proposals for the renewal of the welfare state which encompass the transnational level at which, they argue, global capitalism must now be regulated. In other words, they present projects for a Social Europe and, in several cases, relate this to the mobilization of social movements within Europe and to the wider GJM. This writing is consistent with the earlier work presented in chapter two in that it identifies 'new' social subjects such as the unemployed, insecurely employed and migrants as the agents of a 'new' social settlement required to civilize the 'new' global capitalism. I characterize this work as a 'new reformism' which describes how it amounts to an attempt to renew the social democratic project in the age of neoliberal globalization.

I then return to the work of Pierre Bourdieu, one of the main proponents of a European social movement, whose analysis, I argue, shared some of the assumptions of the 'new reformism' while departing from it by proposing the renewal of labour as a social movement. This goal of revitalizing labour as the civilising agent of the 'new'

---

14   Bandy, J. & Smith, J. (2005) 'Factors Affecting Conflict and Cooperation in Transnational Movement Networks', in J.Bandy & J.Smith (eds) *Coalitions Across Borders* (Lanham, Maryland: Rowman & Littlefield).

15   A similar distinction in aims and other differences at the levels of strategy and discourse within the European Marches are discussed in Chabanet, D. (2002) 'Les Marches européenes contre le chômage, la précarité et les exclusions', in R. Balme, D. Chabanet & V. Wright (eds) *L'action collective en Europe* (Paris: Presses de Science Po).

capitalism was also adopted by Peter Waterman whose proposal for a renewed trade unionism was based on the sociological analysis of writers such as Giddens, Beck, Castells and Gorz and therefore shared some of its limitations. These ideas have also been influential in the development of a 'new' social democratic politics whose limitations, I argue, have opened up a space for the advance of more radical political alternatives for the development of the European Marches and the broader GJM.

I consider these radical alternatives through the work of, firstly, Tony Negri as the main theorist of autonomist anti-capitalism which I assess as a radicalized version of the 'new reformism'. This is because it accepted its main tenets of the formation of new social subjects mobilizing on a new and privileged transnational terrain. I then consider the socialist alternative by outlining the argument for a democratic socialist version of a Social Europe advanced by André Brie MEP. I then present the revolutionary socialist alternative through the work of Ernest Mandel and Alex Callinicos which, in contrast to the 'new reformism', placed the organized working class at the centre of an anti-capitalist social movement aimed at the revolutionary transformation of society. Their work sought to promote the radical implications of the demands arising from the European Marches and the GJM whose anti-capitalist logic challenged the capacity of the state to deliver such a programme of reforms. This alternative analysis raised the question of the impact of the sociological thinking evident in the 'new reformism' on the development of projects for a Social Europe and on the formation of a social movement capable of bringing about their realization. Therefore, I conclude chapter seven by asking 'What kind of social movement'? By this I mean to highlight the possibilities for a course of development for the European Marches and the GJM which would take them beyond the limitations imposed on them by the sociological thinking of the 'New social democratic Left'.

In particular, I argue how the identity of European citizens suggests a broader conception of the working class than that assumed by the 'old' social democracy which is being formed around a needs-based politics. In addition, I suggest that the identification of the movement's opponent as neoliberalism may restrict the development of a project for a Social Europe whereas a truly Social Europe would eliminate the market mechanism and replace it by socialist planning. Moreover, recognizing that globalization has amounted to a new imperialism problematizes the emergence of a transnational social settlement institutionalized through the EU while prioritizing the development of a new internationalism which is not limited by territorial borders.

To conclude the book, I have included a Postscript which attempts to bring the reader up to date with developments in the type of Social Europe propagated by the institutions of the EU as well as in the maturation of a social movement to oppose it. This focuses specifically on the way that national trade unions engaged in mass mobilizations and general strikes in opposition to the reform of social protection systems and how this highlighted the increasing polarization of organized labour between the proponents of social partnership in modernization and the mobilization of an autonomous and oppositional social movement. This distinction was also apparent at the transnational level at which the ETUC mobilized in support of the Constitutional Treaty while the European Marches and the wider GJM opposed it as a mechanism for advancing neoliberal globalization.

Chapter 2

The Decline of Labour and the Rise of the New Social Movements in the Work of the New Social Democratic Left

In this chapter I provide an outline of the earlier work from the writers from the 'New social democratic Left' which, as I will show more clearly in chapter seven, has been proposing a new social settlement whose main agency is not labour, but a new social subject. This earlier work was highly influential in the development of a dominant paradigm in the sociology of social movements.[1] This paradigm argued for the newness of contemporary 'new' social movements that were beyond class-based 'old' social movements and were not comprehensible through a class analysis. This paradigm also suggested therefore that labour was no longer a progressive social actor and therefore a new social actor (such as the NSMs) must carry the task of civilizing the new social order.

The writers from the 'New social democratic Left' underpinned this analysis in two main ways. Firstly, the ascendancy of the NSMs was regarded as the result of a shift from an industrial to a post-industrial order (Touraine, Melucci, Gorz, Castells) and secondly, as the outcome of the crisis and reformation of modernity (Habermas, Offe, Beck, Giddens). After outlining the work of each writer and describing the model of social movements to which it gave rise, I then begin to develop a criticism of the dominant paradigm to which their work contributed. This leads me to argue for a class analysis of contemporary social movements which is the basis for reasserting the centrality of labour to the formation of a successful movement capable of halting, and of advancing an alternative to, neoliberal globalization.

The Post-Industrial Argument

Touraine

Alain Touraine began to formulate his ideas in the wake of the defeat of the student-led uprisings in France that culminated in the events in Paris in May 1968. Rather than wholeheartedly supporting the students' demands for radical social change, the organizations of the worker's movement remained largely tied to the immediate question of improving material living standards within the confines of the existing

---

1   This idea of a dominant paradigm is based on the idea put forward in Barker, C. & Dale, G. (1998) 'Protest Waves in Western Europe: A Critique of 'New Social Movement' Theory, *Critical Sociology,* 24 (1–2) pp. 65–104.

institutions.[2] The effect of such experiences was to persuade Touraine to reconsider his earlier Marxist analysis fundamentally and to develop a new analysis of contemporary society as post-industrial[3] and thereafter a new account of the kind of social movement activity to which it gave rise.

For Touraine, social movements remained central to social conflict and social change. Indeed, it was the 'decline of the workers' movement' (p. 11) that was the first stage in the transition from the industrial to the programmed or post-industrial society.[4] Touraine argued that the shift to a post-industrial society was resulting in the worker's movement being replaced as the central social movement. He stated that

> we are living through the transition from industrial society to programmed society and hence experiencing the decline of a certain type of class relations and conflicts and the emergence of a new generation of social movements ... which tomorrow will take over the central role that the workers' movement held in industrial society (p. 9).[5]

Such a statement was based on Touraine's analysis that industrial society based on the manufacture of material goods had given way to a 'programmed' society based on the production of symbolic goods. The main conflict was no longer over ownership of the means of production but over control of knowledge that was now the major source of social power. Conflict was no longer centred on material questions, but had been displaced onto cultural or ethical questions and therefore the new movements that have arisen take more of a cultural than a political form.[6]

The post-industrial society engenders a highly reflexive condition and therefore social movements struggle for control over 'historicity': the ability for society to recreate itself in a conscious fashion. However, social projects are no longer to be realized through conquering state power as, although a powerful technocracy can be identified, power is more diffused. Civil society is consequently the terrain of the post-industrial social movement: a field which labour has vacated due to its institutionalization. Due to its relationship to knowledge production, the technocratic élite has replaced the capitalist class as the leading social actor. However, technocratic control gives rise to opposition in a number of fields and to calls for self-management. But it is specifically the role of a new central social movement to define the technocratic enemy and to develop an alternative to the technocratic vision of society.[7] But as yet it was not clear which new social movement would take

---

2   Sauvageot, J., Geismar, A., Cohn-Bendit, D. & Duteuil, J-P. (1968) *La Révolte Etudiante* (Paris: Editions du Seuil); Cohn-Bendit, G. & Cohn-Bendit, D. (1969) *Obsolete Communism the Left-Wing Alternative* (London: Penguin Books).

3   Touraine, A. (1974) *Post-Industrial Society* (London: Wildwood House).

4   Touraine, A. (1981) *The Voice and the Eye. An Analysis of Social Movements* (Cambridge: Cambridge University Press).

5   *Ibid.*

6   Touraine, A. (1985) 'An Introduction to the Study of Social Movements', *Social Research,* 52 (4) pp. 749–88.

7   Touraine (1981) *op cit.*

over this role after 'the encumbering rubble of the old social movements' (p. 18) had been cleared away.

By the early 1990s, Touraine argued that society was undergoing a shift from a vertical society to a horizontal society.[8] Vertical societies were characterized by a division between social classes which were an expression of the social inequalities arising from exploitation. The main social division in horizontal societies is between the centre and the periphery which is tending to produce social segregation. Therefore, while horizontal societies produce a massive middle class, they also generate social exclusion due to the disadvantages of lack of work, money, education and social ties.

According to Touraine, French society was undergoing a shift towards the more liberal societies seen in the USA and the UK and was therefore experiencing an increasingly wide divide between those 'in' and those 'out' of society (p. 8). However, all citizens were experiencing increasing insecurity which was particularly acute amongst young people that were experiencing high rates of unemployment and were therefore at a particularly grave risk of social exclusion. The new social problems could not be remedied by solutions emanating from the traditional types of social movements which had been the significant force in the 'society of production' (p. 9) such as trade unionism which was no longer relevant along with the old ideas, politics and ideologies. As yet, Touraine could not identify a social movement capable of generating new answers, but he did argue for new forms of political action and participation. These would apparently be generated by a 'new social democracy' (p. 12).

Touraine's analysis rendered the idea of a labour movement anachronistic and suggested that labour organizations would become opponents rather than supporters of progressive social change. This idea was vindicated by Touraine's analysis of the strike wave in France in 1995 which he argued did not show signs of a true social movement. He assessed these strikes as largely a defensive reaction by privileged securely employed workers to the insecurities produced by France opening itself up to economic globalization. It seems that for Touraine, this episode of collective action reinforced the 'old' interests within the state rather than expressing the demands of 'new' social actors that could be the agents of a socially just process of modernization.[9] Nevertheless, Touraine's analysis suggested that the mobilization of a social movement around a new social project was possible while sidelining labour from such a movement.

Melucci

Much of Alberto Melucci's research was conducted in Italy in the wake of the defeat of the economic and social struggles of the late 1960s and 1970s. The disintegration of the movement led to the growth of 'terrorist' groups and a retreat into neo-

---

8   Touraine, A. (1991) 'Face à l'exclusion', *Esprit*, February pp. 7–13.
9   Touraine, A. (1996) 'L'ombre d'un mouvement', in A. Touraine, F. Dubet, D. Lapeyronnie, F. Khosrokhavar & M. Wievorka *Le Grand Refus: Réflexions sur la grève de décembre 1995* (Paris: Fayard).

religious sects that was accompanied by rising consumption of hard drugs. Melucci also identified the growth of new small groups of mainly young people concerned with 'self-realization', 'expressiveness' and 'affective communication' (p.58) that were based in social centres. These 'hidden networks' were the 'latent' dimension of social movement activity and Melucci identified in them the embryos of the 'New Social Movements' that engaged in a new wave of 'visible' mobilization that focused around specific cultural issues rather than on offering a direct political challenge to the state.[10]

Melucci's work was largely consonant with Touraine's argument that the rise of the NSMs was a product of new forms of information-based production in a post-industrial society. The labour movement as a central agent of fundamental social change was also regarded as an out of date idea. He stated clearly that,

> The working class performed an antagonistic role in capitalist development when the society's vital problems still arose centred around industrialization, the conquest of nature, and the subjugation of the workforce to the requirements of large-scale industrial production. But in societies that must confront the complexity of human systems, ... the image of a compact and homogeneous workers' movement assuming responsibility for global transformation ... belongs to the realm of ritual celebration (p. 209).[11]

Melucci, however, broke with Touraine who he argued maintained incorrectly that social movements were a 'personage': a unified social actor with a coherent societal project. He argued that post-industrial societies were complex systems in which totalizing change was rendered impossible and transformation was limited to specific levels. This too made the labour movement's aim of instituting citizenship rights through the state a project of a previous age that was not replicable in the present epoch.

> In the industrial age, social conflicts were incorporated into struggles for citizenship, just as in the history of the workers' movement anticapitalistic social struggle and the fight against the bourgeois state coincided. When these two levels separate, as they do in contemporary societies, movements lose their character as personages engaged in a confrontation-clash with a state for citizenship rights. Instead, they form themselves into social networks, where a collective identity is negotiated and given shape (pp. 116/7).[12]

This focused attention on the way that the formation of a collective identity in a complex society was a matter of negotiating a fleeting unity out of the multitude of differences existing amongst a plurality of fragmented identities. The transitory character of unity also suggested that social movements were capable only of articulating demands for specific reforms and not of developing a totalizing project.

---

10   Melucci, A. (1989) *Nomads of the Present* (London: Hutchinson Radius) pp. 58–60, pp. 70–73.

11   Melucci, A. (1996) *Challenging Codes: collective action in the information age* (Cambridge: Cambridge University Press).

12   Melucci, A. (1994) 'A Strange Kind of Newness: What's 'New' in New Social Movements?' in E. Larana, H. Johnston & J.R. Gusfield (eds) *New Social Movements: From Ideology to Identity* (Philadelphia: Temple University Press).

This was also in tune with the nature of change in a complex society which was a question of system adaptation. Consequently social movements were engaged in a process of renewal rather than transformation. They did this by producing cultural innovation, by providing new elites for institutions and by achieving institutional reforms.[13] These were the products of the symbolic power of social movements that made problems visible and offered alternative ways of solving them.

This analysis may be applicable to a movement mobilizing around material issues in that it may deliver a symbolic challenge to the values embodied in institutional policies and practices and serve to reveal possible alternative answers to the questions of unemployment, job insecurity and poverty. However, Melucci's perspective precluded the formation of a stable social movement capable of formulating and mobilizing around a coherent social and political alternative to neoliberalism.

Gorz

André Gorz developed his argument in the context of the emergence of mass unemployment in France in the early 1980s that was particularly severe in the industrial sector. Rather than embrace a new 'Strategy for Labour',[14] the labour movement remained tied to a defence of the goal of full employment. Gorz embraced the post-industrial perspective to argue that the introduction of new technologies into the production process was resulting in the inevitable abolition of work: an inherently progressive process of which mass unemployment was merely the negative consequence of its capitalist form.[15]

This analysis made demanding that the state guarantee the right to work (the main response of a labour movement still dominated by the industrial proletariat) at best a defensive strategy and at worst a reactionary one that was doomed to defeat. The main issue was not the maintenance of work, but rather how to control its abolition. Its abolition within capitalism was leading to mass unemployment whereas a renewed post-industrial socialist strategy could abolish work in a way that ended wage labour as a means to an end and give way to autonomous, self-directed activity that would be an end in itself. In this sense, the answer to the social question was no longer a matter of meeting of needs through the right to waged work ensured as a citizenship right, but was rather about meeting needs through the 'right to autonomous production' (p. 4) outside of capitalist social relations and state regulation. For Gorz, this could not be achieved through gaining control of the state apparatus, but would rather be the product of a new extra-institutional politics of a new progressive social actor that would be the subject of the abolition of work.

Through the onset of post-industrial society, the radicality of the industrial proletariat had been displaced onto 'non-workers' (p. 7) who did not positively identify themselves with their work and sought their liberation beyond and not

---

13   Melucci, A. (1985) 'The Symbolic Challenge of Contemporary Movements', *Social Research,* 52 (4) pp. 789–816.

14   Gorz, A. (1967) *Strategy for Labour: A Radical Proposal* (Boston: Beacon Press).

15   Gorz, A. (1982) *Farewell to the Working Class: an Essay on Post-Industrial Socialism* (London: Pluto Press).

within wage labour. This actor was a 'non-class' (p. 7) in that it was not a universal subject capable of taking over the production of society, but was rather a non-subject that was concerned with developing areas of individual autonomy in opposition to the logic of capitalist society. From this perspective, the 'non-class of non-workers' (p. 6) took over from the disappearing industrial working class as the progressive social force thus rendering labour organizations a defensive, if not a reactionary force. Gorz argued that:

> the 'social subject' of the abolition of work will not be the stratum of skilled workers who take pride in their trade and in the real or potential power that this confers on them. The main strategic goal of this social stratum, which has always been hegemonic within the organised labour movement, will remain the appropriation of work, of the work tools and of power over production. ...Protecting jobs and skills, rather than seeking to control and benefit from the way in which work is abolished, will remain the major concern of traditional trade unionism. ... I have used the term of 'non-class of non-workers' to designate the stratum that experiences its work as an externally imposed obligation in which 'you waste your life to earn a living'. Its goal is the abolition of workers and work rather than their appropriation. And this prefigures the future world. ... a society based on the liberation of time (p. 6–7).

Gorz's analysis that class was no longer a salient social and political category, led him away from considering organized labour as a focus of social and political mobilization. He replaced it with a focus on environmental movements which he saw as rejecting the work ethic and expressing the values of caring for the self, other people and the planet. Subsequent work by Gorz concerned itself with developing practical steps on the way to the utopia of a society in which the sphere of material necessity would be subordinate to the sphere of autonomy.[16] He called for the Left to develop a project which would unite the stronger core group of workers with the weaker marginalized groups around a common set of demands.[17] Thus while dismissing the demand for full employment and a social wage as 'labourist conservatism' (p. 34), he advanced demands for the lifelong right to an income in return for 20,000 hours of work. Such a demand was part of 'the new agenda' (p. 37) which could unite workers demanding a shorter working week with the post-industrial proletariat's requirement of a basic income.[18] As we will see in subsequent chapters, these were two of the central demands advanced by the European Marches, while the ETUC remained firmly in favour of a return to full employment. This might therefore suggest that the new European mobilizations were under the influence of Gorz's new social subject.

Castells

The work of Manuel Castells has been wide-ranging in its empirical focus and its theoretical claims. His earlier work on urban social movements in Latin America,

---

16   Gorz, A. (1985) *Paths to Paradise: On the Liberation from Work* (London: Pluto Press).

17   Gorz, A. (1989) *Critique of Economic Reason* (London: Verso).

18   Gorz, A. (1990) 'The New Agenda', *New Left Review*, 184 pp. 37–46.

the USA and France highlighted the growth of 'collective consumption trade unionism' (p. 319) in response to the economic and cultural transformation of the city.[19] Castells more recent study located the decline of the labour movement and the rise of the NSMs within a far-reaching analysis of the new 'information age' and an international study of contemporary social movements.

For Castells, the emergence of the network society marked a new epoch of 'information capitalism' (p. 18) that is distinctive in that it is globalized and networked. Capital accumulation and valorization occur in global financial markets that function through information networks. Rather than an identifiable global capitalist class, capital exists as a global network in the 'space of flows' and functions according to the 'instant time of computerized networks'. Labour has become 'disaggregated', 'fragmented', 'diversified' and 'divided' and exists in the 'space of places' and functions according to the 'clock time of everyday life' (p. 475). Rather than assert that capital is powerful vis-à-vis labour, Castells argued that they have become disconnected as capital exists in hyperspace and labour no longer possesses a collective identity. The labour movement, rooted in the space of places and therefore tied to the territorial nation state, has been 'historically superseded' (p. 360) as is its old ideology of 'labor-based socialism' characterized as one of the 'dusty flags of forgotten wars' (p. 355). Labour has ceased to be a social movement and has become 'a political agent integrated into the realm of public institutions' (p. 354), but this has been a largely ineffective strategy as the state has been deprived of much of its influence by the power of global flows.[20]

In relation to the formation of social movements in network society, Castells stated that the main social conflict in the information age is between the instrumental logic governing the flow of information in networked capitalism and the cultural codes rooted in everyday life.[21] As with Touraine and Melucci, this analysis asserted that social movements are key agents in the battle over the production and dissemination of cultural codes. Social movements arise around a defence of cultural particularity against the networking logic: 'resistance identity' (p. 8), or take the form of proactive movements that challenge the logic of the space of flows and out of which new social subjects can develop: 'project identity' (p. 8). Organized labour, however, has been tied into attempts to construct a new hegemony with government and business: 'legitimizing identity' (p. 8) and therefore has not been a source of a new progressive project. Castells concluded that

> new project identities do not seem to emerge from former identities of the industrial era's civil society … identity projects emerge from communal resistance rather than from the reconstruction of institutions of civil society … because of the structural features and historical processes I have tried to convey … the labor movement does not seem fit to generate by itself and from itself a project identity able to reconstruct social control and rebuild social institutions in the Information Age (pp. 357/358/360).

---

19   Castells, M. (1983) *The City and the Grassroots* (London: Edward Arnold).
20   Castells, M. (1996) *The Rise of the Network Society* (Oxford: Blackwell).
21   Castells, M. (1997) *The Power of Identity* (Oxford: Blackwell).

It was amongst the NSMs such as ecologists, feminists and 'insurgents against the global order' (p. 362) such as the Zapatistas that Castells identified evidence of an emergent project identity. Moreover, he argued that these movements took the network form of organization that was necessary to engage with the new forms of networked power.

Despite this focus, Castells' analysis suggests examining the European mobilizations for traces of an emergent project identity. In the popular opposition in France to welfare cuts and labour market flexibilization he identified a tendency towards the defence of cultural identity that articulated opposition to global market forces and 'Eurocrats' in nationalist terms. He also made out the embryo of a European project identity around such shared values as 'the defense of the welfare state; of social solidarity; of stable employment; the concern about universal human rights and the plight of the Fourth World; the reaffirmation of democracy (p. 333).[22] While, unlike Touraine, Castells acknowledged the progressive nature of such resistance, his analysis too suggested that organized labour would, at best, be a highly unlikely or peripheral player in the formation of such resistance into a social movement.

The Crisis and Reformation of Modernity Argument

The writers from the 'New social democratic Left' that took this perspective argued that the NSMs were not the product of a shift to a society beyond modernity, but were in fact a product of the crisis tendencies of modernity itself. They also represented the emergence of a new politics that amounted to a rescue of the modernist project. This new politics overlaid the old politics of the earlier phase of modernity, but amounted to a qualitative departure from it that gave the NSMs an importance as a potentially progressive social force that the labour movement had lost.

Habermas

For Habermas, social conflict over the question of material distribution was institutionalized through the administrative mechanisms of the welfare state: mechanisms that provided the material compensations through which such conflict was assuaged. The organizations of the labour movement had eschewed mobilization and had become mechanisms for channeling grievances. However, while the old material social conflict was allayed it was overlaid with new conflicts over the 'grammar of forms of life' (p. 392).[23]

The activities of the NSMs were to be understood in terms of a defence or restoration of lifestyles and identities that were threatened by 'tendencies to colonize the life-world' (p. 35) by the processes of commodification and state domination which were mediated through the mechanisms of money and power.[24] The new conflicts were consequently not amenable to alleviation through the machinery of the welfare

22   Castells, M. (1998) *End of Millennium* (Oxford: Blackwell).
23   Habermas, J. (1987) *The Theory of Communicative Action. Volume Two: Lifeworld and System: A Critique of Functionalist Reason* (Cambridge: Polity).
24   Habermas, J. (1981) 'New Social Movements' *Telos*, 49 pp. 33-37.

state and therefore produced the new forms of protest, occurring beneath and beyond institutional politics, which were associated with the NSMs. Although diverse, the NSMs were held together by their common challenge to the focus on economic growth. Habermas recognized amongst the NSMs the potential for a reactionary defence of tradition, but also identified a progressive potential for liberation whereby elements such as feminism could develop new values and lifestyles that offered a communicative challenge to the instrumental rationality of the system.

Habermas also identified a division between employers and workers that were located at the core of the production process and supported the 'old politics' of economic, social and military security and those peripheral to production that supported the 'new politics' of 'individual self-realization' and the quality of life (p. 33).[25] He stated that,

> A line of conflict forms between, on the one hand, a center composed of strata *directly* involved in the production process, and interested in maintaining capitalist growth as the basis of the welfare-state compromise, and, on the other hand, a periphery composed of a variegated array of groups ... that are further removed from the 'productivist core of performance' in late capitalist societies, ... The bond that unites these heterogeneous groups is the critique of growth. ... Alternative practice ... takes aim at the monetarization of services, relationships and time, at the consumerist redefinition of private spheres of life and personal life-styles. Furthermore, the relations of clients to public service agencies is to be opened up and reorganized in a participatory mode, along the lines of self-help organizations (pp. 392/3, 395).[26]

Habermas' distinction between 'old' and 'new' politics suggests two distinct strategies for developing an alternative to neoliberalism which could be applicable to the division between the strategies advanced by the ETUC and the European Marches. Supporters of the 'old' politics would support a growth-based strategy resulting in a quantitative increase in the total amount of work and of the numbers in employment. This strategy would tend to give rise to a demand for a return to full employment.

Supporters of the 'new' politics would tend to be critical of such a strategy based on an appreciation of the quality of life. This would result in approaches to unemployment based on more people working less and so tend towards demands such as a shorter working week. Without wishing to stray too far into his later work, this call for a redistribution of work was the approach supported by Habermas as the alternative to market based solutions to mass unemployment.[27]

Offe

Offe argued that the NSMs were signs of new conflicts, arising around the 'perverse effects' (p. 854) and broken promises of economic and political modernization that could not be resolved according to the institutional mechanisms of the 'old politics'

---

25   *Ibid.*
26   Habermas (1987) *op cit*
27   Habermas, J. (1998) 'There Are Alternatives', *New Left Review* 231 pp. 3–12.

(p. 824).[28] He suggested that these new forms of non-institutional conflict appeared when working class interests were institutionalized and its organizations operated according to the maxim of class collaboration as opposed to class conflict. Thus rather than pursuing the goal of socialist transformation, the unions and socialist parties operated as mechanisms for ensuring the loyalty of the working class to the Keynesian welfare state (KWS) settlement by enabling some limited redistribution of the fruits of economic growth.[29]

While Offe's analysis was similar to that of Habermas, he emphasized that the significance of the NSMs was not as socio-cultural movements that mounted a defence of the lifeworld. They were rather socio-political movements that mobilized support for binding claims, but utilized means of action that were not deemed legitimate by political authorities. Offe argued that the NSMs were part of an emerging new political paradigm that operated in a new space of non-institutional politics and could be understood as a constellation of collective 'actors', 'issues', 'values' and 'modes of action' (p. 828).[30]

The new middle class were the central actors of an alliance that included sections of the old middle class as well as 'peripheral and decommodified groups', such as students, pensioners and unemployed and marginally employed youth, that were 'not (presently) defined directly in their social situation by the labor market' (p. 834).[31] The 'new' actors mobilized around the issues of 'peace, environment, human rights and unalienated forms of work' (p. 832) that were the 'forgotten agenda' (p. 836) of a labour movement that had abandoned these issues in return for institutional recognition and political exchange around core issues of material distribution and social security.[32] The NSMs espousal of the values of identity and autonomy represented a modernist critique of a modernization process that was overly reliant on instrumental rationality.[33] It therefore produced perverse consequences such as ecological destruction that provoked mobilization.[34] The NSMs were also notable for 'informal', 'spontaneous' and 'egalitarian' forms of internal organization and engaged in forms of protest politics.[35]

This new political paradigm was also beyond the old political paradigm in the sense that class was no longer the central salient factor. Offe argued that,

> In several senses, it can be said therefore that the pattern of social and political conflict that we find expressed in new social movements is the polar opposite of the model of class conflict. First, the conflict is not staged by one class but by a social alliance that consists, in varying proportions, of elements coming from different classes and 'nonclasses'. Second, it is not a conflict between the principal economic agents of the model of production but

---

28   Offe, C. (1985) 'New Social Movements: Challenging the Boundaries of Institutional Politics', *Social Research*, 52 (4) pp. 817–869.

29   *Ibid.*

30   *Ibid.*

31   *Ibid.*

32   *Ibid.*

33   Offe, C. (1984) *Contradictions of the Welfare State* (London: Hutchinson).

34   Offe (1985) op cit

35   *Ibid* pp. 829–30.

an alliance that includes virtually every element *but* these principal classes. Third, the demands are not class-specific but rather strongly universalistic or, to the contrary, highly particularistic, and thus in any case either more *or* less inclusive or 'categorical' than class issues (p. 835).[36]

For Offe, this form of the end of class politics suggested that the labour movement was incapable of adapting to encompass the new politics due to its core working class constituency being largely unaware of, or unaffected by, the new contradictions arising from the modernization process. Although the peripheral groups involved in the NSMs did display a tendency to retreat into premodern irrationality, the new middle class element represented a critique of modernization from the perspective of the 'universal and emancipatory values' (p. 856) of modernity itself. It was precisely this new middle class that was most aware of the risks and perverse effects of further modernization. This would be the element of the NSMs that would form a progressive alliance with the social democratic Left to take up the new central issues of the 'redistribution of work', 'disarmament', 'environmental protection', and 'economic democracy' (p. 860).[37]

From this perspective, the European Marches, with its support for the redistribution of work alongside a wider set of issues, might suggest the emergence of Offe's 'new' European Left. This would replace the 'old' European Left whose constituency, Offe argued, has largely evaporated and whose organizations remain tied to defending the welfare state and to demands for full employment. While the 'old' European Left lacks a plausible mobilizing programme and a vision of an alternative project, an emergent 'new' European Left might be developing a new programme and project based around the demands and issues of the 'new' politics mobilized around by its 'new' social basis.[38]

Beck

Like Habermas and Offe, Beck was also influenced by the development in Germany of strong peace and environmental movements. He wrote his earlier work in the context of the late 1980s and early 1990s that saw rising levels of affluence and lifestyle differentiation alongside record levels of unemployment and poverty that placed a growing strain on welfare systems. The response of the German labour movement was, however, one of relative acquiescence.

For Beck, the process of reflexive modernization had dissolved industrial society that was based on the production of material goods and replaced it with a risk society central to which was the production of 'bads' (p. 3): global hazards that threatened the lives of humans and the integrity of the natural environment. Late modernity was beyond the material culture of early industrial society and the process of individualization had dissolved the old identities of status and class and individuals were 'set free' (p. 87) to create new identities in a reflexive manner. However,

---

36   Offe (1985) *op cit.*

37   *Ibid* pp. 864–8.

38   Offe, C. (1996) *Modernity and the State: East and West* (Cambridge: Polity) pp. 147–82.

individualization was also accompanied by a tendency towards standardization that engendered new institutionalized dependencies and risks. Thus the NSMs were both the expressions of the new identities formed in a non-traditional culture and responses to the new risks arising in risk society. In late modernity, the workplace was no longer a significant location for social conflict and therefore class based collective action waned. New arenas of struggle emerged which resulted in the growth of the NSMs that addressed new risks such as ecological destruction and new central conflicts such as that arising around gender roles.[39] The labour movement has been superseded as the agent of progressive social change. It has become a conservative force incapable of developing a vision of a different social order.

> The achievements of the workers' political and trade union movement were great, so great that they have even undermined its former role as leader into the future. It has become more a preserver of what has already been attained and is being eroded by the future, than a course of political imagination that seeks and finds answers to the hazards of the risk society (p. 48).

For Beck, in the new individualized society class is not a basis for the formation of social and political action as classes have lost their self-understanding as such and can no longer develop 'to become a formative political force' (p. 100). Moreover, it has become increasingly difficult to mobilize social actors around social problems such as unemployment which have appeared increasingly as individualized risks and have been experienced as an individual crisis and as individual failings. Where mobilization has occurred, it has not followed model the old class model, but has taken the form of a series of pragmatic temporary alliances which have been formed around single issues. However, Beck's work does highlight the emergence of the new issue of job insecurity as a possible focus of mobilization and also how labour has failed to recognize or mobilize around it.

Beck argued that a 'counter-industrial rationalization process' (p. 140) has been producing a 'destandardization of labour' (pp. 139–149) manifested as the flexibilization of contracts, working hours and workplaces. This has been resulting in a shift from the visible problem of standardized unemployment towards the new invisible issue of job insecurity in a labour market characterized increasingly by 'flexible and pluralized underemployment' (p. 140). This shift has created 'new social insecurities and inequalities' (p. 143) which have been experienced by a new peripheral sector of the workforce populated in particular by the young, women and migrants.

Beck argued that the consequences of this trend for political consciousness and action have as yet been incalculable. However, the suggestion is that organized labour has been tied to the old industrial order and its solutions and has therefore been focused on resisting change as opposed to developing and demanding policies more in tune with the new reality. For Beck, an alternative course of action would appear to be to construct a temporary alliance to support the demand for a 'legally guaranteed minimum income for everyone' (p. 149). It is possible, in these terms, to consider the European Marches as just such a temporary alliance. An alliance

---

39   Beck, U. (1992) *Risk Society: Towards a New Modernity* (London: Sage).

that was based around the new peripheral social actors and that focused on the new issue of job insecurity and on the new centrepiece of a modernized system of social protection: a guaranteed minimum income.

Giddens

Giddens developed his argument in the wake of a series of devastating defeats for the British labour movement in the 1980s. This period also saw the failure of extra-parliamentary protest movements to resist successfully the neoliberal agenda of successive Conservative governments.

Giddens presented a picture of a runaway juggernaut of a radicalized high modernity that rendered projects based on controlling social change unrealistically utopian. For Giddens, the development of a globalized, post-traditional and reflexive society not only produced new levels of security, but also manufactured uncontrollable and fundamental risks for modernity across each of its four institutional formations.[40] Knowledge of these risk environments provided the realistic confines within which social movements could engage to develop utopian projects that could steer modernity into post-modernity. Operating within this framework of 'utopian realism' (p. 154) social movements could produce 'models of the good society' (p. 156) utilizing the freedom from inequality achieved by the 'old' emancipatory politics to develop projects that articulate the 'new' life politics of freedom to self-actualize.[41] In such a late modern context, class as the basis for collective action has gone out of the game[42] and other individual and collective agencies such as the NSMs have come into play.[43]

Giddens analysis severed the link between labour and the development of a new social order while also forestalling attempts to replace labour with the NSMs as the primary agents of social change. He argued that, while in the early phases of modernity the labour movement, through its close association with the demands for civil and political rights, appeared as the central movement, it did and still does not in fact play the central role in modernity and its transformation. Empirically, other movements contesting the various dimensions of power can be traced back to early modernity. Analytically, there remains a separation between the various movements due to the multi-dimensionality of modernity. The separation of modernity's institutional complexes militates against the formation of a social movement that could act as a unified and unifying force for social change.[44] Moreover, Giddens stated that,

> the new social movements are not 'totalizing' in the way that socialism is (or was), promising a new 'stage' of social development beyond the existing order ... they don't

---

40   Giddens (1990a) *The Consequences of Modernity* (Cambridge: Polity Press).

41   *Ibid.*

42   Giddens, A. (1994) *Beyond Left and Right: The Future of Radical Politics* (Cambridge: Polity Press).

43   Giddens, A. (1991), *Moderntiy and Self-Identity* (Cambridge: Polity Press).

44   Giddens, A. (1990b) 'Modernity and utopia', *New Statesman* 2 November.

envisage seizing control of the future in the way the more ambitious versions of socialism have done (p. 3).[45]

In terms of developing an alternative to neoliberalism, Giddens' argument seemed to place less emphasis on direct state intervention to correct the market and more emphasis on encouraging counselling and self-help groups that would play an important role in developing life political responses to risks. However, social movements may retain an important role in bringing about social change through the development of broader life political projects that promote self-actualization and an engagement with the narrower political sphere to articulate demands for life political rights.[46]

For Giddens, the global 'South' illustrated how, at the community level, social movements and self-help groups have been constructively engaging with the risk of poverty by developing the informal economy that challenges productivist ideology and also prefigures an alternative 'post-scarcity society' (p. 163).[47] At the political level, Giddens suggested that the KWS is a 'lapsed historical endeavour' (p. 150).[48] Therefore, Giddens suggested that welfare was in need of modernization to rise to the challenges of the late modern epoch. While the neoliberal Right demanded that the welfare state gave way to the market and the Left stood for the defence of the existing forms of state provision, Giddens developed an agenda for welfare reform which he argued was 'beyond Left and Right'.[49] As we will see in subsequent chapters, this idea of a 'Third Way'[50] has been one that has actually had more influence on social democratic parties that have accommodated to neoliberal globalization than on the grass roots social movements that have challenged it.

The Dichotomy of 'Old' and 'New' Social Movements

The two sets of writers discussed so far in this chapter offered differing accounts for the decline of the labour movement and the rise of the NSMs. However, they shared common themes thereby producing a dichotomy between 'old' and 'new' social movements that has become central to sociological studies of social movements. This dichotomy can be represented in terms of ideal types with contrasting elements of actors, issues, location, forms of action and organization and social change.[51]

In terms of actors and issues, the dominant paradigm has operated with a model of the labour movement based on an industrial working class actor engaged in class

---

45   Giddens (1994) *op cit.*
46   *Ibid.*
47   *Ibid.*
48   *Ibid.*
49   *Ibid* pp. 180–97.
50   Giddens (1998) *The Third Way: The Renewal of Social Democracy* (Cambridge: Polity Press).
51   These elements have been derived partially from Scott, A. (1990) *Ideology and the New Social Movements* (London: Unwin Hyman); Dalton, R.J. & Kuechler, M. (1990) 'Introduction' in R.J. Dalton & M. Kuechler (eds) *Challenging the Political Order* (Cambridge: Polity).

conflict over issues relating to material distribution. The social question is a matter of material want that is most extreme for those without work. That labour movement politics has been superseded is a testament to the way that material want has given way to material affluence and that this has provided the basis for new needs and conflicts that have been engaged in by individualized new and non-class actors. The social question has been displaced by, or transformed into, a post-material question that has given rise to the politics of lifestyle choice.

Beck, for example, argued that overcoming material immiseration meant that the class basis for collective action has disappeared as labour market individualization built on material affluence and underpinned by the welfare state has led to 'capitalism without classes' (p. 88).[52] This position was echoed by Giddens who argued that the process of individualization has meant that class is no longer experienced as a 'collective fate' (p. 143), but in terms of a changeable individual biography.[53] Gorz and Touraine grounded their assertion of the end of class politics in the declining numbers of industrial workers that has eroded the basis for a mass movement united around a working class identity.[54]

Melucci argued that basic needs have largely been met and that this provided the basis for a new post-material politics based around the 'freedom to be' (p. 178) rather than the 'freedom to have' (p. 177).[55] For Offe, the new middle class that formed the progressive base of the NSMs have enjoyed the 'relative economic security' (p. 833) that has enabled them to develop post-material concerns with the quality of life that have been articulated in non-class specific terms.[56] This link between material well-being and the NSMs was also evident in Inglehart who argued that the increasingly affluent post-war Western societies expressed a growing attachment to 'Post-Materialist needs' (p. 41) around which the NSMs mobilized.[57]

The 'old' labour movement developed a strategy that aimed to realize its material aspirations by addressing demands to the nation state. Mobilization has thus been geared to 'political exchange'[58] resulting in institutional forms of action. The labour movement has also tended towards representative, hierarchical and centralized forms of organization with a clearly specified leadership that has engaged in the institutional mechanisms of political exchange. The NSMs, in contrast, have eschewed state-based strategies in favour of reforming and politicizing civil society as a sphere that is independent of both state and market.[59] The NSMs concern with developing and defending civil society initiatives has given rise to informal, egalitarian forms of

52   Beck (1992) *op cit.*
53   Giddens (1994) *op cit.*
54   Gorz (1982) *op cit*; Touraine, A., Wieviorka, M. & Dubet, F. (1984) *Le Mouvement Ouvrier* (Paris: Fayard).
55   Melucci (1989) *op cit* pp. 177–8.
56   Offe (1985) *op cit.*
57   Inglehart, R. (1977) *The Silent Revolution: Changing Values and Political Styles among Western Publics* (Princeton: Princeton University Press).
58   Pizzorno, A. (1978) 'Political Exchange and Collective Identity in Industrial Conflict', in C. Crouch & A. Pizzorno (eds) *The Resurgence of Class Conflict in Western Europe since 1968* (Basingstoke: Macmillan).
59   Offe (1985) *op cit.*

organization that function through participation rather than representation.[60] They have engaged in forms of non-institutional action that are either directly expressive of a social alternative[61] or articulate a politics of protest against institutional initiatives.[62]

The dominant paradigm has presented the labour movement as seeking to achieve social change through political mobilization and organization in order to realize its aim of socialism as an 'all embracing project' (p. 21) that has sought transformation across the dimensions of modernity.[63] The NSMs, in contrast, have tended to have disparate and even opposed objectives[64] and have lacked an encompassing vision and a consistent ideological perspective which could form the basis of a different societal project. For the NSMs, social transformation is focussed on developing a project at the cultural as opposed to the political level. This has been more of an individual project of personal development than a collective political project.[65] The NSMs have operated according to a 'self-limiting radicalism' (p. 664)[66] that has recognized the autonomy of each movement, has accepted the existence of the market economy and has developed new democratic institutions that have operated within the framework of formal democratic politics. In this sense, the NSMs have functioned as a force for cultural[67] and political[68] renewal rather than for social transformation through gaining political power.

Challenging the Dominant Paradigm

Class and Class Politics

Having outlined the work of the writers from the 'New social democratic Left' and how this contributed to the formation of the dominant paradigm of the sociology of social movements that developed in the 1980s and 1990s, I will now move on to develop a criticism of it. I will also identify the ramifications for understanding the supposed distinction between 'old' and 'new' social movements. This begins with a critique of its conception of class and class politics.

It has been argued that NSM theorists operate with a gradational Weberian conception of class as an economic/market category thereby limiting class politics to intermittent collective action over questions of material distribution. However, class is more fruitfully understood in Marxist terms as a social relation and class politics as a struggle for working class self-emancipation that arises from a continuous

---

60   *Ibid.*

61   Melucci (1989) *op cit.*

62   Offe (1985) *op cit.*

63   Giddens (1990b) *op cit.*

64   Giddens (1994) *op cit.*

65   Melucci (1989) *op cit.*

66   Cohen, J. (1985) 'Strategy or Identity: New Theoretical Paradigms and Contemporary Social Movements', *Social Research*, 52 (4) pp. 663–716.

67   Melucci (1989) *op cit.*

68   Offe (1985) *op cit.*

and ubiquitous social struggle that is 'rooted in a clash of opposed needs' (p. 75).[69] This position is supported by the work of Edward Thompson who demonstrated historically that class is a not a static category, but a dynamic social relation. Classes stand in an internal antagonistic relationship that is characterized by a constant yet surmountable struggle whose product may be the formation of a class with a consciousness of its contradictory existence to capital:[70]

> ... class formations and class consciousness (while subject to determinate pressures) eventuate in an open-ended process of relationship – of struggle with other classes – over time. ... Classes arise because men and women, in determinate productive relations, identify their antagonistic interests, and come to struggle, to think, and to value in class ways: thus the process of class formation is a process of self-making, although under conditions which are 'given' (p. 298–9).[71]

Therefore the formation of classes is usefully comprehended as a 'structured process' (p. 98).[72] Class struggle is not a struggle between classes that are already constituted, but is a perpetual struggle to decollectivize workers' control over the labour process and thereby constitute the worker as an independent labourer subject to capitalist exploitation.[73] Its two tendencies are the reproduction of an apparent (non)-class of atomized workers geared to the needs of capital accumulation and a class of collective labourers that is conscious of how its needs are opposed to continued capital accumulation.[74]

Understanding class as a social relation rather than as an economic category and class formation as a contested process suggests that social movements are not simply the expressions of ready made classes, but are in fact staging posts in their production.[75] This suggests that the labour movement has never been a straightforward expression of a clear-cut working class identity and interest. It has rather been an important element of the process through which such an identity and interest have been formed in ways that either confirm or challenge the maintenance of capitalist social relations. Such a conception suggests that attributing 'instrumental' interests

---

69   Barker & Dale (1998) *op cit.*

70   Thompson, E.P. (1966) *The making of the English working class* (New York: Vintage).

71   Thompson, E.P. (1978) *The Poverty of Theory* (London: Merlin Press).

72   Wood, E. M. (1995) *Democracy Against Capitalism: Renewing Historical Materialism* (Cambridge: Cambridge University Press).

73   Clarke, S. (1991) 'The State Debate' in S. Clarke (ed) *The State Debate* (Basingstoke: Macmillan).

74   Lebowitz, M. A. (1992) *Beyond Capital: Marx's Political Economy of the Working Class* (Basingstoke Macmillan). A similar analysis of class formation through class struggle has been expounded in Holloway, J. (2002) *Change the World Without Taking Power* (London: Pluto). However, it is important to state that Holloway's argument that 'working class' is a non-identity fails to follow the logic of his own argument that suggests that working class is a self-negating identity. In other words that through identifying itself and taking power the working class lays the foundations for abolishing itself as a class thereby liberating itself and humanity as a whole from exploitation and oppression.

75   For a more detailed outline of this perspective see Barker & Dale (1998) *op cit.*

to labour renders the labour movement an 'old' movement and any departure from instrumentalism as evidence of the 'new'. This negates an historical approach to examining labour movement dynamics.[76] This analysis suggests that the purported decline of labour and the rise of the NSMs may not have signalled the end of class politics, but rather marked a particular phase in its development.

'New' Movements for a 'New' Society?

The argument that the declining labour movement has been superseded by the NSMs has also been underpinned by the assertion that there has been a disjuncture in the socio-structural conditions that, it has been argued, determine the character of social movements. These conditions have been periodized into an 'old' period of nationally organized industrial capitalist societies in which social movements operated according to a class-based logic. This has been superseded by a 'new' period that has been variously characterized as post-industrial, post-modern, high/late modernity, late and/or disorganized capitalism, Post-Fordism, post-national and so on in which the 'old' logic of class based action is no longer operative.

The outcome of such an approach has been largely an emphasis on the apparent stability of periods of socio-structural conditions and an identification of the 'old' and 'new' social movements that mobilize on these stable terrains. The essential features of these movements can then be identified and on this basis 'old' and 'new' paradigms can be constructed.[77] In terms of agency, social movements have been relegated to the role of responding to changing objective social conditions that may result in a crisis to which social movements may provide an answer thereby ushering in a new period of stability. For example, writers such as Hirsch[78] who still referred to class struggle (albeit it without a class subject) relegated it to the role of delivering a stable mode of regulation to the new Post-Fordist structure.[79]

However, an emphasis on the dialectical rather than dualistic relationship between 'subjective' human agency and 'objective' social structure serves to reveal the inherent instability of structural conditions. It also suggests that social movements are not understandable as static reified categories that operate according to the logic of socio-structural conditions to which they have an external and subordinate relationship. Social movements are rather comprehensible as dynamic social forms that arise and develop with the process of crisis and restructuring of the capital relation.[80]

---

76   Tucker, K.H. (1991) 'How New are the New Social Movements?' *Theory, Culture & Society,* 8 pp. 75–98.

77   Offe (1985) *op cit.*

78   Hirsch, J. (1991) 'Fordism and Post-Fordism: The Present Social Crisis and its Consequences', in W. Bonefeld & J. Holloway (eds) *Post-Fordism & Social Form: A Marxist Debate on the Post-Fordist State* (Basingstoke: Macmillan).

79   Bonefeld, W. (1991) 'The Reformulation of State Theory', in Bonefeld & Holloway (eds) *op cit.*

80   Holloway, J. (1991a) 'The State and Everyday Struggle' in Clarke (ed) *op cit*; Holloway, J. (1991b) 'The Great Bear: Post-Fordism and Class Struggle. A Comment on

The contribution of such writing is that it demonstrated theoretically that human agency is not subordinate to purportedly objective social structures, but that such structures are the products of the human creative practices that they contain. Understanding capitalism in such a way suggests that it cannot be periodized satisfactorily along the lines of the thesis of a radical disjuncture proposed by writers from the dominant paradigm. Proponents of such a thesis have tended to articulate an evolutionary theory of historical development that has privileged either the development of technology or reason with the result that capitalism has been rendered as an invisible and natural state of affairs.[81] Therefore, an evolutionary leap in technology (informationalism) or rationality (late/postmodernity) has resulted allegedly in a qualitatively new social order, but one to which capitalist social relations are in fact still of fundamental importance.

Challenging such a conception of historical development suggests that the apparent distinction between 'old' and 'new' social movements has not been the product of a disjuncture in socio-structural conditions. It should rather be considered in conjunctural terms and therefore as arising in a particular phase of an ongoing process of capitalist crisis and restructuring. A further corollary of this argument is that it opens up the possibilities for a social movement to develop a social and political project that goes beyond the limits set by apparently objective socio-structural conditions and to articulate a fundamental challenge to capitalist social relations.

Keynesianism and Crisis: From 'Old' to 'New' Social Movements?

The particular conjuncture that produced the model of the labour movement as an 'old' social movement was the period of post-war reconstruction that led onto sustained growth in the 1950s and early 1960s. Restructuring of production was largely achieved without widespread and overt conflict through the 'socialization of consumption' (p. 272) associated with the KWS.[82] The worker's instrumental orientation reflected and reproduced the virtuous circle of rising wages, welfare and employment, but also their subordination to the goal of increased productivity that ensured sustained economic growth and rising profitability. Collective action was limited largely to supporting these instrumental ends and disconnected from broader but limited political goals that were to be achieved through electoral

---

Bonefeld and Jessop', in Bonefeld & Holloway (eds) *op cit*; Boncfeld, W., Gunn, R. & Psychopedis, K. (1992) 'Introduction', in W. Bonefeld, R. Gunn & K. Psychopedis (eds) *Dialectics and History: Open Marxism Volume One* (London: Pluto); Bonefeld, W. 'Social Constitution and the Form of the Capitalist State' in Bonefeld et al (1992) *op cit*; Holloway, J. 'From Scream of Refusal to Scream of Power: The Centrality of Work' in W. Bonefeld, R. Gunn, J. Holloway & K. Psychopedis (eds) *Emancipating Marxism Volume Three* (London: Pluto Press).

81   Wood, E.M. (1996) 'Modernity, Postmodernism or Capitalism?', *Monthly Review,* 48 (3) pp. 21–39.

82   Clarke, S. (1988) *Keynesianism, Monetarism and the Crisis of the State* (Aldershot: Edward Elgar).

means. Mobilization was largely channelled through the centralized bureaucratic organizational machines through which class conflicts were 'resolved'.

That these forms of collective action can be presented credibly as *the* model of the labour movement only serves to highlight the extent to which class struggle in the Keynesian era was successfully contained within forms that did not threaten capital's profitability. Therefore, the dichotomy of 'old' and 'new' social movements described the real sense in which labour, under the hegemony of social democratic ideology and organizational forms, was incapable of responding positively to the 'new' economic and social struggles that emerged as the apparent stability brought to capitalism by the KWS was plunged into crisis.

The term 'New Social Movements' was coined by Melucci in response to the activities developing out of the social centres of Italy in the period immediately following the decline of the wave of economic and social struggles spanning the period from 1968–1977. He identified the suspicion and hostility that existed between the new generation of activists organized informally in the network of social centres and the established hierarchical institutions of the labour movement.[83] This was also the case for the upsurge in workers discontent in the 'hot autumn' of 1969 that was expressed through absenteeism, sabotage, and wildcat strikes around issues for factory workers such as health and safety, production line speed and tight discipline. These were issues that were dealt with inadequately by established union and Communist Party officials.[84]

Resistance to state restructuring was also manifested through 'new' forms of collective action such as non-payment of rent and utility bills and free shopping and free transport actions. Such social struggles were carried out by workers, but organized outside of the factory, and also involved other neighbourhood-based actors identified as women, youth, and the unemployed. Links between workplace (economic) and neighbourhood (social) struggles developed and crystallized around the demand for a social wage.[85] This link was theorized in terms of the 'social worker' (p. 219) that was regarded as the new social subject emerging through social struggles occurring beyond the workplace over the liberation of time.[86] However, there were divisions between those focussing on the 'old' factory based struggles and those highlighting the role of the 'new' struggles at the level of society. Moreover, there was another tendency that favoured armed struggle at the expense of mass mobilization. Such divisions in the movement contributed to its defeat and this was followed by a period of industrial and state restructuring.[87] The fallout from this defeat was severe repression alongside the incorporation of some of the movement's leaders, organizations and initiatives that were celebrated by Melucci as the sources

---

83   Melucci (1989) *op cit.*

84   Fleming, J. (1991) 'Editor's Preface' in A. Negri *Marx Beyond Marx: Lessons on the Grundrisse* (New York: Autonomedia).

85   Ryan, M. (1991) 'Introduction' in A. Negri *op cit.*

86   Negri, A. (1988) *Revolution Retrieved* (London: Red Notes).

87   *Ibid*; Red Notes (1979) *Working Class Autonomy and the Crisis* (London: Red Notes).

of systemic renewal. There were also the various forms of retreatism into alternative lifestyles, religious groups and hard drugs.[88]

The lesson drawn by others engaged in social struggles around the issues of housing, health and transport was that they offered a viable possibility for linking with organized labour to form a political movement capable of successfully confronting the crisis of the KWS.[89] This position was underpinned by a theoretical critique of writers such as Offe and Hirsch that asserted a rigid separation of the 'economic' and the 'political', and thereby the autonomy of the state, as the basis for displacing class politics with that of the NSMs. The autonomy of the state was actually a real illusion which expressed but obscured the class relations underpinning the capitalist state. This suggested that the struggle against the capitalist state was a struggle against the forms through which it divided and channelled discontent and resistance. This analysis suggested that the diversity of 'new' social struggles did not herald the end of class politics, but were rather partial and fragmented forms of class struggle. The task was to broaden class politics by linking the hitherto largely fragmented economic and social struggles into a totalizing movement with the goal of gaining state power and transforming it into a mechanism through which the working class could wield power.[90]

Therefore, to respond positively to the crisis of Keynesianism, labour had itself to undergo a process of change as its existing organizations were inadequately addressing the issues being raised by the actors engaged in these struggles. For example, it was argued that the existing organizations expressed a 'labour interest' (p. 161) based on the narrow interests of male workers at work. The choice for labour was between its organizations being institutionalized as an interest within capitalism or the 'remaking of a social movement which begins from primary human needs … needs which the capitalist social order cannot adapt itself to' (p. 173).[91] The NSMs were potentially a major resource for developing such a movement and the necessary links between the NSMs and organized labour were, it was argued, already beginning to take place on the fringes of the main organizations.

Neoliberal Restructuring and the Rise of the Dominant Paradigm

In the context of the UK, the leadership of the official labour organizations regarded such a tendency as a threat rather than an opportunity for renewing labour's project of social change. They rejected the development of a project of radical social transformation on the basis of a united working class movement

---

88   Melucci (1989) *op cit.*

89   Conference of Socialist Economists State Apparatus and Expenditure Group (CSE-SAEG) (1979) *Struggle Over The State: Cuts and Restructuring in Contemporary Britain* (London: CSE Books); London to Edinburgh Weekend Return Group (LEWRG) (1979) *In and Against the State* (London: Pluto Press).

90   Clarke (1991) *op cit*; Holloway (1991a) *op cit*; Holloway, J. & Picciotto, S. (1991) 'Capital, Crisis and the State' in Clarke (ed) *op cit.*

91   Williams, R. (1983) *Towards 2000* (London: Chatto & Windus/The Hogarth Press).

preferring instead a strategy of managing the crisis which involved containing and demobilizing discontent. The outcome was that it was the Labour Party that began the implementation of austerity programmes that paved the way for monetarism and marketization.[92] Elsewhere in Europe, such as in France where popular discontent translated into the election of a socialist government, any progressive reforms and socialist rhetoric soon gave way to 'realism' (p. 17).[93] This produced national plans for economic and social modernization that, while presented as progressive, were translated into conservative policies aimed at growth through competitiveness.[94] It seems that whichever party was in office; the 'old' policies of Keynesian planning were abandoned and 'new' policies that favoured the free market were introduced. The late 1970s can therefore be regarded as the early days of a phase of class struggle that was focussed on the restructuring of capital and the state along neoliberal lines that itself gave rise to a 'new' politics.

In the 1980s and early 1990s, as the conjuncture of neoliberal restructuring developed, the tendency to link economic and social struggles into a united movement to resist it remained relatively marginal and politics appeared as an unconnected set of single issues. The radical potential of the 'new' social struggles was channelled mainly into specific claims for equal opportunities or dissipated into a disparate politics of alternative lifestyles. Organized labour largely remained tied to attempting to defend its core constituency through a strategy of 'new realism' that accommodated to, rather than challenged, restructuring. The result was a period of outright defeat (the UK) and retreat (mainland Europe) that was expressed as a crisis of the labour movement in the period of flexibility.[95] Whereas defeat in the UK led to some concern that the UK would follow the USA in the direction of business unionism,[96] the trend in mainland Europe was towards the extension of corporatist social pacts that allegedly traded pay restraint for job creation.[97] However, neither these labour strategies nor identity politics challenged the restructuring of industry and the public services that was leading to rising unemployment, job insecurity and poverty.

The dominant paradigm of the sociology of social movements came to prominence in this period of retreat and defeat in the face of restructuring. The working class was said to be disappearing at the same time as unemployment was soaring due to the rationalization and relocation of production. Identity politics had its heyday as women and migrant workers were over-represented in the growing number of

---

92   Clarke (1988) *op cit* pp. 287–351.

93   Liebman, M. (1986) 'Reformism Yesterday and Social Democracy Today' in R. Miliband, J. Saville, M. Liebman & L. Panitch (eds) *Social Democracy and After: Socialist Register 1985/6* (London: Merlin Press).

94   Kesselman, M. (1986) 'Whither French Socialism?', in Miliband et al *op cit.*

95   Regini, M. (1992) 'Introduction: the Past and Future of Social Studies of Labour Movements', in M. Regini (ed) *The Future of Labour Movements* (London: Sage).

96   Cohen, S. (1991) 'Us and Them: business unionism in America and some implications for the UK' *Capital & Class* 45 pp. 95–127.

97   Pochet, P. & Fajertag, G. (1997) 'Social pacts in Europe in the 1990s. Towards a European social pact?', in G. Fajertag & P. Pochet (eds) *Social Pacts in Europe,* (Brussels: ETUI).

low paid service sector jobs and hardest hit by cuts in public service provision. The failure of organized labour to lead a generalized opposition to restructuring and the fragmentation of resistance appeared to confirm the assertion that the social democratic project no longer had a credible class basis.

Consequently, it was argued that socialism needed to be revised into a democratic project with a new social basis in the NSMs.[98] This analysis translated into a populist electoral strategy that increasingly found favour in social democratic and labour parties that increasingly favoured policies that advanced market based solutions to economic and social problems.

Here we can see clearly the real social and political repercussions of the dominant paradigm: retreat in the face of neoliberalism and the demobilization of any social and political force capable of advancing a social and political alternative. However, the 1990s saw the emergence of a new wave of collective action against the social consequences of neoliberalism of which the crucial moment in Europe was the strikes over austerity programmes and public sector reform in France in 1995. These strikes marked a shift from sectional resistance to the mobilization of a broader current which allied public and private sector workers and gained support from organizations of students, the unemployed and illegal migrants who themselves had begun to mobilize.

While sociologists such as Touraine denigrated the strikers as opponents of modernization, Bourdieu addressed a mass meeting in the *Gare de Lyon,* and characterized their struggle as one 'against the destruction of a civilization' (p.24) and for a new vision of public services.[99] He also recognized the need to co-ordinate this struggle across the countries of Europe which is the matter to which I turn in chapter four. Before this, chapter three sets out the methodological underpinning for this investigation of the struggle for a Social Europe.

---

98   Laclau, E. & Mouffe, C. (1985) *Hegemony & Socialist Strategy: Towards a Radical Democratic Politics* (London & New York: Verso).

99   Bourdieu (1998) *op cit.*

Chapter 3

Investigating the Struggle for a Social Europe

At the end of chapter two, I mentioned how Bourdieu addressed a mass meeting at the *Gare de Lyon* during the wave of strikes in France in 1995 over the defence of public services. During this address, Bourdieu declared himself in 'solidarity with those who are fighting to change society' (p, 27).[1] This declaration raised the issue of the relationship between intellectuals and social movements against neoliberal globalization which is the starting point for outlining the methodological approach adopted for my investigation of the struggle for a Social Europe.

Intellectuals and Social Movements against Neoliberal Globalization

In the conclusion to 'Beyond Neoliberalism',[2] Touraine noted approvingly that intellectuals have emerged from their silence of the 1980s to intervene once again in social and political life. Touraine identified four different types of intellectual: the 'accuser' (p. 106), the interpreter, the 'ideologue' (p. 107), and the utopian. The accuser focuses on developing a critique of the existing order and powers. S/he does so by revealing the interests hidden behind the dominant discourses and by making visible the suffering of the socially excluded. The ideologue declares him/herself in solidarity with these victims of the social and political order and bears witness to their plight by participating in demonstrations and marches and by signing petitions and by so doing provides them with the voice in public life that they lack. The ideologue, however, identifies closely with particular social struggles and political forces and therefore is unable to assess objectively their social and political significance and thereby aid their development.

In contrast, although the 'interpreter-intellectuals' (p. 110) may be sympathetic to the plight, protests and demands of social actors, s/he maintains a distance from them. This is to be able to analyze them objectively and identify the primary meaning of their social action which assists in their formation into a coherent social movement. This interpretation of social movements is shared largely by the 'utopians' (p. 109) who are most concerned with identifying and making visible the new personal and cultural developments which may eventually blossom into the social movements that will engage in future social conflicts. Touraine's typology provides a useful

---

1   Bourdieu (1998) *op cit.*
2   Touraine (2001) *op cit.*

template for considering the role of intellectuals in relation to the development of a social movement mobilizing for a Social Europe.

Gorz thinking suggests he is a utopian intellectual.[3] He identified the cultural change which has been occurring in relation to the value of work in peoples' lives and sought to decipher its meaning so as to assist the subjects to develop a consciousness of their desire for autonomy. This led him as an intellectual to engage others in an examination of those 'exemplary experiences which explore other forms of productive co-operation, exchange, solidarity and living' (p. 78) so as to develop an alternative to the dominant technocratic discourse. Moreover, he attempted to translate the desire for autonomy into the public sphere so as to promote its inherent political radicalism. This required the intellectual to argue that the public should adopt a viewpoint based on a vision of a 'radically different society and economy' (p. 78). This utopian perspective also led Gorz to call on politicians to provide the necessary resources to fund initiatives which lead society 'out of capitalism' (p. 79). This intellectual role suggests to me a division of labour between the development of a utopian project which appears to be the primary task of the intellectual and the activities of the social movement. These activities would be to mobilize around the specific set of policies which would advance such a project so as to popularize them with the public and place the necessary pressure on politicians to adopt and implement them. A closer collaboration between intellectual and social movement was proposed by Bourdieu who also combined the development of a utopian project with the intellectual critique of the currently dominant neoliberal ideology.

Touraine[4] identified Bourdieu as the 'exemplary representative' (p. 107) of the intellectual accuser. This, however, recognized only the 'negative functions' (p. 20) which Bourdieu[5] ascribed to intellectuals which focused on challenging symbolic domination and was centred on developing a critique of the dominant discourse. Bourdieu[6] himself undertook this task in relation to the apparent inevitability and superiority of neoliberalism. Neoliberal thinking masquerades as a scientific and therefore progressive set of ideas which liberates the people from the overbearing power of the state, but actually amounts to a 'conservative revolution' (p. 35) which liberates the economic sphere from democratic social and political control. The consequences of this are the enrichment of the financial and commercial sectors and interests along with the empowerment of the repressive 'right hand' (p. 2) of the state. This is at the expense of the economic insecurity and social suffering of the majority of the population and the withering of the 'left hand' (p. 2) of the state that is concerned with their welfare.

In addition to exposing the real interests behind neoliberal ideology and its economic and social consequences, Bourdieu[7] also identified a 'positive function' (p. 21) for intellectuals which was to engage in a collective project to develop social

---

3   See Gorz, A. (1999) *Reclaiming Work: Beyond the Wage-Based Society* (Cambridge: Polity Press).
4   Touraine (2001) *op cit.*
5   Bourdieu (2003) *op cit.* pp. 17–25
6   Bourdieu (1998) *op cit.* pp. 29–44
7   Bourdieu (2003) *op cit.*

and political alternatives to neoliberalism understood as 'realistic utopias' (p. 21). For Bourdieu,[8] however, this meant that intellectuals should not adopt an overtly political role as 'figureheads' (p. 56) or remain as 'experts' (p. 56) who lecture social movement activists or indeed act as 'prophets' (p. 56) providing the social movement with its highest meaning. He rather proposed a more modest role for intellectuals in developing structures through which social scientists and social movement activists could come together and develop collective research projects and through which research findings useful to the social movement could be disseminated. In this sense, Bourdieu rejected not only the role of organic intellectual, which he too feared could all too easily become that of ideologue or 'apparatchik' (p. 56), but also that of intellectual interpreter which was promoted by Touraine and which he attempted to adopt.

For Touraine,[9] the intellectual interpreter assists the victims of neoliberalism to transform themselves into conscious social actors who recognize the highest meaning of the social conflict in which they are engaged. However, the main task of this kind of intellectual is to decide which elements of the demands advanced by a social movement are actually translatable into policy. This role for intellectuals requires them not only to understand and interpret the actors and their actions, but also to engage in a critique of their analysis and strategy. This is to enable the social actors to achieve an accurate understanding of their situation and to adopt the correct course to realize the necessary social and political changes. This role puts the intellectual interpreter in an awkward relationship with the social movement in that s/he may be sympathetic to it, but also be critical of it. This is even more the case as the interpreter intellectual must expose the political ideologies which contaminate the social movement and its demands. This also leads the interpreter intellectual to wage a fight against the ideologues who prophesy disaster and seek to dominate social actors and stifle the development of an independent social movement by manipulative political intervention.

Touraine's process of intellectual interpretation amounts to exactly the kind of manipulative intervention from outside of the social movement for which he condemns the revolutionary 'ultra-left' (p. 78). He recognized the 'reformist' (p. 3) character of those in the early part of the last century who rejected a radical break with capitalism and celebrated their role in the formation of industrial and social democracy and the welfare state. He condemned the radicals on the grounds that their revolutionary orientation inevitably leads to a renewal of domination and not liberation. His juxtaposition of democracy and revolution equated the self-activity of social actors around their immediate social conditions as alien to revolutionary activity that rendered social actors passive victims requiring representation by socialist intellectuals.

However, he was condemning a stream of Marxism that has been already discredited amongst all but a few die-hard defenders of the politics of the old Soviet bloc. The current conjuncture has seen a renewal of Marxism that takes as its starting

---

8   Bourdieu (1998) *op cit.*
9   Touraine (2001) *op cit.*

point the self-activity of the working class as the basis for its emancipation.[10] A small, but significant number of Marxist intellectuals have been involved in the movement against neoliberal globalization and, for the most part, they have combined the promotion of their particular political perspectives with practical contributions to the mobilization of the movement. Touraine's work showed no evidence of such an insider engagement and indeed argued for maintaining a distance between intellectual and social movement so as to offer a more telling critique of it. His method of sociological intervention was akin to what he was criticizing in that he stood outside, and indeed above, the movement supporting those elements that conformed to his reforming doctrine and condemning those that sought to go beyond its limits.[11]

Touraine[12] accepted that intellectual ideologues can demonstrate their solidarity with social movements in a 'perfectly honest way' (p. 107) by bearing witness yet he rejected their more direct political intervention as somehow dishonest. However, his interpretation was clearly an ideological intervention into the social movement in that it was an attempt to influence its acceptance of a particular political position and its rejection of another. Nevertheless, the resurgence of resistance to neoliberalism has been accompanied by the emergence of overtly ideological intellectuals who do identify themselves with particular political parties such as Callinicos or are identified with particular political currents such as Negri while also allying themselves with the whole oppositional movement to neoliberal globalization.

As I suggested above, this development has been associated with the renewal of Marxism as an emancipatory political ideology. The reemergence of this type of intellectual means that Touraine was inaccurate in dismissing them with the label of 'ideologue' and more accurate with the term 'organic intellectual' (p. 17). This term suggests they may actually be more or less firmly rooted in the social and political struggles in which they wish to intervene. Indeed, there has been a growing interest in the growing links between academics and social movement activism.

------

10   Amongst the most interesting and politically useful of the attempts at Marxist theoretical renewal is that provided by 'Open Marxism'. See Bonefeld, W., Gunn, R. & Psychopedis, K. (1992) 'Introduction', in W. Bonefeld, R. Gunn & K. Psychopedis (eds) *Dialectics and History: Open Marxism Volume One* (London: Pluto).

11   The negative effects of Touraine's attempts to interpret social movements can be seen in his work on the opposition to nuclear power in France. In an attempt to create the social movement along the lines of his analysis, Touraine and his research colleagues set up intervention groups in which they emphasized everything which separated the different positions. This was resisted by the activists who even perpetrated a hoax on the researchers so as to demonstrate their unity against the attempt by the researchers to divide them. This only intensified the campaign by the researchers who worked 'aggressively' on some of the activists and made personal pleas to convert them to their position. This led to even the cooks launching an attack on the sociologists for trying to 'manipulate the militants' (p. 140) and to an accusation by a leading ecologist that Touraine had 'driven a score of unfortunate ecologists up the wall and round the bend' (p. 153). The outcome of Touraine's intervention was to splinter the group with which he had had contact. See Touraine, A. et al (1983) *Anti-nuclear protest: the opposition to nuclear energy in France* (Cambridge: Cambridge University Press).

12   Touraine (2001) *op cit.*

An interesting early contribution was made by Routledge[13] who described the development of a 'third space as critical engagement' (p. 405) between academia and activism in which 'social relations of conversation' (p. 414) were developed. More recently, Johnston & Goodman[14] have highlighted how such a dialogue is one of several key principles which underpin a Freirean model for academic engagement with 'global justice campaigns' (p. 9). I have recently argued for such an engagement through ethnographic research of social struggles understood in terms of solidarity and praxis.[15] This argument was based partially on my experience researching the European Marches. What was peculiar about this project (and that of my co-author in his research with a Columbian trade union) was that I was not only researching the struggle for a Social Europe, but also participated in it as an activist. This role of 'activist-researcher' is somewhat akin to the role of 'organic intellectual' in that it is based on roots in the social movement which is being researched while retaining a capacity for critical intervention into its development. In the subsequent sections, I describe the development and practice of this role, but before this I describe the theoretical perspective on which the investigation of the struggle for a Social Europe was based.

Critical Ethnography

While sharing the conventional ethnographical concern with uncovering facts and meanings through observing human experience the methodological approach adopted for this study (critical ethnography) overcame the problems arising from the nominalism of conventional ethnography by incorporating ethnographic methods of data collection into a dialectical analysis. The key phrase whose examination reveals the differences between critical and conventional ethnography is: observing human experience.[16]

Observing the social world through whatever techniques may fall foul of the same problem faced by observation of the natural world in that appearances may be deceptive. For example, observation may indicate that the earth stands still and that the sun revolves around it leading to the generation of theories that place the earth at the centre of the universe.[17] Social observation may find a lack of overt indications of economic and social conflict and on this basis construct a model of capitalism without class struggle. This suggests that mainstream sociology is akin to a 'theory of society' (p. 156) which observes the forms in which the contradictions of capitalist

13   Routledge. P. (1996) 'The Third Space as Critical Engagement', *Antipode*, 28 (4) pp. 399–419.

14   Johnston, J. & Goodman, J. (2006) 'Hope and Activism in the Ivory Tower: Freirean Lessons for Critical Globalization Research', *Globalizations*, 3 (1) pp. 9–30.

15   Mathers, A. & Novelli, M. (2007) 'Researching Resistance to Neoliberal Globalization: Engaged Ethnography as Solidarity and Praxis', *Globalizations*. 4(2)

16   For another outline of the differences between conventional and critical ethnography, see Harvey, L. (1990) *Critical Social Research* (London: Unwin Hyman).

17   This analogy is made by Marx but is taken from Callinicos, A. (1983) *The Revolutionary Ideas of Karl Marx* (London: Bookmarks).

society appear to generate theories which attempt to erase them. However, what is required is a 'theory against society' (p. 156) which analyzes the resistance to these forms of domination through a critical process so as to produce critical knowledge and liberationary theory which can assist in bringing about social change.[18]

To penetrate beneath these forms of appearance and thereby locate observed human experience within its concrete material social reality requires a different process of abstraction to that seen in conventional sociology. This process is outlined by Marx who traced the concrete instance of population to its most abstract contradictory determination and then on this basis reconstructed a very different conception of it as 'a rich totality of many determinations and relationships' (p. 72).[19] The radical implications of this approach can be most fully appreciated by his analysis of Capital. On the basis of the contradiction between exchange-value and use-value contained in its simplest determination of the commodity, Marx reconstructed the totality of capitalism as a fundamentally exploitative social system that gave rise to a pervasive class struggle.[20]

This understanding of concrete material social reality as a complex and contradictory totality indicates how conventional ethnography has a tendency to explore subjective individual meanings independently of the objective totality of structured social relations within which they are experienced. However, particular instances of human experience are not only located as parts of a social totality, but their meaning also cannot be analyzed in isolation from this totality. Moreover, the social relations that compose this social totality are historically specific. For example, the social relation of labour and capital is specific to the capitalist mode of production. Therefore the facts and meanings established through empirical investigation are only comprehensible in relation to 'a structural and historical whole' (p. 21).[21] However, the process of history is not comprehensible in terms of the development of structures according to external objective laws, but rather in terms of the development of a central contradiction that produces changing social forms.[22] In other words, there is no duality between structure and agency, but rather it is human practice that constitutes the social structures that condition it. This enables an understanding of human experience that renders men and women active subjects, not in the sense of the autonomous individuals of positivist and interactionist sociology but,

> as persons experiencing their determinative productive situations and relationships, as needs and interests and as antagonisms, and then 'handling' this experience within their consciousness ... and then ... acting upon their determinate situation in their turn (p. 164).[23]

---

18   Holloway, J. (1995) *op cit.*
19   Cited in Carvell, T. (1975) *Karl Marx Texts on Method* (Oxford: Basil Blackwell).
20   Marx, K. (1976) *Capital Volume 1* (Harmondsworth: Penguin).
21   Harvey, L. (1990) *op cit.*
22   Bonefeld et al (1992) op cit; Bonefeld (1992) *op cit.*
23   Thompson, E.P. (1978) *op cit.*

This is an understanding of human experience as practical, active and negating and contrasts with the passive empiricist view of experience that positively endorses the status quo. It enables a focus on human experience as inseparable from capitalist exploitation and domination thereby offering a way of theorizing the specific forms of resistance that arise through opposition to the everyday realities produced by capitalist social relations.[24] The implication for my investigation of the struggle for a Social Europe is that the products of my empirical observation must be understood in relation to the specific historical social forms of the capital relation; itself understood as a contradictory totalizing social relation. In other words, the specific instances of the emerging European social movement and its component economic and social struggles must be examined in relation to the current historical conjuncture of the restructuring of capital and state understood as a total social process.

The European Marches as a Critical Case Study

Burawoy's 'extended case method' (ECM)[25] provides an excellent framework for an examination of the European Marches as a specific episode of social movement activity in relation to the broader historical and transnational context of neoliberal globalization. Indeed, Burawoy highlighted how the ECM utilizes ethnographic techniques so as to be able to generate data on 'everyday life' and locate it in its 'extralocal and historical context' (p. 4). By so doing, the ECM's focus on resistance in the localities 'challenges the postulated omnipotence of the global, whether it be international capital (or) neoliberal politics' (p. 30).

The ECM is based in a reflexive model of science whose central principle is dialogue and is premised on 'intersubjectivity between participant and observer' (p. 14). Reflexive science is sensitive to the contexts of research and the ECM positively embraces the effects of context. For Burawoy, the ethnographic interview is an 'intervention' into the life of the interviewee and it is through the 'mutual reaction' (p. 14) between interviewer and interviewee that meaningful knowledge is generated. Moreover, the knowledge generated is situational and reflects the various social locations of different social actors. This knowledge must therefore be aggregated into 'social processes' which themselves must be comprehended in relation to the 'social forces that impress themselves on the ethnographic locale' (p. 15). This 'structuration' (p. 15) is a dialectical process in that social forces not only shape the everyday life of social actors, but are also shaped by them. Finally, the ECM extends out from the specific social actors, social processes, and social forces to produce generality through a critical engagement with, and the 'reconstruction' (p. 16) of, social theory.

The elements of relating the European Marches to broader social forces and the critical engagement with social theory are, I trust, evident throughout the book.

---

24   Bonefeld, W., Gunn, R., Holloway, J. & Psychopedis, K. (1995) 'Introduction: Emancipating Marx', in W. Bonefeld, R. Gunn, J. Holloway & K. Psychopedis (eds) *Emancipating Marx: Open Marxism Volume Three* (London: Pluto Press) ; Holloway (1995) *op cit.*

25   Burawoy (1998) *op cit.*

Therefore, in the following section, I focus on how I actually intervened in the European Marches and how this intervention extended across time and place so as to produce knowledge of it in terms of its social processes. I also show how this intervention took the form of 'activist research' in the sense that I participated in the European Marches both as an activist and as a researcher.

Critical Ethnography in Practice

The methodological outlook outlined in the previous sections suggests that my investigation was not carried out in such a way as to apply a set of objectives social scientific techniques. This would suggest a distance between the researcher and the researched.[26] My approach was to attempt to overcome the gap between the researcher as the subject and the researched as the object of the research process through adopting the role of 'activist-researcher' that expressed how I was actively engaged in the struggles that I was investigating. Adopting this role meant that not only did I take part in the social movement struggling for a Social Europe, but also developed a dialogical relationship between myself and the other activists.

The monological/dialogical distinction has been usefully conceptualized as one between the researcher as 'miner' (p. 4) and 'traveler' (p. 5). Whereas the miner seeks the most productive seam from which to extract nuggets of information, the traveller gains new knowledge and experiences that are influenced by the people that they meet and engage in dialogue along the way. Neither the route nor the destination is fixed and both traveller and respondent are changed by the relationships formed.[27]

This conception of the researcher as dialogical traveller is also one that aptly describes the way that I investigated the social movement through travelling within the UK and mainland Europe. It also reflects the way that the research process affected my own outlook towards current economic and social struggles and thereby my involvement within them. The 'activist-researcher' label was not one that I originally coined myself, but was how I was introduced to a meeting in Paris in September 1999. For me, the part of activist was not a question of taking on an unfamiliar role and learning about a strange environment. It flowed from my involvement in the same kind of grass roots economic and social struggles as the militants who I met. It also expressed how I already held similar goals and values that were crucial to enabling me to enter the same 'critical plane' (p. 8) as the activists with whom I came into contact.[28] This affinity was also reinforced by common experiences of punitive social security regulations and of insecure employment.

---

26   Neary, M. (1997) *Youth, training and the training state* (Basingstoke: Macmillan).

27   Kvale, S. (1996) *Interviews: An Introduction to Qualitative Research* (Thousands Oaks, CA: Sage).

28   Harding, S. (1987) 'Is there a Feminist method' in S. Harding (ed) *Feminism and Methodology* (Milton Keynes: Open University Press).

Gaining Access and Snowballing

Hammersley & Atkinson have highlighted that, although the problem of gaining access is most acute at the start, it actually persists throughout the process of data collection. They also emphasized how overcoming the obstacles to access in fact provides useful insights into the social organization in question.[29] My initial concerns about who could in fact grant permission to study the European Marches were almost immediately allayed when I realized that without a formal membership and officers there was in fact nobody who could formally grant or withhold permission. In the absence of formal 'gatekeepers', I relied on establishing contacts who acted as 'sponsors'; opening doors to interviews with key informants and organizational meetings.[30] As I became more involved and more familiar with the social movement, the possible number of activists to meet and events to take part in grew rapidly and this method of gaining access to informants and opportunities for participant observation was akin to 'snowball sampling' (p. 50).[31]

I met the first activist from another country with whom I spoke during the demonstration in Cardiff. I approached her as I was impressed with the files of information that she was distributing about the activities of the European Marches in Munich. When our discussion was curtailed, we decided to exchange contact details and agreed to keep in touch. Gitti Götz kept me informed about the mobilization in Vienna and we met again in Cologne in January and June 1999 before I interviewed her in Munich. This trip to Munich also enabled me to meet local activists and to carry out a second unscheduled interview. Through the European Marches, Gitti became a close friend with Michel Rousseau and she introduced me to him at the evaluation meeting that followed the Cologne counter-summit events and strongly encouraged him to do an interview with me when I visited Paris.

I first spoke briefly to Willi Lubkes after he introduced a workshop at the conference held in Cologne and again after talking at the 'Parliament'. He arranged for me to visit the unemployed centre (ALSO) in Oldenburg. This trip enabled me to participate in informal discussions about the European Marches and its events and to undertake two further unscheduled interviews. It also provided an opportunity to meet Yvonne Rocomaure who was also visiting Oldenburg on her way back from Cologne and this meeting led to an invitation from her to visit Paris. Willi also recommended attending the evaluation meeting in Cologne and I also accompanied him to the German coordinating committee meeting held during the 'Assembly'. However, by this time I felt that I had gained a more general acceptance amongst the activists as I had already interviewed several of those present at this meeting.

During one of the UK steering committee meetings I suggested the possibility of my writing an article about the struggle for a Social Europe for an academic publication and this met with some enthusiasm amongst the participants. The article

---

29   Hammersley, M. & Atkinson, P. (1995) *Ethnography: Principles in Practice* (London: Routledge).

30   *Ibid.*

31   Jorgensen, D.L. (1989) *Participant Observation: A Methodology for the Human Sciences* (London: Sage).

was published shortly before my trip to Cologne in May 1999.[32] I took several copies of the article that I distributed amongst the activists and subsequently sent to those activists that I interviewed. It is possible that this article helped to establish some credibility and may have facilitated access to interviewing prominent activists in the social movement.

The Extent of Participation

The actual data that I was able to generate not only depended on gaining access to informants and events, but was also determined by my physical and social positioning.[33] It is important to recognize that I was based in the UK that was both politically and geographically marginal to the struggle for a Social Europe during the period of my empirical investigation. The relatively low level of economic and social struggles and the particular political situation vis-à-vis the EU meant that UK organisations and activists played a relatively minor part in the European Marches. However, UK activists' experiences of welfare reform were highly sought after. As well as facilitating my more active participation, this also provided me with something tangible to offer activists thus promoting an element of reciprocal exchange.

My intermittent involvement in events mirrored the participation of many activists in the European social movement and was an indication of the tempo of its organization. It was a minority of activists who marched to Amsterdam and Cologne or who regularly attended European Coordinating Committee meetings. Most activist involvement was centred on the summit meetings that provided the European Marches with periods of intense organization.[34] Taking part in these events and interviewing activists involved travelling long distances that required resources of time and money. My attendance at events held in mainland Europe was funded largely through research expenses, but this was supplemented significantly by cheap accommodation and food supplied by organizations and existing friends and informal contacts made through my involvement in the social movement.

While the European Marches was based on open participation, I had, like the activists, to establish who it was most worthwhile talking to and in which forthcoming events it was most useful to participate. My judgement was that although e-mails, the Internet and written documents would prove useful sources of information, it was most important to participate in, and observe, the main mobilizations and meetings that were held during the German and French presidencies of the EU. I initially considered spending a protracted period of time living in mainland Europe, but this proved financially and practically impossible. I decided instead to undertake several trips that spanned these events and, whenever possible, I scheduled interviews in the

---

32   Mathers, A. (1999) 'Euromarch – The Struggle for a Social Europe' *Capital & Class* 68 pp.15–20.

33   Jorgensen (1989) *op cit.*

34   In relation to international summit meetings such as the EU, G8, WTO, IMF and World Bank, this activity has come to be known as 'summit hopping', see Abramsky, K. (ed) (2001) *Restructuring and Resistance: Diverse Voices of Struggle in Western Europe* Self-published book available through resresrev@yahoo.com pp. 519–21.

period leading up to and following them. Although this strategy proved generally successful in generating informative data, with hindsight I have judged that either the first visit to France or the trip to Belgium could have been combined with participation in a European Coordinating Committee meeting.

The bulk of the empirical investigation was carried out in the period from May 1999 to December 2000. I had originally planned to take part in the march from Brussels to Cologne, but this proved impossible as the postponement of the EU summit led to a delay of the march that resulted in a clash with previously agreed work and personal commitments. The main elements of the investigation were carried out during four trips to mainland Europe. I spent four weeks in Germany in May/June 1999 that spanned the EU and G8 summit events in Cologne. This was followed by a week in Paris, in September 1999 and a week in Brussels leading up to the demonstration at the UNICE conference in June 2000. The final element was a week in France in December 2000 leading up to the EU summit in Nice. These trips involved participating and observing in the entirety or parts of the events listed in the appendix. I have subsequently been able to attend the ESFs held in Florence in 2002, in Paris in 2003 and in London in 2004 which assisted in writing the Postscript.

As well as participating in, and observing, these events, they provided an opportunity to collect primary and secondary written and visual materials and to take part in numerous informal conversations. During the overseas trips, I was also able to carry out unstructured interviews with prominent activists and other key informants as well as participants in the social movement and the locally and nationally based organizations out of which the social movement was formed. The trip to Brussels also allowed me to interview MEPs that had been, or were still, sympathetic to the European Marches as well as representatives of other European level organizations of trade unionists and NGOs.

In addition to the trips that were funded by my research expenses, I was also able to carry out the interviews in Amsterdam during a trip to an academic conference. Moreover, in December 1999, I was involved with a group in Bristol organizing an action against the New Deal and this event formed part of the decentralized European Day of Action against Workfare. Activists from Brighton, who I had met in Cologne, also participated in this event and I was able to engage them in informal conversations and interviews. In January 2000, I took part in a day conference organised by the UAG after which I interviewed a participant from the European Marches' UK steering committee and representatives of the WAC from Nazareth. In April 2001, during an academic conference trip to Boston, USA, I stumbled upon a meeting that was evaluating the demonstration in Quebec against the FTAA. The contacts that I made through this meeting and the conference enabled me to discover more about the links that the militants and organizations in the European dimension of the GJM had made with those in North America.

During, and subsequent to, the period studied I kept in touch with the activities of the European Marches and the broader social movement through subscribing to its French and German e-mail lists and journals and by e-mail and telephone contact with militants from France and Germany who provided me with useful background information and materials. These contacts also indicated how I took part in the informal dimension to the movement that involved receiving hospitality from, and providing it to, activists that I met through the events.

Participant Observation as Activist-Researcher

Jorgensen drew attention to how the researcher's self-concept affects participant role performances and data collection.[35] In relation to my role of 'activist-researcher' the part of activist did not require a significant change in self-concept, but was rather an extension of an established identity into the research setting. Rather than consciously engage in managing the impressions of those I met,[36] I found that I shared a similar set of values, experiences and goals that provided a ready basis for genuine interaction. The part of researcher was more difficult to adapt to in that it initially involved more observation and less active participation in events than perhaps would usually have been the case had I remained solely in my activist role. My participation was genuine, but was restrained by what I saw as the requirements of the investigation.

I travelled to the Cologne demonstration with a group from an anti-fascist organization that I had helped set up while living in Germany. However, on arrival we parted company as they headed for the anti-fascist bloc and I stood on the sidelines of the demonstration taking notes and collecting leaflets before marching to attend the rally. Had I remained with them I would probably have gained a different impression of the demonstration, as that particular bloc was involved with skirmishes with the police. However, merely being at the event was enough to experience its more intangible elements such as the sense of collective strength, of camaradarie, the internationalist sentiments, and the resulting feelings of joy and hope as well as the anger induced by the heavy policing.

I adopted the same approach in Nice for the demonstrations, but I decided to take a more active part in the blockade. This partially reflected the different character of the event, but was also an expression of the growing sense of solidarity with the militants taking part in it. This was not only experienced as commitment in the sense of personal choice, but also in the sense of duty. After hearing activists declare '*On reste ici*!' [We're staying put here!] I neither wanted to, nor felt able to leave, and their presence made it possible to face the riot police and tear gas. Such situations may be conceptualized as the 'strains and stresses of fieldwork' (p. 113–120)[37] or as evidence of 'going native',[38] but such notions are based on a separation of researcher

---

35   Jorgensen (1989) *op cit.*

36   Hammersley & Atkinson (1995) *op cit.*

37   *Ibid.*

38   'Going native' has been described as the concern that the scientific researcher would over-identify with and thereby compromise the objectivity of a study by transgressing the distance between him/herself and the 'other' of the researched see Lincoln, Y.S. & Denzin, N.K. (1994) 'The Fifth Moment' in N.K. Denzin & Y.S. Lincoln (eds) *Handbook of Qualitative Research* (London: Sage) p.581/2; feminist researchers have been at the forefront of criticising the concern with 'going native' as one that is based on a rejection of politicized research. For a brief overview see Punch, M (1994) 'Politics and Ethics in Qualitative Research' in N.K. Denzin & Y.S. Lincoln (eds) op cit, pp. 85–6.

and researched. Adopting the role of 'activist-researcher' to tackle this separation meant that there were occasions when I felt that it was appropriate to observe but other times when it was absolutely necessary to participate fully. In this sense, overcoming the gap between researcher and researched was not solely a question of engaging in dialogue thereby ascertaining common values, but was also a matter of engaging in common action for a common goal of a Social Europe.

I adopted a more observational role at the meetings and while some journalists experienced some antipathy from the participants, it seemed that my presence as an activist allowed me to record these events. It also meant that I was called upon to contribute information about the UK even when my intention had been simply to listen and observe. These events were also an opportunity to experience the intangible elements of informal association such as sharing food, singing, and exchanging experiences and opinions. Given my absence from the marches, the mobilizations and meetings were key events of shared experience that helped to build the rapport with participants that is crucial for quality data collection.[39] They also facilitated access to elements of the movement such as the informal dimension that would possibly have remained largely unconsidered and inaccessible had I adopted an approach more closely associated with that of a university based professionalized researcher.

After the summit in Cologne, I undertook a short visit to Munich and to the ALSO in Oldenburg. In addition to carrying out interviews during these trips, I was able to observe and participate in evaluating the Cologne events. In Munich this took place through a meeting of the local coordinating committee while in Oldenburg it was through informal discussions in the unemployed centre and a local bar. In Oldenburg, I was also able to find out about the centre and its place within the local unemployed mobilizations and to locate it more accurately within the wider national and European networks. In this sense I was engaged in the same learning process as many activists who also undertook such visits. Before leaving Oldenburg, I agreed to try and stay in contact with the ALSO and this involved sending and receiving information that was useful in compiling chapters four to six. Such visits involved receiving hospitality from local activists and this enabled access to the more informal dimension of the European Marches.

For my visit to Paris I decided to spend only part of the time staying with old friends and took up Yvonne Rocomaure's offer of hospitality and also spent time with Nassera Abbed who it turned out was well acquainted with several of my friends. Relations in the field are assisted by the researcher being sociable and the collection of quality data can be helped greatly by the formation of trust generated through exchanging personal experiences and opinions.[40] In this sense, as well as offering the chance to visit the AC! and SUD offices and to take part in informal discussions and meetings with local activists, the week in Paris was also an opportunity for sharing experiences of claiming benefits and of insecure work. Such discussions also extended into areas of personal as well as political life. This was also the case when

39   Jorgensen (1989) *op cit.*
40   Hammersley & Atkinson (1995) *op cit.*; Burgess, R. (1994) *In the Field: an introduction to field research* (London: Allen & Unwin).

activists from Brighton, Chrystelle from Paris, and Antonino from Cosenza visited Bristol on different occasions. These contacts were made initially at the counter-summit events and gave rise to cheerful reunions at subsequent events and were maintained in the meantime by sporadic e-mails and phone calls that exchanged information about mobilizations, meetings and more personal information.

Selecting Respondents and Conducting Interviews

Although the fringes of the events provided excellent opportunities to engage in informal conversations, these were often abruptly curtailed as the participants were drawn back into the formal sessions. Nevertheless, they provided a good chance to meet and converse with key informants with whom I could enter into a more in depth dialogue. The answer to the 'crucial issue' (of) 'who should be interviewed'?(p. 133)[41] was governed by practical as well as methodological concerns. In line with my 'snowballing' approach to data collection, the knowledge that I gained of the European Marches from participation and documentary sources enabled me to identify a number of key informants from across the various elements of the social movement and from its main constituent organizations and countries. This initial list was supplemented by a small number of interviewees that were either recommended to me by activists, informally selected by an organization's delegation, or simply invited along by the initially chosen respondent. I provide a chronological list of those interviewed including their affiliations, and the location and language in which the interview was conducted in the Appendix.[42]

Who actually participated in the interviews was also influenced by who was able and available. This may appear a somewhat obvious observation, but there was a question of finding a common language and also of finding a suitable location. My initial strategy of interviewing participants on the fringes of the 'Parliament' fell apart due to the lack of suitable space and the rather hectic character of the event. I promptly decided to arrange the interviews at a later date and in trade union and unemployed centres as well as in workplaces and homes. Consequently, about half of the interviews were with activists from Germany and France where the counter-summit events that I attended took place, but I also interviewed participants from Belgium, Holland and Italy that were amongst the other major participating countries.

In chapters four to six, I use the label 'prominent activist' for participants who took on tasks such as providing the opening address at the 'Assembly', speaking at the press conferences, writing analytical articles and carrying out important tasks such as overseeing the *Canal Marche* video project. Other activists were identified due to the prominent role they took in a particular event such as chairing a session of the conference in Cologne (Willi Lubkes) or the 'Parliament' (Laurent Guilloteau) or in the national and local march support committees (Andy Robertson, Barbara Trowe). I also emphasized interviewing the European Marchers (Nassera Abbed,

---

41   Hammersley & Atkinson (1995) *op cit.*

42   The extracts from the interviews that appear in the text of chapters four, five and six were translated from the original language into English by the author.

Denise Wood) as well as the locally based grass roots activists that took part in the European mobilizations and meetings (Yvonne Rocomaure, Andi Dallmann). Most of those interviewed were approached face to face while others were initially contacted by e-mail, post or phone. Of all those activists approached, only one failed to reply, one refused outright, and one MEP suggested a more appropriate party contact. This high rate of positive response was indicative of the openness of the movement and of the general enthusiasm to share information, experiences and ideas.

Six of the respondents were interviewed in pairs otherwise the interviews were on a one to one basis and in the case of the representatives of the WAC it was agreed that other activists sit in on the discussion. With the agreement of the respondents, the interviews were recorded on mini-disc and ranged in length from about forty five minutes to about two hours forty five minutes. During the longest interview it was the participants that stressed the need to continue the interview with reassurances that I would catch the last tram back to my accommodation.

In accordance with my methodological approach the interviews were both dialogical and interventionist.[43] Although I developed some preliminary ideas for matters to raise during the interviews based around themes arising from my initial investigation, my outlook was that these must not serve to limit or suppress the participant's agenda. This meant that I tried to be open to the possible discrepancies between my initial conceptions and the participants' accounts of the European Marches and its place in the wider struggle. As a result of earlier interviews, I was able to develop more useful lines of questioning and to address the themes that had been raised.

I also presented as many of the participants as possible with a photocopy of my journal article on the struggle for a Social Europe and subsequently with a list of conference papers and received several requests for copies. This was an indication that while the interviews were focused mainly around the participants' descriptions and explanations of situations and events there was also a discussion element that attempted to evaluate the broader social and political situation. Ailko van der Veen, for example, admitted that he had partially agreed to do the interview as it provided him with an opportunity to reflect on these issues and this was the reason why he had invited Piet van der Lende to contribute. The role of 'activist-researcher' facilitated such a discussion in that it attempted consciously to counteract the hierarchical structure of the conventional researcher-respondent relationship.[44] However, actually operationalizing this approach did not necessarily involve challenging the researcher's authority,[45] in that this implies a passivity and respect for such authority that was by no means evident amongst the participants.

---

43   Burawoy, (1998) *op cit.*
44   Harvey (1990) *op cit.*
45   Wasserfall, R.R. (1997) 'Reflexivity, feminism, and difference', in R. Hertz (ed) *Reflexivity and Voice* (Thousand Oaks, CA: Sage).

Documentary Sources

In contrast to the mobilizations at the summits of global institutions such as the WTO, the G8 and the IMF, I was unable to unearth many secondary sources such as newspaper reports or journal articles reporting or analyzing the mobilizations at the EU summits. This was particularly the case in the English language publications to which I had primary access and orientation. However, there were more such reports and articles relating to the unemployed mobilizations in France and to a lesser extent in Germany. My empirical investigation drew more heavily on primary documentary sources including printed leaflets, booklets, journals and declarations and electronic communications such as e-mails and the websites of the European Marches and its constituent organizations. I also made use of the materials through which the European Marches represented itself to a wider audience such as the videos produced by the *Canal Marche* project and its published books. When writing chapters four to six on the European Marches and the wider movement struggling for a Social Europe, to which I now turn, I attempted to make reference to as many materials as possible that are available on the Internet. This is in order to provide the reader with the possibility to verify their accuracy and to read them in more detail.

Chapter 4

Protesting Europe: the European Marches to Amsterdam, Cologne and Nice

What has it added to you being involved in something European wide? Or what would you lose if you stayed in Belgium?

What we would lose is the understanding that this is something that goes on worldwide. That the EU is one of the key actors in what goes on in our lives everyday and it influences a great deal of what our future will be like if we let it. So I think we would feel more isolated as we feel much stronger when we have a lot of other people telling us that we are living the same shit and we are fighting the same shit. And we know we are right because everybody else in the other countries are doing the same and thinking the same. Also it can help to create the resistance by having new ideas of how to fight.[1]

In this chapter I focus on the European Marches, and the transnational mobilizations at the EU summits in Amsterdam, Cologne and Nice at which they culminated. I present them as the products of a process of internationalizing protests against the social consequences of neoliberal globalization that were already occurring within nation states. In this sense, the construction of these mobilizations showed some similarity with the formation of other similar transnational alliances which, it was argued, have only been possible when and where there are already significant mobilizations and pre-existing organizations on which the successful construction of transnational alliances has been reliant.[2]

Therefore, this chapter not only examines the transnational mobilizations around the EU summits, but also outlines the national mobilizations out of, and through which, they developed. This also enables an appreciation of how the complex multi-level structure of the EU works in relation to social movement mobilization. As Lahusen argued,[3] the European level does not replace the national and local, but operates alongside them thereby producing a complex multi-level political opportunity structure (POS). This means that the European Marches provides an interesting example of how the high profile and highly mediatized political events of the EU summits might have provided a structural opportunity for contentious mobilizations to be developed.[4] Moreover, it also shows the possibilities and limits for

---

1   Excerpt from interview with Corinne Barella.
2   Bandy & Smith (2005) *op cit.*
3   Lahusen, C. (2004) 'Joining the Cocktail Circuit: Social Movement Organizations at the European Union', *Mobilization*, 9 (1) pp. 55–71.
4   *Ibid.*

'modeling' across borders the goals and forms of protest found in the mobilizations in France out of which the European Marches originated.[5]

However, this chapter is not only concerned with how the POS of the EU is facilitating the production of transnational mobilization and the diffusion of protest across borders, it is also about its agents. These include the '*entrepreneurs politiques*' [political entrepreneurs] (p. 464) who succeeded in achieving a paradoxical situation in which those deemed least able to engage in collective action (the unemployed) led the way in developing the Europeanization of protest action around social issues.[6] What is notable about these individuals and their organisations is that they were precisely those who were not part of the 'cocktail circuit' (p. 57) which characterizes the way that social movement organizations are encouraged to operate as dependent lobbyists in the EU.[7] In other words, they were not enmeshed in its integrationist project, its ideology of social pacts and social dialogue and its institutional machinery of patronage. Indeed, they saw the opportunity for mobilizing around key social issues presented by just such an integration of the ETUC that was largely reliant on lobbying and expressed little dissent from the competitiveness agenda advanced by its social partner of business which was dominating the integration process.[8] The ETUC was also thereby linking itself to EU officialdom and denying itself the 'tactic of mobilization that is the most familiar and powerful weapon its constituents possess at the national level' (p. 250). Moreover, the European Marches also filled the real mobilization gap left by the prevalence of 'virtual representation' (p. 235) of the unemployed and other 'excluded' groups at the EU level which also privileged the lobbying tactic.[9]

The successful movement of the unemployed in France gave its leaders the legitimacy to play a decisive role in the European Marches.[10] This legitimacy was the first characteristic of successful 'brokerage' which, Tarrow argued, has been one of the key mechanisms through which transnational networks around international institutions have been formed. Brokerage is the capacity for 'making connections between otherwise unconnected domestic actors in a way that produces at least a temporary political identity that did not exist before' (p. 248).[11] Various characteristics of skilled brokerage[12] were evident in the process of internationalizing protests further evidence of which is manifested in subsequent chapters.

Leading activists were involved in the translation of grievances and action forms across sectors and borders which was expressed in the multiple foci and participation of the marches and other protest events and the variety of actions they encompassed. The common events such as the *Assises* as well as the demonstrations, days of action, and the marches themselves enabled a process of education and socialization

---

5   Tarrow (2001) *op cit.*

6   Chabanet (2002) *op cit.*

7   Lahusen (2004) *op cit.*

8   Mazey, S. & Richardson, J. (1997) 'Policy Framing: Interest Groups and the lead up to 1996 Inter-Governmental Conference', *West European Politics*, 20 (3) pp. 111–133.

9   Tarrow (2001) *op cit.*

10   Chabanet (2002) *op cit.*

11   Tarrow (2001) *op cit.*

12   see Bandy & Smith (2005) *op cit.* pp. 240–2.

of participants into a common framework of a Social Europe. The *Assises* at which the European Marches were launched were also important 'coalition forums' (pp. 243–4)[13] at which the commitment of constituent organizations was codified through the formulation of common documents and declarations. Finally, the coalition brokers did not so much manage internal conflict as seek to avoid it through focusing attention on practical organizational tasks as well as by developing a supple form of organization which could encompass the plurality of perspectives amongst the participating organizations.[14]

The European Marches were an early example of the formation of a transnational network which developed the 'flexible, democratic, organizational culture' (pp. 244–5) which has contributed to the successful practice of transnational coalition building.[15] However, this was a network with a centre: a European Co-ordinating Committee which provided some strategic direction and fulfilled functional tasks. Nevertheless, the network was loose enough to allow the largely autonomous functioning of the marches and to enable the participation of the grass roots activists involved in local and national social movement organizations (SMO) that played a significant role in the mobilizations. In this sense, the experience of the European Marches confirmed the argument that 'organisations do, indeed, matter' (p. 116) in the formation of transnational mobilizations in that they play a crucial role in enlisting the participation of non-local protestors.[16]

This networked mode of organization was not without its tensions and its problems, yet the attempt to formalize the network and thereby make progress towards becoming a transnational social movement organization (TSMO) was unsuccessful. This centralization did not mobilize additional material resources and also, perhaps, jeopardized the mobilization of the non-material resources that the network form had facilitated. This weak institutional capacity was one of the main difficulties which militated against the durability of the European Marches Network.[17]

The lack of sufficient funding associated with this institutional weakness remained a significant ongoing problem for the European Marches especially in relation to overcoming the practical barriers to transnational collective action. However, the European Marches did prove adept in finding innovative ways of addressing the 'practical' (p. 41), 'psychological' (p. 42) and 'political' (p. 42) barriers to transnational mobilization.[18] The practical issues of distance, time and cost were tackled by deploying an innovative repertoire of action.

The European Marches were regarded as paradoxical in that they combined a traditional form of action whilst utilizing modern communication technologies.[19]

---

13   *Ibid.*

14   Chabanet (2002) *op cit.*

15   Bandy & Smith (2005) *op cit.*

16   Fisher, D. R. et al (2005) 'How do Organizations Matter? Mobilization and Support for Participants at Five Globalization Protests', *Social Problems*, 52 (1) pp. 102–121.

17   Chabanet (2002) *op cit.*

18   Bédoyan, I. , Van Aelst, P. & Walgrave, S. (2004) 'Limitations and Possibilities of Transnational Mobilization: The Case of EU Summit Protestors in Brussels, 2001', *Mobilization*, 9 (1) pp. 39–54.

19   Chabanet (2002) *op cit.*

The marches mobilized the time resources of the unemployed while the internet and emails facilitated the affordable exchange of information across distance. The 'free train' actions addressed the problem of mobilizing participants across distance, while the 'decentralized days of action' mobilized participants in their locality using the internet to overcome the distance between them. The openness of the network form to the grass roots activists proved very effective in mobilizing non-material resources. The European Co-ordinations and the *Assises* generated goodwill and commitment to the mobilizations while tapping into and revitalizing the latent spirit of internationalism present amongst activists. These events and the marches were formed not only through formal networks, but also inter-personal networks (see chapter 5) whose affective quality served to reinforce the capacity to mobilize.

These inter-personal networks also began to address the deficit of personal interaction amongst activists from different countries which was a manifestation of the 'psychological distance' (p. 42) which impeded transnational mobilization.[20] The 'lack of a transnational European public' (p. 42) was also tackled by the march form which generated deliberative spaces in the localities they passed through in which the question of a Social Europe was debated. The strongly symbolic character of the marches and the forms of action they adopted also drew the media attention which was required to assist in the framing of social issues in European terms. Moreover, the adoption of a discourse of rights was a powerful 'cross-cultural frame' (p. 42) which further enabled transnational mobilization. This framing process was reliant upon the generation and exchange of information amongst activists and in this sense resembles the kind of 'information politics' practised by transnational activist networks (TANs).[21] This and other forms of politics associated with TANs also appeared to be adopted by the European Marches to overcome the political obstacle of the EU's lack of openness to contentious forms of politics.

The European Marches adopted '*une logique d'exposition*' [a logic of exhibition] (p.475) which utilized the media to make the experiences and the demands of the unemployed visible in the public sphere.[22] This was reinforced by the films (see chapter 5) which documented the forceful emotional experience of the marches so making use of testimony, a notable element of 'information politics' (pp. 18–22), which served to humanize and thereby politicize issues which had been presented as technical matters by international institutions.

The European Marches also resembled the 'symbolic politics' (pp. 22–3)[23] of TANs in that they utilized the Intergovernmental Conferences (IGCs) as highly symbolic events around which to mobilize and thereby intervene in the framing process through which the central 'European' problems were defined. In this sense, the European Marches were engaged in the production and dissemination of a 'rival meta-idea' (p. 125) to the 'competitiveness' (p. 123) frame which was dominant at

20   Bédoyan, I. et al, (2004) *op cit.*

21   Keck, M. E. & Sikkink, K. (1998) *Activists beyond Borders: Advocacy Networks in International Politics* (Ithaca & London: Cornell University Press).

22   Chabanet (2002) *op cit.*

23   Keck & Sikkink (1998) *op cit.*

the IGCs in the late 1990s.[24] In other words, the European Marches were a strongly symbolic manifestation of a 'solidarity' frame for future European development (see chapter 5).

It has been argued that the main organizers of the European Marches chose deliberately *'la voie de la respectabilité'* [the route of respectability] (p. 476) mobilizing a small yet highly symbolic group of excluded citizens so as to appeal to public opinion.[25] This focus on the moral dimension of 'leverage politics' (pp. 23–4) through shaming institutional actors[26] was a central element of the European Marches. The marches made it evident that unemployment was not a matter of individual culpability and therefore individual shame, but a matter of state culpability and therefore government shame over collective inaction. However, this moral dimension of mobilization did not limit unduly the action repertoire of the European Marches. The mobilization of moral outrage enabled the deployment of more militant forms of action. Capturing the moral highground enabled the marchers to push against the boundaries of legality and also challenged the state's capacity for severe repression. Therefore, the European Marches while encompassing the 'conventional' and at times veering close to the 'violent' repertoires of action, focused mainly on developing 'disruptive' forms of protest action.[27]

The more large-scale mobilizations at the summit meetings and the popular assemblies which were held alongside them can also be considered as forms of 'accountability politics' (pp. 24–5)[28] which attempted to hold powerful yet undemocratic decision-making bodies to account and also embodied an alternative more democratic and popular mechanism. This could also be seen in the way that the European Marches utilized the mechanism of 'institutional appropriation' (p. 248) to bolster its own legitimacy.[29] It did so by making links with sympathetic Members of the European Parliament (MEP) active in the 'Convention for Full Employment' (see chapter 6).

The Road to Amsterdam

The first set of European Marches was born out of the nationally based economic and social struggles against rising levels of unemployment and poverty that came to be associated with the process of EMU and in particular with the austerity measures related to the application of the convergence criteria. These measures not only led to increasing public disenchantment with the idea of 'Europe', but also resulted in outbreaks of intense social unrest across the continent in opposition to welfare

---

24   Mazey & Richardson (1996) *op cit.*

25   Chabanet (2002) *op cit.*

26   Keck & Sikkink (1998) *op cit.*

27   Tarrow, S. (1998) *Power in Movement* (Second Edition) (Cambridge: Cambridge University Press), pp. 93-100.

28   Keck & Sikkink *op cit.*

29   Tarrow (2001) *op cit.*

reform and public sector pay limits.[30] In Germany, austerity programmes contributed to the production of social polarization on a scale not seen since before the war.[31] Unemployment soared to five million, but the *Bundnisse für Arbeit* [Alliance for Jobs] was abandoned in the face of widespread strikes opposing welfare reforms and a three hundred and fifty thousand strong demonstration in Berlin in June 1996.[32] The DGB also voted to support the largest ever protests by students against underfunding, cuts and overcrowding in education.[33] The Italian Government's plan to reform pension provision was opposed by a month long series of militant protest demonstrations that expressed discontent with the response of established trade unions as well as with the reforms.[34] There was also opposition to privatization and public sector pay restraint that saw the emergence of rank and file trade union organisations such as the COBAS that were at the forefront of organizing strikes in the public sector.[35] Even in the UK, where economic and social struggle had taken a serious downturn, there were unofficial disputes in support of sacked workers and campaigns by the unemployed against welfare reforms.[36]

The most profound and widespread opposition was seen in France in 1995. The Juppé plan to reform social security and a public sector pay freeze resulted in a wave of one day public sector strikes involving up to five million workers and indefinite strikes concentrated in the transport, communication and energy sectors. There were also massive street demonstrations that drew support from over two million participants.[37] Solidarity rallies with the French strikers were organized in Rome, Athens and Berlin and the French influence on the German protests led to their participants displaying a willingness to go beyond the usual orderly forms of action.[38] The French strikes displayed a tendency to link up with other sectors involved in resistance[39] and the strikers received the active support of militants from networks like AC! that was mainly composed of local associations of unemployed

30   Taylor, G. & Mathers, A. (2002) 'The politics of European integration: a European labour movement in the making?' *Capital & Class* 78 pp. 39–60.

31   Callinicos, A. (2001b) 'The Contradictions of European Monetary Union' in W. Bonefeld (ed) *The Politics of Europe: Monetary Union and Class* (Basingstoke: Palgrave).

32   Schauer, H. (1997) 'Protest und Verwirrung', in P. Bourdieu, C. Debons, D. Hensche, B. Lutz u.a. *Perspektiven des Protests* (Hamburg: VSA-Verlag).

33   Budd, A. (2001) 'Western Europe', in E. Bircham & J. Charlton (eds) *Anti-Capitalism: a guide to the movement* (London: Bookmarks).

34   Behan, T. (1999) 'The return of Italian Communism?' *International Socialism* 2 (84) pp. 101–8.

35   Gall, G. (1995) 'The emergence of a rank and file movement: the Comitati di Base in the Italian worker's movement *Capital & Class* 55 pp. 9–20.

36   Levidow, L. (2000) 'UK trade unions: resisting or legitimizing flexploitation' available at <*http://www.cseweb.org.uk/past/globe.html#levidow* > accessed on 20/7/2000.

37   Jeffreys, S. (1996) 'France 1995: the backward march of labour halted? *Capital & Class* 59 pp. 7–21.

38   Schauer (1997) *op cit.*

39   Wolfreys, J. (1999) 'Class struggles in France' *International Socialism* 2 (84) pp. 31–68.

militants that had grown out of a set of national marches against unemployment in 1994.[40]

Leading militants in AC! and its union ally SUD became increasingly aware of the European dimension to the problems faced by the French unemployed and workers and the limits this placed on nationally based campaigns. In response they decided that mobilizing at the European level was necessary and therefore in 1996 they took up the idea for the European Marches to Amsterdam. The proponents argued that such an initiative was necessary due to the lack of an effective response to unemployment and poverty by the established institutional actors such as the trade unions. Michel Rousseau, an official in the French union SUD and a prominent activist in the European Marches recalled that,

> After the various national experiences like that of AC! in France the need was felt to go beyond the national borders to find how to organize together at the European level. … But it's true that up to the European Marches very little had been done in relation to unemployment at the European level. Well it has to be stated that the unions at the European level, and that includes both national unions and the ETUC, have either been surprised by it or they haven't known how to respond to it. But we haven't had any strong mobilizations at the European level against the neo-liberal policies that have brought us twenty million unemployed and almost sixty million living in poverty. So it's the lack of a response from what existed before which has brought about the European Marches and above all to do something about this scandal of unemployment.[41]

Representatives of AC! made the initial proposal for the European Marches to Amsterdam at a small meeting in Turin on the occasion of the EU summit in early 1996. Apart from AC! those in attendance included representatives from the unemployed information centre of the Italian union CGIL, from the Spanish union CGT, as well as a writer from the German trade union journal 'Express'.[42] After national consultation, the decision to launch the marches was finally taken at a meeting of approximately twenty five representatives of supporting organizations in Florence on the occasion of the EU summit in June 1996.

The Florence Appeal was signed subsequently by organizations from across the continent representing a range of social and political forces. These included the British network of unemployed centres; the Spanish union CGT and association 'Baladre'; the Italian unions CGIL and COBAS and the political organization RC; the German Greens and PDS; and in France three of the four national unemployed associations, AC!, MNCP, APEIS as well as union federations such as the G10, the FSU and the left wing of the CFDT. At the European level, NGOs such as the ENU and Kairos Europe also made known their support.[43] Despite these declarations of

---

40   Schmitt, B. & Spadoni, P. (eds) (2000) *Les sentiers de la colère* (Paris: L'esprit frappeur).

41   Excerpt from interview with Michel Rousseau.

42   'Euromarches – Appel européen de Turin pour une initiative de grande ampleur contre le chômage' available at <*www.euromarches.org/francais/96/turina1.htm*> accessed on 17/01/2001.

43   'Le point après la réunion de Florence fin juin 96' available at <*www.euromarches. org/francais/96/flo2.htm*> accessed on 17/01/2001.

support there was a major concern with funding the marches, as the budget for the French legs alone was approximately a million francs.[44] Money was not forthcoming at the European level because, while the ENU conference had voted to support the marches, this network did not possess the funds necessary to finance them.[45] The main avenue for financial support, the large trade unions and federations, remained closed off. Emilio Gabaglio, the General Secretary of the ETUC, sent a memo to affiliates stating that groups opposed to ETUC policy were supporting the marches and that therefore affiliates should keep their distance.[46]

The decision to hold the marches was taken almost a year prior to their planned starting date and in the interim period the necessary political and logistical infrastructure was put in place. The sheer size and scope of the initiative, and the antipathy shown by the ETUC, meant that there was no single organization that had the resources to shape the marches or the capacity to control their message. Indeed the strategy that was articulated by prominent activists such as Michel Rousseau was that to ensure a successful mobilization it was necessary to overcome ideological and policy differences and so develop a broad alliance of participating organizations:

> The concept of the European Marches Network has always been to say that even if there are tensions it is necessary to find the spaces where we can work together. Our goal was, in the absence of action against the neoliberal policies in Europe, to find a place where trade unionists, people in associations and people in parties could join together to mobilize against unemployment.[47]

In the run up to the Amsterdam marches such a space was indeed developed. The various committees that sprung up to support the marchers at the European, national and local levels were notable for the plurality of participating organizations and for generating a discernible spirit of goodwill for the project. Although the broad parameters for the marches were agreed at the European level, there was a great deal of organizational and political space left for the grass roots activists to mould the character of the marches in their locality. Indeed the lack of resources at the European level meant that the participation of activists from locally based organizations was vital to the success of the marches.

The first European level organizational meeting, held in Paris on 21–22 September 1996, enabled a wide-ranging debate on the basic objectives of the European Marches. It was agreed that the marches would be politically independent and open to all organizations concerned with its main issues. A working group drawn from participants from several countries made suggestions for developing the Florence

---

44   'European Marches against Unemployment, Job Insecurity and Social Exclusion March Organisation Preliminary meetings of 22/23 February 1997' available at <*www- pluto. informatik.uni-oldenburg.de/~also/eusepa64.htm*> accessed on 07/08/2001.

45   'Minutes of the European Co-ordination Meeting held in Brussels on November 30 1996' available at <*www.euromarches.org/english/96/brup1.htm*> accessed on 20/08/2001.

46   'European Marches against unemployment. Memo from ETUC General Secretary, Emilio Gabaglio, to General Secretaries of affiliated unions'. Copy of memo taken from EuroMarsch-Komitee (Duisburg) *Euromarsch in Duisburg* Unpublished document.

47   Excerpt from interview with Michel Rousseau.

Appeal that was formulated into a draft manifesto. This was subject to debate and amendments by the final plenary session.[48] The spirit of goodwill that existed in the initial meetings was recognized by one activist who took part in the first official European Coordinating Committee meeting held in Paris in November 1996:

> In the November we went to Paris and there were about forty people there and from the beginning there was a climate of co-operation. In my experience it is particularly the case for left wing groups that they are normally quite inward looking and here it was really different. There were people from different ideological positions and they entered into a dialogue and found a form of working together. And that was the spirit that it began with.[49]

The forty participants came from eight countries (Belgium, Holland, Ireland, UK, Germany, Switzerland, Spain, and France) ranging from unions like the Spanish CGT and the French SUD, through unemployed associations such as the Irish INOU, and Swiss ADC, to political organizations such as the German PDS. According to the minutes the meeting was to deal with technical issues and focused on making decisions on matters such as adopting a common logo of a white foot on a black background and ensuring that each march had an international participation. In line with its co-ordinating role, a lot of time was spent exchanging information about the progress made in organizing the marches in each of the countries and decisions were made about the dates and rendezvous points for the various marches. The initial arrangements for the first *Assises* were made and it was decided that its function was to enable the militants to explain about their particular situation, to engage in debate and to organize the marches jointly.[50]

Before the marches departed, a final European Co-ordinating Committee was held in Brussels on 22 March 1997. It was agreed to open an office in Paris staffed by French militants and funded by their associations and this office produced and distributed posters, badges, and t-shirts. However, the plans for more complicated initiatives such as a multilingual European journal and website were not carried through largely due to the lack of resources available at the European level to fund the necessary translations. Information was also exchanged about the negative response of the trade union movement to the marches at the European level and the more positive links made with some of the national unions within the five countries represented at the meeting (Belgium, France, Germany, Finland and Netherlands).[51] Despite European co-ordination, prominent activists considered the marches as a leap in the dark and their success relied heavily on an impulse from the grass roots activists in the various countries, regions and localities. Angela Klein, a leading militant in the German European Marches recollected that,

---

48   'Communique concerning the Florence Appeal' available at <*www-pluto.informatik. uni-oldenburg.de/~also/eusepar3.htm*> accessed on 07/08/2001.

49   Excerpt from interview with Joachim Glund.

50   'Minutes of the European Co-ordination Meeting held in Brussels on November 30 1996' available at <*www.euromarches.org/english/96/brup1.htm*> accessed on 20/08/2001.

51   'Courrier du 27 mars 1997' available at <*http://eurplace.org/diba/cig/marcia5corr. html*> accessed on 26/08/1998.

We said that it was good to have a central initiative but we had little or no idea what it would mean to carry through the marches and who we would work with. We discovered all this. In any case the idea struck a chord especially amongst the unemployed and there was a bit of a spontaneous movement and a kind of snowball effect.[52]

The Florence Appeal called for national and local march support committees to be set up and the first national committee meetings in the UK and Germany were held in late October 1996. Their first task was to decide on the number of marches and marchers that it was feasible to mobilize and then to raise funds to support them. The first UK national committee meeting was held in Manchester and was attended by fifty two people drawn from unemployed associations, trade unions and left wing parties. The meeting elected a national steering group that met periodically to co-ordinate the marches and fundraising.[53] However, the steering group worked with limited resources with the result that sympathetic local TUCs were relied upon heavily to provide accommodation for the marchers. This meant that the organizers even had to change the route of the marches to avoid areas showing insufficient support or hostility.[54] This response was due partially to a withdrawal of support by the TUC backed Unemployed Workers Combine after TUC General Secretary, John Monks, labelled the marches as 'anti-Maastricht'.[55]

The initial German Co-ordinating Committee meeting in Hanover brought together twenty participants from unemployed and migrants associations, trade unions, and left wing and Green Parties. It agreed to aim to mobilize a broad spectrum of supporters in order to build a 'Europe from below'. It set up a national secretariat to manage the organization and the funding of the marches and a national conference to give a political dynamic to the campaign.[56] After regional consultation, the second national meeting agreed to hold four marches, but this was later reduced to three as the lack of central funding meant that where there was little local support the marches were not carried through.[57] There were similar funding problems in Germany to those experienced in the UK as the DGB withheld support on the grounds that the marches were 'anti-European': because they were supported by groups in France and Spain that were allegedly 'anarchist, nationalist and right wing extremists'.[58]

In France, where mobilization was most developed, the marches received support from radical union federations such as the G10 Solidaires as well as critical

---

52   Excerpt from interview with Angela Klein.

53   'Report and Decisions of Meeting to Discuss the European Marches against Unemployment, Job Insecurity and Exclusion' available at <*www-pluto.informatik.uni-oldenburg.de/~also/eusepa31.htm*> accessed on 07/08/2001.

54   Information from interview with Andy Robertson.

55   'Extract from TUC Executive Committee Document – 19 February 1997', Copy of document taken from EuroMarsch-Komitee (Duisburg) *op cit.*

56   'Infos der BRD-Koordination. Protokoll vom 1. Treffen' available at <*www-pluto.informatik.uni-oldenburg.de/~also/eusepa13.htm*> accessed on 08/08/2001

57   Information from interview with Angela Klein.

58   'Europäische Märsche gegen Erwerbslosigkeit, ungeschützte Beschäftigung und Ausgrenzung'. Letter from IG Metall Executive to all branches 18 April 1997. Copy of document taken from EuroMarsch-Komitee (Duisburg) *op cit.*

tendencies within the more mainstream CFDT. However, the CGT informed the French Co-ordinating Committee that it would not support the marches as it wished to become an affiliate of the ETUC and as a result its unemployed committees did not participate in the marches. Nevertheless, the other main unemployed associations were involved alongside other associations representing the 'excluded' such as DD! and DAL.[59] The marches also received support from Left and Green political parties as well as an appeal signed by intellectuals.[60] The French Co-ordinating Committee raised funds from its union supporters, by individual sponsorship and by the marchers selling copies of the journal that publicized the European marches titled *À Amsterdam* [To Amsterdam] and through sales of a book titled *Europe: Modes D'Emploi* [Europe: Ways of Working]. This funding enabled it to provide administrative and political support for the marches elsewhere with French militants travelling to join the marches from Bosnia and the UK and Christophe Aguiton, a leading militant in SUD, travelling to Ireland to address the rally at which the march was launched.[61]

The marches were launched on 14 April 1997 with departure points as far spread as Ivalo (Finland) in the North, Dublin (Ireland) in the West, Tuzla (Bosnia) in the East and Tangiers (Morocco) in the South.[62] In the UK, a veteran of the 1930s hunger marches greeted the marchers as they passed through Jarrow and the French militants too recalled the march in 1933 from Lille to Paris.[63] The UK marches were launched in London at the 'March for Social Justice' that brought trade unionists supporting the sacked Liverpool dockers together with ravers and environmental activists. This was an early indication that the 'Euromarchers' also aimed to link wider issues to their initial core concern with unemployment, job insecurity and exclusions. In Tuzla, a wreath was laid at the site of the ethnic cleansing of seventy one Bosnians and as the marches crossed over national borders there were actions to oppose immigration controls.[64] There were eventually eleven marches that snaked their way through Europe crossing countless borders before converging in Amsterdam.[65] Each leg had an international participation and was composed of between ten and a hundred permanent marchers. The marchers were mainly unemployed and in France included a contingent of homeless people.[66]

---

59   'Informations sur les marches' available at <*www-pluto.informatik.uni-oldenburg. de/~also/eusepa77.htm*> accessed on 07/08/2001.

60   Balibar, E. et al (1997) 'Appel De Soutien aux Marches en France', in Marches Européenes *Europe: Modes D'Emploi* (Paris: Editions Syllepse).

61   'Minutes of the European Co-ordination Meeting held in Brussels on November 30 1996' available at <*www.euromarches.org/english/96/brup1.htm*> accessed on 20/08/2000; Schmitt & Spadoni (eds) (2000) *op cit.*; 'Carnets des Marches Européenes' available at <*www. euromarches.org/francais/97/carnet.htm*> accessed on 17/01/2001.

62   Canal Marche (1997a) *Ils sont partis* No.2 (Paris: Canal Marche).

63   Dreyfus, M. (2000) 'Les marcheurs de la faim', in Schmitt & Spadoni (eds) *op cit.*

64   'Les Marches Européenes – Chronologie', available at <*www.euromarches.org/ chr.htm*> accessed on 17/01/2001; 'Carnets des Marches Européenes', available at <*www. euromarches.org/francais/97/carnet.htm*> accessed on 17/01/2001.

65   Canal Marche (1997b) *À Amsterdam* No.4 (Paris: Canal Marche).

66   Schmitt & Spadoni (eds) *op cit.*

As the marchers passed through the towns and cities en route they supported local economic and social struggles and carried out numerous actions. To oppose unemployment the marchers showed solidarity with workers struggling against job losses. They joined a picket line in Darlington, UK[67] and a rally by striking Renault carworkers in Vilvoorde, Belgium.[68] There were also more spectacular actions like that at Palencia in Spain where the 'Euromarches' blocked all the tills in a supermarket demanding a boycott of the products of a Belgian company that had recently made workers at its nearby chicken factory redundant.[69] There were also numerous occupations of job centres to oppose policies resulting in benefit cuts and the proliferation of low paid jobs. These spectacular actions were particularly widely employed in France where the marches were most strongly supported and these included a three hundred strong occupation of the *Château de Versailles* to protest about a new law on social cohesion. Banners demanding an end to inequalities were draped from the very balcony where in 1789 an end to privileges had been declared.[70] The 'Euromarchers' also generated local street demonstrations that attracted fifteen hundred people in Madrid, two to three thousand people in Barcelona, and a thousand people in Bayonne.[71]

Actions, meetings and social events to mark the passing of the marches through each locality were organized in liaison with local march support committees made up of grass roots activists. These committees also tended to involve a plurality of individuals and representatives of organizations. In Frankfurt, those involved came from unemployed organizations, left wing parties and unions, but there were also representatives from the Greens, a café for the homeless and a Turkish cultural association.[72] In Eindhoven, the committee was drawn from representatives of progressive churches, womens' organizations, migrant, youth, anti-racist, refugee and retired peoples' groups.[73]

These committees operated with a considerable degree of autonomy in that they were largely self-organized and self-funded. In Dortmund, Barbara Trowe, an unemployed activist, remembered asking for donations from local associations, unions, and parties. To mark the start of the marches, the local committee joined the picket line at a factory facing closure and a rally and a party were organized to greet the marchers. She recalled how these local committees were compelled to network with each other in order to keep abreast of the progress of the march and as the

---

67   Canal Marche (1997b) *op cit.*

68   Canal Marche (1997c) *Réunion de Bruxelles 22–23 Février 1997: Panorama des luttes européenes* No.1(Paris: Canal Marche).

69   'European March Diary', available at <*www.snore.org/archief/1997 ... erent-europe/marches/diary.html*> accessed on 30/09/1998.

70   Schmitt & Spadoni (eds) *op cit.*

71   'Carnets des Marches Européenes', available at <*www.euromarches.org/francais/97/carnet.htm*> accessed on 17/01/2001.

72   'Frankfurt Vorberietungen', *quer* August 1997.

73   'Eindhoven: Preparations for receiving the March in full swing' available at <*www.snore.org/archief/1997*> accessed on 30/09/1999.

marches crossed borders this involved creating links with local committees in other countries.[74]

As well as the space for initiatives taken by the local committees, there also proved to be a good deal of autonomy for the marchers to organize the conduct of the marches. There were daily assemblies at which the marchers made decisions about the actions to be carried out and allocated tasks such as speaking at meetings and giving interviews to the press. For the marchers this control over the conduct of the march was experienced as a form of direct democracy:

> The march was a real experience of democracy. That is to say that you found yourself in a situation in which you were directly confronted by democracy at the most concrete level. … It was necessary for us to learn how to regulate life on an everyday level. … For all of the small posts that I call the posts of power, it was necessary to decide who should occupy them and how.[75]

The grass roots control of the marches led, on occasions, to conflict between the marchers and their political supporters. In Chambery, France where the mayor, an ex-socialist minister, had arranged a reception in the town hall, the marchers threatened to camp in front of it in support of a tenant threatened with an eviction notice issued from the Mayor's office.[76]

The situation of the marches and related initiatives in each country was exchanged and discussed at the final meeting of the European Co-ordinating Committee in Amsterdam on May 10 with delegations from France, Spain, Italy, Belgium, Holland and Germany. The final arrangements for the Amsterdam demonstration such as speakers and stewarding were made.[77]

The idea of pan-European mobilization struck a chord with European workers as ten thousand were mobilized in Brussels in support of the 'European Action Day for Full Employment' called by the ETUC.[78] On June 10, the 'Euromarchers' demonstrated in Paris alongside over forty thousand French trade unionists calling for 'Jobs for Europe'.[79] However, organized with many fewer resources, the fifty thousand strong turnout on the demonstration in Amsterdam was the peak of mobilization and much higher than the thirty thousand people expected by its organizers.[80] An important mobilizing role was played by the local march support committees that organized transport to Amsterdam and the diversity of participating

---

74   Information from interview with Barbara Trowe.

75   Excerpt from Interview: Carole Faure: in Schmitt & Spadoni (eds) (2000) *op cit.* p. 79 (author's translation).

76   Schmitt & Spadoni (2000) *op cit.*

77   '10th May minutes of the meeting of the Amsterdam Coordination Group' available at <www- pluto.informatik.uni-oldenburg.de/~also/eusep123.htm> accessed on 07/08/2001.

78   Dekelper, I. (1997) 'Pour une Europe <plus et plus vite> sociale' *L'Echo* 29 May.

79   ETUC (1997) *European Action Day 28/5/1997. The ETUC's Press Coverage* Brussels: ETUC: 18.

80   'Protokoll der 3.Bundeskoordination, 2. Marz in Hannover', available at <www-pluto.informatik.uni-oldenburg.de/~also/eusepa55.htm>, accessed on 08/08/2001.

organizations helped to ensure a broader as well as a larger mobilization. Barbara Trowe remembered that,

> From Duisburg we sent two buses to Amsterdam and the people on them were literally from fourteen year old 'Falken' (SPD youth), to sixty five year old works council members, mothers with kids, disabled. We got all of the relevant social groups involved.[81]

Despite the general feeling of anger amongst the marchers and demonstrators expressed in slogans like *Qui seme la misère, recolte la colère* [Who sows misery, reaps anger] (p. 94)[82] the demonstration was largely good-humoured and ended in singing and dancing in Dam Square.[83] However, there were some minor clashes with the police[84] after a large group of protestors from Italy was hemmed into the railway station by riot police after successfully having demanded free travel to Amsterdam by a mass occupation of Milan railway station. They refused to show their passports en route to assert their right to freedom of movement and to protest over immigration controls. Over a hundred were arrested and photographed before being released back onto the trains which then departed with riot police on board.[85] This action was co-ordinated by the *Ya Basta* [Enough Is Enough] network whose activists on the trains were in contact by mobile phone with their supporters in Italy. Information about the progress of the trains was transmitted via independent radio stations, the Internet and the mainstream media to pressurize for their safe and speedy return.[86]

The demonstration was led by the 'Euromarchers' who carried a huge banner with the slogan 'Against Unemployment, Job Insecurity, and Social Exclusion' written in a multitude of languages.[87] They were joined by trade unionists including the Renault strikers and the sacked Liverpool dockers, young people, pensioners, and environmentalists as well as a wide range of left wing political activists. There were contingents from every EU member state as well as from Eastern Europe, and even from other continents.[88] They had a variety of banners such as *Liberalisme: Chômage et Exclusion: Imposons L'Europe Sociale!* [Neoliberalism: Unemployment and Poverty: Let's Impose a Social Europe!][89] and chanted slogans such as 'People's Europe not Bankers Europe'.[90] This was a large and diverse mobilization bringing together grass roots militants that Piet van der Lende, an activist at an unemployed

---

81   Excerpt from interview with Barbara Trowe.

82   Schmitt & Spadoni (eds) (2000) *op cit.*

83   Paasch, R. (1997) 'Der Sternmarsch der Vergessenen' *Frankfurter Rundschau* 17 June.

84   Conradi, P. (1997) 'Street action: a British demonstrator joins protests over unemployment in Amsterdam?' *The Times* 15 June.

85   Movimento delle Tute Bianche Padova (1999) *'Les 'Invisibles': chomeurs, precaires, sans droits'* January.

86   *ibid*

87   Canal Marche (1997b) *op cit.*

88   *ibid*; Information from interview with Angela Klein.

89   Canal Marche (1997b) *op cit.*

90   Information from interview with Willi Lubkes.

centre based in Amsterdam, argued were united largely around the call for a Social Europe:

> In Amsterdam it was about a Social Europe, there was one focus with many different interpretations and people came from everywhere like 'Women on the Waterfront' and the Renault strikers all came with their own analysis but always with the same focus.[91]

At the rally, a speaker representing the Renault strikers stated that they had come to demonstrate for a Social Europe, for a job for all, and to work in and for a different Europe.[92] The rally was marked by speeches that were translated into several languages and a message of solidarity from Zapatista leader 'Marcos'[93] added to the general 'fever of internationalism'[94] expressed in banners such as *Arbeitslose Alle Länder Vereinigt Euch!* [Unemployed of the World Unite!].[95] Activists involved in them considered the European Marches and the demonstration to which they had led up as a new departure that inspired them to continue their particular struggle with a new elan. Piet van der Lende stated that his experience of the European Marches in Amsterdam,

> ... was very inspiring because of the international dimension, because of the necessity to seek coalitions with other groups, trade union groups, environmental groups, anti-racist groups. Because of the awareness of the necessity to make a total analysis of the social situation and the fact that the response was so big from other countries was also very inspiring.[96]

A fortnight after the demonstration in Amsterdam, a European Co-ordinating Committee meeting to evaluate the events was attended by about forty people from seven countries (Belgium, Holland, Germany, Spain, United Kingdom, Luxembourg, and France). The assessment was largely positive in that the aim of successfully mobilizing a joint European action on the themes of unemployment, poverty and a Social Europe with a high level of mobilization amongst the unemployed had been achieved.[97] However, the level of union involvement had been restricted by the unsympathetic attitude towards the marches displayed by the ETUC and some of its affiliates. Consequently, both the UK and German committees wrote to their respective trade union federations to clarify that the European Marches were not nationalist, but rather aimed to promote international action.[98] They were also not

---

91   Excerpt from interview with Piet van der Lende.

92   Canal Marche (1997b) *op cit.*

93   'Message du Commandant Marcos: La marche européene contre le chômage, la précarité, et les exclusions. Europe rebelle', available at <*www.multimania.com/ras/marches/fzln*> accessed on 23/11/1998.

94   Information from interview with Michel Rousseau.

95   'Euromarsch Nachlese', *quer* August 1997.

96   Excerpt from interview with Piet van der Lende.

97   'European Coordination Committee – Paris – Saturday 28 June 1997' available at <*www-pluto.informatik.uni-oldenburg.de/~also/eusep138.htm*> accessed on 07/01/2000.

98   EuroMarsch-Komitee (Duisburg) *op cit.*

opposed to the participation of the ETUC, but rather wished to work alongside it to mobilize at future EU summits:

> If such a poorly financially and organizationally resourced initiative such as the European Marches succeeded in mobilizing a mass demonstration of 50,000 people from across the whole EU, how many could the ETUC with more than 40 million people in its union federations mobilize for example in Luxembourg? ... We would bring our very weak force into such a European wide demonstration.[99]

The Road to Cologne

Following the success of the Amsterdam campaign, it was decided to formalize the European and national committees into the European Marches Network against Unemployment, Job Insecurity and Exclusions. Angela Klein recalled how this was not envisaged as a membership based organization based on subscriptions, but as a loose participatory network.

> The (Amsterdam) demonstration was a breakthrough and afterwards we had a European meeting and we decided to stay together. It was decided in Luxembourg how the Network should work and it had a very open form. The Network did not have a fixed structure. It was not an association. We could simply say that so and so was taking part, but it was open and they could leave at any time.[100]

Approximately a hundred people from eleven countries (Belgium, Denmark, France, Germany, Greece, Italy, Luxembourg, Netherlands, Spain, Sweden, and the UK) were present at a meeting in Luxembourg on 4–5 October 1997 at which it was agreed to set up a formal European Marches Network.[101] A constituent motion was adopted that committed the participants to an open and plural network with the aim of mobilizing all the unemployed and other grass roots associations alongside unions and other groups committed to the struggle against unemployment, job insecurity, and exclusions. It was decided to adopt a loose structure with decision-making by consensus rather than by majority voting and any decisions taken would not be enforceable upon organizations participating in the network. Major decisions for the network were to be taken by a European Co-ordinating Committee; attendance at which would be open and any administrative work would be ensured by a secretariat: a role taken on by the French Co-ordinating Committee. However, it was emphasized that the network did not amount to a new organization and in no way did it aim to replace existing European organizations such as the ENU or the ETUC.[102]

---

99   'Bundeskoordination Euromarsch an den DGB-Bundesvorstand sowie an die Vorstände der Einzelgewerkschaften vom 22.7.97' available at *<www-pluto.informatik.uni-oldenburg.de/~also/eusep141.htm>* accessed on 07/08/2001. (Author's translation.)

100   Excerpt from interview with Angela Klein.

101   'Coordination européene 4 & 5 octobre 1997/Luxembourg' available at *<www.euromarches.org/francais/97/luxp1.htm>* accessed on 17/01/2001.

102   'Marches Européenes/NEWS. October 1997' available at *<http://eurplace.org/diba/cig/marcia20.html>* accessed on 07/01/2000.

This declaration and the success of the Amsterdam campaign appeared to allay some of the concerns of the ETUC that tempered its initial unfriendly reaction and made no attempt to exclude a distinct European Marches contingent from the demonstration that it called at the 'Jobs Summit' in Luxembourg.[103] Thirty thousand trade unionists were mobilized,[104] and the European Marches formed its own contingent that, in contrast to the nationally grouped trade unionists, marched in an international block. Its supporters numbered about three thousand[105] some of whom were protected from the rain by bright yellow plastic ponchos bearing the logo of a foot on a black disc with the slogan underneath of *Chômage, ya basta!* [Unemployment, Enough is Enough!].[106]

Without the backing of the ETUC, there were much smaller demonstrations of a thousand people in Cardiff in June 1998[107] and two thousand people in Vienna in December 1998.[108] A sizeable group of French unemployed campaigners made the trip to Cardiff where the main slogan was '*No* to big business Europe! *Yes* to Jobs, Public Services and Democracy!'[109] In Vienna, a contingent of German unemployed activists braved the sub-zero temperatures alongside demonstrators from both Western and Eastern Europe and claimed *Es gibt genug für alle da!* ['There's enough there for everyone!'].[110] The relatively high level of French and German involvement in the European demonstrations indicated a growing consciousness of the European dimension amongst activists involved in significant national campaigns against unemployment and poverty and this provided a new impetus to the development of the mobilizations at the European level.

A wave of occupations of social security offices broke out in France in December 1997 in response to a cut in the traditional 'Christmas Bonus' for the unemployed. Beginning in Marseille, where the actions gained mass support, the occupations spread across the country and involved all of the four main organizations representing the unemployed. The campaign intensified with the declaration of a week of 'social emergency' that included mobilizations against homelessness and utility disconnections. The actions became major news through to the New Year and were reportedly supported by more than 70% of the population. In early January, Prime Minister Jospin made a T.V. appearance promising emergency aid, a new law

---

103   Information from interview with Angela Klein.

104   ETUC, '30,000-plus turnout to ETUC's call for jobs', *ETUC Report 30–97*, Brussels.

105   'Admin. Meeting held on Saturday 28 February 1998', *Euromarch Liaison Committee* Photocopied document, Undated.

106   'Succès numérique de la manifestation de Luxembourg', available at <*www.multimania.com/ras/marches/bilan20*> accessed on 23/11/1998.

107   Information from notes taken during participant observation of the Cardiff demonstration on 13 June 1998.

108   'The European movement goes on!', *Marches Européenes News (English version)* No.11 February 1999.

109   'Cardiff call for a demonstration, available at <*www.euromarches.org/english/98/Cardiff1.htm*> accessed on 20/08/2001.

110   'All together to Vienna', available at <*www.euromarches.org/english/98/vienna.htm*> accessed on 20/08/2001.

on social exclusion, and recommitted the Government to a 'society based on work'. This actually helped to intensify the campaign that increasingly placed demands for the right to an income alongside the right to work.

The main slogans heard on the local and national demonstrations became: *un revenu décent pour tous, sans conditions* [a decent income for all, without any strings] and *Un emploi c'est un droit, un revenu est un dû* [a job is my right, an income is my due]. The central demands, supported by all the main organizations representing the unemployed, focused on benefit increases and a right to an income for the under twenty fives. These demands were supported by actions that highlighted income inequalities such as occupying chic cafés, blocking supermarket tills to demand the free distribution of products, and repossessing goods seized by bailiffs. These spectacular actions were extended to support demands for rights to free access to transport, health care, and culture. Occupations extended to hospitals, cinemas, and even to railway lines to block the circulation of high-speed trains.[111]

The longer the unemployed mobilizations lasted the more links were made with other groups engaged in economic and social struggles and this contributed to a recognition amongst mainstream commentators that the mobilizations were taking the form of a 'popular movement' (p. 13).[112] In January 1998, the unemployed associations demonstrated alongside unions in favour of the thirty five hour week. Both trade unionists and the unemployed gave practical and political support to the church occupation by the *Sans Papiers* [without papers] migrants to avoid deportation. Unemployed activists organized alongside associations against homelessness to occupy vacant buildings. There were also joint occupations of universities by students alongside the unemployed. As the campaign became broader and more generalized the demands were formulated increasingly in terms of universal social rights at the forefront of which was the unconditional right to an income.[113]

The French campaign was relatively widely reported in other countries and in Germany it was instrumental to inspiring the trade union unemployed sections (KOS) to call for a series of monthly action days against unemployment that ran from February to September 1998.[114] The action days mustered consistently more than forty thousand people across four hundred towns and cities around the slogan of *Endlich auf der Strasse: die neue A-Klasse* [Finally on the streets – the new A-Class].[115]

---

111   Levy, C. & Aguiton,C. (1998) 'Les chômeurs desserent l'étau' *Le monde diplomatique* Février; Royall, F. (1998) 'Le mouvement des chômeurs de l'hiver 1997', *Modern & Contemporary France* 3 pp. 351–365; Le bande à 35h par jour (1998) *Le Lundi au Soleil: Recueil de textes et de récits du 'mouvement des chômeurs* cahier no.1 novembre 1997 – avril 1998 Paris.

112   Henley, J. (1998) 'Fight for French jobless 'becoming popular movement', *The Guardian* 15 January.

113   Le bande à 35h par jour (1998) *op cit.*; Levy & Aguiton (1998) *op cit.*

114   KOS (1998)*Info-Rundbrief Nr.39* Februar; Information from interviews with Gitti Götz, Joachim Glund & Andi Dallmann.

115   'Die 'neue A-Klasse' ging wieder auf die Strasse', *Frankfurter Rundschau*, 6 March 1998, afp/dpa/rtr/ap.

The initial action days focused mainly on record post-war unemployment figures and many of the actions were rather orderly affairs rallying the unemployed in front of job centres to demand work.[116] However, the increase in disciplinary and control measures on benefit receipt was also an issue and resulted in such slogans as *Meldepflicht woll'n wir nicht!* [We don't want to have to sign on! lit. obligatory registration].[117] As the campaign progressed other issues were brought into the limelight such as the link between mass unemployment and the growth of right-wing extremism[118] and demands similar to those arising in France were adopted. By action days six and seven the main slogans had become *Recht auf Arbeit und Recht auf Einkommen!*[119] [Right to Work and Right to Income!] and *Umverteilung von Arbeit und Reichtum!*[120] [Redistribution of Work and Wealth!]. This was supported by a number of spectacular actions inspired by the French movement such as that in Oldenburg where a 'free shopping' action was carried out successfully.[121] A job centre entrance was bricked up in Nurnburg in protest against the SPD's slogan of *Arbeit vor Sozialhilfe*[122] [Work before Benefits] and free cappuccinos were drunk in the Frankfurt Stock Exchange café before the building itself was 'stormed'.[123] The campaign culminated shortly before the general election in a series of regional demonstrations, but an attempt to restart the campaign early in 1999 was largely unsuccessful possibly as the result of the election of the SPD led government.[124]

Mobilization around employment and social issues was also developing in other EU member states. Italian unemployed associations organized sit-ins in front of job centres to demand legislation enforcing a thirty five hour week and public sector employment programmes to tackle mass youth unemployment.[125] In April 1998, fifteen thousand *Lavoratori Socialmente Utili* (LSU) [socially useful workers] demonstrated in Rome. The LSU were unemployed people that were employed temporarily by public authorities to provide 'additional' services. The reality turned out to be insecure employment at wage levels that undercut those paid to public sector workers and resulted in their displacement. Mass weekly demonstrations took place in towns and cities across the country demanding permanent public sector employment for the LSU at union rates of pay.[126] Unemployed associations were also particularly active in towns and cities in the South of Italy and helped to organize

---

116   Rein, H. (1998) 'Wir waren lange genug höflich!' *Express* August.

117   KOS (1998) *Info-Rundbrief Nr.39* Februar.

118   KOS (1998) *Info-Rundbrief Nr. 42* Mai.

119   KOS (1998) *Info-Rundbrief Nr.44* Juli/August.

120   KOS (1998) *Info-Rundbrief Nr.45* September.

121   KOS (1998) *Info-Rundbrief Nr.43* Juni and information from interview with Andi Dallmann.

122   'Erwerbslosenproteste' *quer* Juni 1998.

123   KOS (1998) *Info-Rundbrief Nr.44* Juli/August.

124   'Aktionen', *quer* April 1999.

125   'Italie: 'In Marcia' pour la réduction du temps de travail', *Marches Européenes/ NEWS (French version)* Décembre 1998 No.8.

126   'Ca bouge en Italie', <marches97-info.fr@ras.eu.org>, sent on 27/04/98 07:50; Information from interviews with Paolo Iafrete and Antonino Campenni.

mass demonstrations, road blocks and occupations of local authority buildings in support of demands for work and a basic income.[127]

Later the same year in the month of November, the first day of action organized by the *Tute Bianche* [White Overalls] network was held. Demands such as a citizenship income and free access to public services mobilized students alongside the unemployed and insecure workers. Actions included occupations of government buildings and social security offices as well as free transport actions. In Milan, an action was held in front of the stock exchange to argue for financing a universal citizenship income through the Tobin Tax on capital transfers. The *Tute Bianche* were also involved in challenging the 'Europe of Schengen'. They organized demonstrations against detention centres and for the regularization of illegal migrants and on 12 December 1998 they sailed the 'Boat of Universal Citizenship' to Valona, Albania in remembrance of the migrants who had drowned in the Otranto channel.[128]

In Spain, unemployed associations, left wing trade unions, and the anti-Maastricht committee supported a petition in favour of legislation for a thirty five hour week and a charter of social rights.[129] In April 1999, there were campaigns against employment agencies and government employment schemes organized by local committees against unemployment. This was followed in May by a march in the south of Spain against 'unemployment, poverty, social exclusion and racism' that was supported by the CGT, various associations and a section of the *Izquierda Unida* [United Left]. Its main proposals were for the redistribution of work through the demand for the thirty five hour week and the redistribution of wealth through the demand for citizenship rights such as a basic income.[130]

In Belgium, mobilizations by unemployed associations began with a national day of action on 30 April 1998.[131] Unconstitutional cohabitation regulations were targeted and a play written and acted by the Liège based group *Chômeurs pas Chiens!* [Unemployed not Dogs!] highlighted how more than forty thousand mainly female claimants had to endure home visits and intrusive questioning about their private lives.[132] The group carried out spectacular actions such as 'searching' for cohabiting women in social security offices. On International Women's Day they joined forces with a group from Brussels to cream cake the Employment minister, Ms. Miet Smet, in protest against the indignity of the home visits.[133]

---

127   Information from notes made from recording of the 'Assembly' on 3 December 2000.

128   Movimento delle Tute Bianche Padova (1999) *op cit.*

129   'Espagne. 35 heures et salaire social', *Marches Européenes/NEWS (French version)* No.11 Mai 1999.

130   'Marchas Contra el Paro, La Pobreza, La Exclusion Social y el Racismo', Undated Leaflet.

131   'Belgian Unemployed Prepared to take action', *Marches Européenes/NEWS (English version)* No.4 May 1998.

132   'Chômeurs pas chiens!', *Marches Européenes/NEWS (French version)* No.10 Avril 1999.

133   'Belgium's Minister of Labour Cream-caked and Plastered' *Marches Européenes/ NEWS (English version)* No.13 April 1999.

It is notable how the links forged between unemployed activists during the European Marches to Amsterdam served to foster cross-border solidarity action and further networking between these nationally based movements. As early as January 1998, the European Co-ordinating Committee, with participants from Finland, France, Germany, UK, Italy, Luxembourg, Spain, Sweden and Switzerland, issued a declaration of support for the French unemployed movement.[134] A contingent of Belgian unemployed activists marched in support of the French movement at a demonstration in Paris in January 1998 and there were solidarity actions with the French movement in Germany, Spain, Luxembourg and Holland.[135] At the next European Co-ordinating Committee on 12 February, with participants from France, Belgium, Luxembourg and Germany, it was suggested that closer contact between the organizations involved in the French and German mobilizations could be established through exchange visits by delegations.[136]

The visits to Germany were relatively frequent and in the case of AC! involved literally dozens of militants.[137] An indication of the breadth and content of such visits was given by Irène who was invited to Germany to speak on behalf of AC!:

Mostly the invitations were for these monthly action days and each time we met with the people there and I gave a talk about the situation in France and then a small speech at the rally. So I made twelve visits in total. I went to Frankfurt to an unemployed centre, to Nurenburg on Mayday and that was to the 'Autonomen'. I went to Kassel and that was to the university students, to Marburg and that was the DGB group. I was in Berlin with the claimant's group and I was in Hamburg once and that was an invitation from the Evangelical Church. So quite different people and I tried to describe the situation in France, the types of mobilization, and the structure of the unemployed movement, what sort of initiatives, what sort of network, to what extent we are organized and how and so on.[138]

These links contributed to the mobilization of joint actions by French and German unemployed activists and to a growing consciousness of the European dimension to social affairs. These were exemplified by the linking of the two campaigns by a joint demonstration that blocked the *Europa* bridge between Kehl, Germany and Strasbourg, France on 8 May 1998 that was the anniversary of the Second World War armistice.[139] The KOS commented that 'the message has jumped over from France to Germany' and the speakers at the rally argued for further international actions in

---

134 'Minutes of the European Marches Coordination meeting, Paris, January 10, 1998' available at *<www-pluto.informatik.uni-oldenburg.de/~also/eusep136.htm>* accessed on 07/08/2001.

135 *Ibid.*

136 '2 Bruesseler Konferenz EM 18./19.4 – Tagesordnung' available at *<www-pluto. informatik.uni-oldenburg.de/~also/eusep204.htm>* accessed on 07/08/2001.

137 Information from interviews with Michel Rousseau, Patrice Spadoni & Irène Bonnaud.

138 Excerpt from interview with Irène Bonnaud.

139 KOS (1998) *Info-Rundbrief Nr.42* Mai.

support of social protection in the EU.[140] Growing European awareness amongst French activists contributed to a successful national mobilization in Perpignon to combat a proposed local scheme that the associations argued resembled a 'Workfare' programme.[141]

The forms of action adopted by the unemployed movement in France were particularly disruptive. Speaking at the 'Assembly', Eric, representing AC!, explained that the aim of their actions was to 'block society' at locations other than the workplace in order to achieve a redistribution of wealth. He highlighted how the occupations of the administrative offices of electricity providers and social security offices and blockading motorways and railway lines were effective in momentarily disrupting the usual routine of business and administration.[142]

Although it was agreed at the 'Assembly' that such disruptive forms of direct action were the preferred mode of action of the unemployed, the attempt to transmit these disruptive forms of action across borders was met with varying degrees of success. Where the political culture was similar, the transmission process was more straightforward and worked both ways. For example, both Italian and French associations reported at the 'Assembly' the widespread deployment of the tactic of occupying buildings. They were also both engaged in blockading railway stations as a way of generating pressure to enforce their demands for free transport to the demonstrations in Amsterdam and Nice.[143] However, where the political cultures were distinctly different, such as in France and Germany, it was not so straightforward and the adoption of innovation required a more direct channel than that provided by the media. The process of diffusing forms of protest across this border was less a matter of direct adoption than of a loose translation.

German activists related how the media reporting of the unemployed mobilizations in France had an inspirational effect on them. The often repeated message was *Wir müssen Französisch mit dem Kapital reden* [We must speak French to Capital].[144] However, a simple transmission of action forms seen in France to Germany not only did not work, but also proved to be counter-productive. At the beginning of the days of action in Germany described above, attempts were made to copy the 'free shopping' actions, but when carried out as organized shoplifting they were ill received by the media and also amongst the unemployed themselves.[145]

However, the image of the actions that had come across in the media was largely inaccurate whereas meetings between French and German activists enabled a clearer

---

140   'Deutsche und französische Arbeitslose besetzen <Europabrücke>' 4. Protesttag – Meldungen Nachrichten-Agenturen *C/DATEN/ATEX/TICK/PROTEST4.DOC* 11/05/98 18:38 (Printed Document).

141   'French Unemployed stop Workfare in its tracks!' *Marches européenes/NEWS (English version)* No.7 September.

142   Information from notes taken from recording of the 'Assembly' on 3 December 2000.

143   Movimento delle Tute Bianche Padova (1999) *op cit.*; <Geronimo@easynet.fr>(2000) 'Communiqué du Collectif Trans Gratuits', AC! list, sent 06/12/2000, viewed 12/12/2000.

144   Information from interview with Gitti Götz.

145   Information from interview with Angela Klein.

picture to be established.[146] These meetings focused on the questions of how actions like occupations and 'free shopping' were actually organized and presented, but there were also broader discussions and debates about the 'illegal but legitimate' [*illégales mais légitimes*] (p. 34)[147] character of some of these actions.[148] In France, these disruptive actions were presented as an assertion of citizens' rights, whereas in Germany they fitted more comfortably within a tradition of civil disobedience seen for example in anti-nuclear protests.[149]

With a clearer picture about these spectacular actions and a greater understanding of the differing protest cultures, it proved possible to make more effective decisions about if and how to carry out such actions during the later protest days.[150] The general conclusion drawn by leading militants was that imposing uniform action was not possible and this led onto the idea for adopting decentralized days of action which had a common focus but encompassed diverse forms of action. Michel Rousseau concluded that,

> The experience that we have had in the European Marches is that if you simply translate one form of action from one country to another, well it often doesn't work. It doesn't work because the traditions aren't the same, the way of understanding things is not the same and it can turn out to be counter-productive. So we need to make it understood that what can be done in one country may not be done in another. But we can explain how we do things to people from another country and they can say well perhaps we can do the same thing, but with some differences. So, in each country it is necessary to find the best way.[151]

There were in fact numerous formally and informally organized cross-border contacts and meetings between the activists from the organizations involved in the mobilizations, with French militants particularly engaged in participating in visits to Spain, Italy and Germany.[152] These and other activists congregated at the second *Assises* held at the 'Free University of Brussels' on 18-19 April 1998 that proved to be a showcase of the renewed militancy amongst the unemployed in Europe that had also found expression at the ENU conference earlier the same month.

Christophe Aguiton, representing AC!, claimed that the increasing influence of the French and German associations in the ENU was leading to a new orientation around collective action.[153] This changing orientation also provided further impetus for mobilization at the European level with organizations that were absent in Amsterdam, such as the French CGT unemployed committees and the German KOS, starting to become involved in the networking process for mobilizing the demonstration in Cologne.

---

146 Information from interviews with Gitti Götz and Irène Bonnaud.
147 Schmitt & Spadoni *op cit.*
148 Information from interview with Patrice Spadoni.
149 Information from interview with Gitti Götz.
150 Information from interviews with Angela Klein and Andi Dallman.
151 Excerpt from interview with Michel Rousseau.
152 Information from interviews with Laurent Guilloteau & Patrice Spadoni.
153 Sotscheck, R. (1998) 'Für Arbeit, gegen Zwangsarbeit', *Die Tageszeitung,* 8 April.

The process of organizing for the events in Cologne began more than a year beforehand with national meetings of activists in Germany. The second meeting agreed that the European Marches Network would take overall responsibility for the preparations for the demonstration at the EU summit.[154] A draft appeal for the demonstration and an agenda for the conference in Cologne were debated at the European Co-ordinating Committee meeting held in Paris on 26-27 September 1998. Although many participants spoke out in support of broadening the appeal for the demonstration to include the issue of rising racism, there was also a concern voiced by a representative of the MNCP that this should not obscure what he saw as the primary issues of unemployment and poverty.[155]

Another European planning meeting for the counter-summit events in Cologne was held over the weekend of 31 October to 1 November. It attracted one hundred and twenty people including representatives of European networks such as 'Towards a Feminist Europe', global networks like PGA, as well as European Marches delegations from Belgium, France, the UK, and the Netherlands.[156]

The Conference held at Cologne over the last weekend in January 1999 assembled in excess of five hundred activists from sixteen countries involved in organizations as diverse as trade unions, unemployed, migrant, and women's associations and campaigns around the issues of education, health, and housing. The Conference enabled a wide-ranging debate over the content of the appeal for the demonstration and the forms of action appropriate for the occasion. As well as a debate over full employment, (see chapter 6), there were also proposals that the appeal was too 'defensive' and should include stronger anti-capitalist statements. Female activists also expressed concern that the particular interests of women had not been fully integrated into the appeal.

In a memorable discussion, an Italian activist proposed that with so many journalists in Cologne to cover the summit, to attract media attention a group of people should strip naked and write 'unemployed' on their genitalia. A German activist advised that such an action would not be well received in Germany where there was a more modest culture of protest. This was followed by a debate amongst the Italian contingent about the efficacy of repeating the 'free train' action. Members of the union CGIL asserted that, although such actions created publicity, they did not express the spirit of the movement that was to contact the mass of workers in the localities.[157] Despite these debates and disagreements a common declaration for a European demonstration was issued stating:

> We call on men and women from all countries who rebel against unemployment, job insecurity, all forms of exclusions and racism, ... to join a very big street demonstration.

---

154 'Köln '99: EU- und G8-Gipfel' available at <*www-pluto.informatik.uni-oldenburg. de/~also/eusep252.htm*> accessed on 07/08/2001.

155 *'Meeting Coordination of EM Secretariats on 26/27 September'* European Marches Photocopied Document Undated.

156 *'Cologne 99: Kick off!'* European Marches, Photocopied Document, Undated.

157 Information from notes made during participation in the Cologne Conference on 24 January 1999.

Together we will make them hear our anger and express our demand for a Europe and a World of social justice and liberty. ... Cologne will become the capital of our anger.[158]

One militant who was heavily involved in organizing the Cologne campaign explained that such unity was a necessity for achieving the difficult task of a successful European mobilization:

It's very difficult to have a social movement at the European level, but if we want to achieve that then we must absolutely reach very different forces and that's the task of the European Marches Network. In the European Marches in Italy you find communist and anarchist influenced trade unionists and in France there are various unions and political tendencies as well as the unemployed movement and so on. And these are people who would normally never work with each other because in left wing circles it's our speciality to fight amongst ourselves and not against the opponents (laughter). But our task is simply too difficult to dissolve ourselves into political tendencies.[159]

The conference in Cologne, as a space for pan-European assembly, also played an important role in the construction of the various European networks of organizations through which the demonstration was subsequently mobilized. A European network of trade unionists had been developing around for support for common European demands for a shorter working week, a minimum wage and income and support for public service access and provision.

The Amsterdam campaign had enabled cross-national links between unions such as SUD (France), COBAS (Italy), and CGT and CC.OO (Spain).[160] In February 1998 there was a meeting in Rome of the left wing tendencies of the CGIL (Italy), CC.OO (Spain), IG Metall (Germany), and the CGT (France) to discuss a European campaign for the shorter working week.[161] Another meeting was held in Paris in May 1998 attended by both officials and activists from IG Metall, IG Medien (Germany), FGTB (Belgium), CFDT, CGT and SUD (France), and CC.OO (Spain) at which a common text was adopted.[162]

A workshop at the conference in Cologne agreed a trade unionist appeal for the forthcoming demonstration that was signed subsequently by hundreds of individual activists and branches from eleven countries that included unions affiliated to the ETUC.[163] Further collaboration between SUD, COBAS and the Spanish CGT

---

158 'Cologne International Appeal European Demonstration, 29 May 1999: Against Unemployment, Job Insecurity, Exclusions and Racism. For a Europe and a World of Solidarity and of Liberty', available at <*www.euromarches.org/english/99/appeal.htm*> accessed on 20/08/2001.

159 Excerpt from interview with Irène Bonnaud.

160 Information from interviews with Patrice Spadoni & Michel Rousseau.

161 Fischbaker, K. 'Sind die Gewerkschaften am Puls der Zeit?' available at <*www-pluto.informatik.uni-oldenburg.de/~also/eusep244.htm*> accessed on 07/08/2001.

162 'Discussion text proposed by EU trade unionists' available at <*www.labournet. net/1998/may/euroe.html*> accessed on 18/11/1999.

163 'Appel Syndical Pour Manifester le 29 Mai A Cologne' available at <*www. euromarches.org/francais/99/appelsyn.htm*> accessed on 01/07/2001; 'UnterstützerInnen des

enabled a joint leaflet outlining a 'Platform of Demands for an Alternative European Trade Unionism' to be distributed on the demonstration in Cologne.[164]

There were also networks of anti-racists, women and students and youth that began to be formed out of national and even inter-continental mobilizations and that came together at the continental assemblies such as the counter-summit meetings and the conference in Cologne. The contact between individual anti-racist activists and organizations from across the continent made at border camps held in 1998 and 1999 led in late 1999 to the formation of the 'Noborder network' bringing together groups from eight EU countries.[165] The formation of this formal network was facilitated by the workshop on immigration held at the conference in Cologne and by the European anti-racist meeting held as part of the Cologne counter-summit. A European wide demonstration against racism was held in Paris on 27 March 1999 and called for a European network of migrants' organizations and anti-racist groups to oppose the increasing number of deportations resulting from the EU's policy of 'Fortress Europe'.[166]

Support for the proposal for the Worldwide Women's March (WWM) led to the formation of a European network to organize it. This project was also assisted by the workshop for women held at the conference in Cologne and by meetings at the Cologne counter-summit on women in the EU and on the march itself.[167] An initiative for a meeting of European youth in Venice in 1997 was followed by a workshop for students and young people at the conference in Cologne.[168]

This coalescence of European networks was reflected in the diversity of the mobilization in Cologne and contributed to the sense that an international social movement was in the course of being constructed: a mood reflected in the call for a second European March from Brussels to Cologne.

> Movements active in the fight against unemployment and job insecurity have emerged throughout Europe. They have their own demands, propositions, and projects. We demand that in Cologne, governments finally listen to them. However, we know that only a strong social movement, co-ordinated and international, will bring together the unemployed, the young, those in insecure jobs and wage earners, and bring about real social transformations

GewerkschafterInnenaufrufs zur Euromarsch-Demonstration am 29. Mai in Köln' available at <*www.euromarches.org/gewaufr.htm*> accessed on 20/08/2001.

164   'Suggested Platform for Alternative European Trade Unionism: The European March against Precariousness on May 29 in Cologne' Leaflet distributed on the Cologne demonstration on 29 May 1999.

165   'About the noborder network' available at <*www.noborder.org/network.html*> accessed on 26/07/2001.

166   'For an Open Europe. European demonstration in Paris on March 27th, 1999', available at <*www.bok.net/pajol/manifeurop27-03-99.en.html*> accessed on 06/08/1999.

167   'European Conference Against Unemployment 23/24 Jan' <*g.goetz@link-m.de*> sent on Sat 09 Jan 1999 11:25; 'Ende der Bescheidenheit, Gipfel stürmen: 28. Mai – 2. Juni EU-Alternativgipfel', Pamphlet produced by AstA der Universität Köln 25-8 Mai 1999.

168   'European Coordination Committee – Paris – Saturday 28 June 1997' available at <*www-pluto.informatik.uni-oldenburg.de/~also/eusep138.htm*> accessed on 07/08/2001; 'Les jeunes pour la manifestation des Marches européenes du 29 mai 1999 à Cologne' in *Marches Européenes/News (French version)* Février 1999 no.9.

with a massive redistribution of wealth. By marching to Cologne we are also preparing for the struggles and the projects of a future society.[169]

The second European March began in Brussels on 24 May 1999 and arrived in Cologne on 28 May. The originally planned size of the march was scaled down due to a lack of finance with Belgian unions preferring to support an expected demonstration by the ETUC that was not forthcoming.[170] Nevertheless, there were in excess of two hundred and fifty marchers with the mainstay being unemployed. The largest contingents came from France and Spain, but there were also small groups from the UK, Germany, Sweden and Denmark.[171]

The first day's march was to the European Commission buildings in Brussels and a delegation of 'Euromarchers' met with the German Employment minister, Walter Riesler, who was the acting President of the Council of Ministers for Employment and Social Policy. Patrice Spadoni of AC!, and a prominent participant in the European Marches, explained that the marchers refused to enter into a dialogue with Riesler as they stated that this would have no effect upon the actual decisions that were going to be made in Cologne. Spadoni stated that the marchers simply delivered the set of common demands agreed at the second *Assises* (see chapter 6) to which they gave him the five days of the march to respond. The marchers were not expecting a positive response, but evaluated the meeting as an advance on Amsterdam where no such meeting occurred.

On Wednesday 26 May there was a march to a detention centre in Vottem. On arrival the asylumseekers were immediately returned to the cells, but showed their support for the marchers by waving their teeshirts through the barred windows. The marchers waved their flags in reply but were frustrated by being denied contact with the asylumseekers and angered by the prison like conditions in which they were being held. A number of the marchers uprooted fence posts using them to bang on the main gates leaving several large dents.[172]

The next day in Liège, the Euromarchers followed a rally with local trade unionists by joining militants from local unemployed associations in occupying the top floor of the regional employment office. Amidst much excitement and exchange of tactics, local activists attended a stormy midnight meeting with the Director and put their demands for an end to the home inspections. The occupation lasted overnight with more of the building taken over and slogans were daubed on the walls. The atmosphere was festive as the occupiers not only discussed and debated strategy and tactics, but also entertained themselves with music and consumed prawns, salmon, and champagne discovered in the Director's fridge. After a sleepless night

169 'Cologne International Appeal European Demonstration, 29 May 1999: Against Unemployment, Job Insecurity, Exclusions and Racism. For a Europe and a World of Solidarity and of Liberty', available at <*www.euromarches.org/english/99/appeal.htm*> accessed on 20/08/2001.

170 Information from notes taken during participation in the German Co-ordination Committee meeting on 20 June 1999. Minutes in German available at <*www.euromarches. org/deutsch/99/0620p.htm*> accessed on 01/07/2001.

171 Schmitt & Spadoni (eds) (2000) *op cit.*

172 *ibid*; Canal Marche (2000) *On va marcher sur Nice!* (Paris: Canal Marche).

the occupation ended peacefully the next morning and for those involved it remained the highpoint of the march.[173]

Crossing the border into Germany was the low point of the march as inadequate provision had been made for the marchers who also suffered from a lack of basic amenities. The relatively small scale welcome they received in Aachen disappointed some of the marchers and there existed some concern that the political autonomy of the marches had been compromised by the rally being held amidst stalls and banners supporting the PDS.[174] There was also an altercation with the German police after some of the marchers blocked a main road and several marchers narrowly avoided the attempts made to arrest them.[175] It was decided subsequently to carry out a 'free transport' action and the marchers took the train directly to Cologne to participate in the demonstration at the Summit meeting.[176]

Saturday 29 May 1999 was a blazing hot midsummer day and the demonstrators were noticeably relieved to get out of the packed trains that brought most of them to Cologne and to make their way past the cathedral towards the assembly point. The demonstration proved to be large, lively and loud with around thirty thousand participants from across the countries of the EU and further afield including Poland, Russia, Brazil, India, and South Korea.[177] The 'Euromarchers' led the demonstration holding a banner with the symbol of the foot and the main slogans in many different languages. The unemployed associations were particularly strongly represented and their banners read: *Wir wollen keine Arbeit, wir fordern Geld* [We don't want work, we demand money], *Existenzgeld statt Arbeitszwang* [Basic income instead of forced work] and *Arbeitshaus Europa ohne uns!* [Workhouse Europe. Without Us!].[178]

Trade unionists were also well represented with members of the French SUD, Spanish CGT, and Italian COBAS distributing a joint leaflet detailing a European platform of demands for an alternative trade unionism including a European minimum wage and an immediate thirty five hour week.[179] There were contingents of anti-fascists 'Fighting Fortress Europe', anti-racists supporting the Caravan for the Rights of Refugees and Migrants, the Intercontinental Caravan of Indian Farmers and other movements from the South, feminists supporting the WWM and many banners opposing war in the Balkans.

---

173   Schmitt & Spadoni (2000) *op cit.*; 'L'etape de Liege de la 'Grande' Marche' *Marches Européenes/NEWS (French version)* No.12 Juin 1999; Information from interviews with activists; Canal Marche (2000) *op cit.*; Information from notes taken from recording of the 'Parliament' on 31 May 1999.

174   Information from interviews with Patrice Spadoni & Denise Wood.

175   Information from interview with activist.

176   *Cologne 99*, Report produced for the Euromarch Liaison Committee by the Unemployed Action Group, undated.

177   Müller Münch, I. (1999) 'Zwei Europas tummeln sich im überfüllten Köln' *Frankfurter Rundschau* 31 May.

178   Information from notes taken during participation in the Cologne demonstration on 29 May 1999.

179   *'Suggested Platform for Alternative European Trade Unionism: The European March against Precariousness on May 29 in Cologne'* Undated leaflet.

Towards the rear of the demonstration came supporters of political organizations that included the German Greens and PDS, a large contingent of the Italian RC, the French Greens and PCF as well as Trotskyist and anarchist organizations drawn mainly from Germany.[180] Activists from these political organizations distributed leaflets of which some were multi-lingual. The anarchist CNT explained how the source of unemployment, exclusion and war was the capitalist system. The Danish 'Red-Green Alliance' called for new European councils to replace the capitalist EU. The Trotskyist 'Fourth International' called for a coming together of the 'new anticapitalist internationalist current' as well as for a 'united, socialist and democratic Europe'.[181]

The demonstrators chanted slogans in many languages including the popular *Hoch die Internationale Solidarität!* [Up with international solidarity!]. There was a theatrical air with some demonstrators in costumes including one dressed as a bishop who blessed the demonstrators with the holy water of the EURO. There was a good deal of drumming and dancing along with singing and music the loudest of which boomed out from a massive sound system that led the anti-fascist contingent. This contingent was singled out for particularly heavy policing by some of the fourteen thousand police officers on duty and after a number of skirmishes the police halted the demonstration. This led to further conflicts as many demonstrators turned around and marched back to stop the demonstration being split, but a full-scale confrontation was avoided and the tail-end of the demonstration was able to proceed towards the rally.

The rally was held in a festive mood and surroundings with the stage draped in colourful banners and the demonstrators milling around the stalls offering German beer alongside Turkish food.[182] The speeches were translated into five languages (German, French, English, Italian and Spanish) and amongst the speakers was Franz-Josef Möllenburg, Chair of the service workers union NGG, who not only spoke out against the proliferation of low paid, insecure 'McJobs', but also against the war in Kosovo.[183] In a similar vein, the European Marches Network issued a press statement that emphasized the link between war, unemployment and impoverishment and a banner at the front of the stage declared 'European Marches against unemployment, job insecurity, social exclusion, racism and war'.[184]

---

180   Information from notes taken during participation in the Cologne demonstration on 29 May 1999; Monnot, C. (1999) 'La marche contre le chômage a rassemblé l'extrême gauche européene à Cologne' *Le Monde* 1 June.

181   Undated Leaflets: *'Le Capitalisme: c'est le chômage! c'est l'exclusion! c'est la guerre!'* issued by the French and Spanish CNT, *'Pour une Europe unie, socialiste et démocratique'*, issued by the Fourth International, *'Europe without the EU – Towards an alternative Europe'* issued by the Danish Red-Green Alliance.

182   Information from notes taken during participation in the Cologne demonstration on 29 May 1999; Information from notes taken during participation in the German Co-ordinating Committee meeting on 20 June 1999.

183   Klas, G. (1999) 'EU-Alternativgipfel in Köln beendet' *Junge Welt* 4 June.

184   *'Presseerklärung Nr.1. Über 30.000 auf der europäischen Grossdemonstration in Köln am 29.5.'* Bundesbüro Euromarsch: Köln, 30/05/1999 Leaflet issued at Press Conference.

After the demonstration in Cologne, evaluation meetings of the German, French and UK Committees concluded that it had been a success.[185] Despite the continued indifference of the ETUC, it had consolidated the achievement of Amsterdam by bringing together a diversity of organizations to mobilize a large demonstration. The general impression amongst activists was that this was a quite different mobilization to that seen in Amsterdam. Whereas in Amsterdam there was a clear focus on unemployment and the lack of a Social Europe, in Cologne the demonstrators highlighted opposition to a whole range of EU policies. In this sense it was seen as less a demonstration against the single issue of unemployment and more of a demonstration of a range of 'social movements' that were voicing their specific demands for a 'different Europe'.[186]

For some activists this was evaluated as an advance on Amsterdam as it represented the establishment of solidarity between hitherto separate networks.[187] For another activist it made it apparent that these networks shared a common struggle against the present course of European integration.[188] However, for another militant, although this unity existed, it was not made sufficiently apparent through the effective communication of shared demands:

> I found the demo to be really nice, very colourful, but perhaps too colourful. There were so many different forces and so many different slogans, 'we're against unemployment', 'we're against insecurity', 'we're against war and racism', and the Kurds were also there. So all possible kinds of people, and on the one hand that was really good to have so many different people coming together, but on the other hand the exact demands that we had were naturally not so clear to the outside world.[189]

Such a situation reflected the fact that the unity expressed in the common mobilizations was not formalized into an effectively functioning transnational organization that had sufficient resources such as finance, equipment and labour or sufficient influence over its constituent organizations. The European Marches Network registered the demonstration, provided police liaison and subsequently held a press conference. However, it lacked the organizational capacity to respond effectively to the splitting of the demonstration by the police. Prominent activists were able to communicate by mobile phone in an attempt to marshal the demonstrators, but there was no international stewarding of the event and the various contingents decided upon their own response to the situation. This suggested that the loosely structured network

---

185 Information from notes made during participation in the German Co-ordinating Committee meeting held in Cologne on 20/06/1999; Information from interview with Michel Rousseau; information from notes made during participation in the UK Euromarch Liaison Committee meeting on 2 October 1999.

186 Information from interviews with Yvonne Rocomaure, Piet van der Lende and Ailko van der Veen.

187 Information from notes taken during participation in the German Co-ordinating Committee meeting on 20 June 1999.

188 Information from interview with Kai Pust.

189 Excerpt from interview with Irène Bonnaud.

was effective in mobilizing the demonstration, but that it did not command the same allegiance as a formally constituted organization.

There were differing opinions expressed as to the underlying causes of such problems. One school of thought asserted that the movement was not sufficiently anchored in local social struggles and that therefore in certain localities there was simply inadequate support. The answer was rather than organize marches with insufficient financial and social support, to form a network out of locally organized unemployed groups and develop common campaigns.[190] A different argument was that the campaign had improved the European coordinating capacity of the network and that this needed to be formalized organizationally. The main problem remained a lack of finance. The union appeal gained hundreds of signatories, but was not matched by the number of financial contributions that were significant, but insufficient to meet all the expenses of a large-scale initiative. In this situation it was proposed to seek out an alternative source of finance while keeping the goal of funding by the unions. Nevertheless, it was judged premature to form a membership or affiliate based organization. It was preferable to continue with a semi-professional campaign structure and, if possible, open a European office.[191]

The Road to Nice

Finland took over the EU presidency for the latter half of 1999 and on 11 December 1999 there was a five hundred strong international demonstration in Helsinki.[192] Partly due to the cost of travelling to this event it had been decided by the 'Parliament' to organize a decentralized 'European Day of Action against Workfare and for a Guaranteed Income'.[193] This occurred on 10 December and actions took place in more than a hundred towns and cities across the continent reports of which were circulated via the Internet and email lists. In Naples, there was a demonstration by three thousand supporters of the LSU. There was a small picket of fifty people in Bristol followed by an occupation organized in opposition to the New Deal programme. In Paris, there was an occupation of the Ministry of Employment building. The occupiers protested that low benefit levels contradicted the theme of *Fraternité* used for a project launched by the Employment Minister. The following day ten thousand people demonstrated in Paris and fifty thousand people participated in events held in towns and cities across France.[194]

---

190 'Erwerbslose Aller Länder – Vereinigt Euch!', *quer*, August 1999.

191 Information from notes made during participation in the German Co-ordinating Committee meeting held in Cologne on 20 June 1999; Information from interview with Gerhard Klas.

192 'European Action Days – Demo in Helsinki', <*marches97-info.eng@ras.eu.org*>, sent on Mon 13 Dec 1999 12:08.

193 'Résolution adoptée par le Parlement européen des chômeurs et précaires en lutte', available at <*www.euromarches.org/francais/99/cologne.htm*> accessed on 24/08/2001.

194 'Press Release: 11/12/99', <*marches97-info.eng@ras.eu.org*> sent on Mon 13 Dec 1999 11:07; 'Europaweiter Aktionstag am 10. Dezember 1999', available at <*www.labournet. de/diskussion/arbeit/berichte/euroact.htm*> accessed on 20/08/2001.

This was the third consecutive winter of unemployed mobilization and alongside the focus on raising benefit levels there was also opposition to new conditions placed on receiving benefits resulting from the reform of the unemployment benefit system initiated by the employer's federation.[195] French activists argued that the employer's federation had developed their proposals for reform in close consultation with the European Commission and in line with its employment guidelines.[196]

It was the influence of the European employer's federation on EU policies that provoked a demonstration at the UNICE meeting in Brussels on 10 June 2000. Belgian unemployed associations and trade unions were joined by delegations from France, Holland and Germany.[197] There were further demonstrations at the summit meetings in Lisbon in March 2000, in Porto in June 2000, and in Biarritz in October 2000.[198] The demonstration in Lisbon was called by the union federation CGTP and mobilized between forty to sixty thousand people.[199]

The demonstration in Porto was called by the ETUC and mobilized twenty five thousand trade unionists to demand a 'Europe of Full Employment' and that the forthcoming European Charter of Fundamental Rights had to include economic and social rights.[200] This demonstration marked a slight shift in the ETUC's strategy away from sole reliance on influence through its role as an institutionalized social partner towards organizing a more sustained series of mobilizations. However, this strategy to engage with other civil society associations in order to mobilize European workers and citizens was largely a top-down process led by paid officials in Brussels that were tied organizationally and financially to the European Commission. This contrasted with the more grass roots approach to constructing a movement out of the diverse economic and social struggles that was resulting in mobilizations around a more radical agenda (see chapter 6). This notwithstanding, the organization of the mobilizations in Nice was also more centralized than had hitherto been the case: a situation that resulted in some criticism and concern that the emerging movement may have been losing its grass roots character.

Some of the prominent activists, such as Michel Rousseau, decided to propose that the joint working that developed during the Cologne campaign should be formalized at the European level:

> We've been in existence now for three years and some groups are saying that it's necessary for you to more clearly define yourselves. We find it difficult to identify ourselves and we

---

195 'UNEDIC. Quelle Refondation de l'Assurance Chômage?', *Marches Européenes/ NEWS (French version)* No.17 Octobre 2000.

196 Canal Marche (2000) *op cit.*

197 'La Societé face à l'UNICE', available at <*www.euromarches.org/francais/00/ unice1.htm*> accessed on 24/08/2001; Information from notes taken after participation in the demonstration on the occasion of the UNICE summit in Brussels on 10 June 2000.

198 'Les Marches d'Amsterdam à Nice en passant par Millau!', *Marches Européenes/ NEWS (French version)* No.16 Juillet.

199 'Anlässlich des EU-Gipfels gab es in Lissabon', available at <*www.euromarches. org/deutsch/00/lissgg.htm*> accessed on 07/08/2001

200 *Full Employment and fundamental rights top ETUC agenda says Gabaglio*, ETUC Report 1-00 (Brussels: ETUC).

know that we want to keep something of this flexibility, but all the same if we want to function at the European level it is necessary to have a minimum of structures. So we feel that it is necessary for us to have what we call 'a facilitating team', a small team of militants that is truly European.[201]

This move led to some criticism voiced by some organizations and militants that decision-making in the organization of European events was becoming over-centralized and that there was a danger that European level structures were becoming distant from grass roots militants. The Spanish union CGT argued that it was the pan-European assemblies that had ensured the success of the mobilizations in Amsterdam and Cologne and on this basis criticized the absence of such an event to launch the Nice campaign.[202] Other activists complained that without such events there had been less opportunity to debate the content of the 'Alternative Charter' issued by a French focussed Collective in whose name the mobilizations in Nice were called·

> Whilst governments are constructing a Europe dominated by the neoliberal logic without and against its citizens, a different Europe is being designed through the struggles of the 'sans' (those without a home, without work, without income, without papers, without rights), citizens mobilizations, the struggles of workers, the struggles of women against violence and poverty. ... This Europe must make itself heard in Nice.[203]

Another key factor affecting the development of the European mobilizations was that, as France took over the EU presidency, events outside of Western Europe contributed to a growing consciousness amongst activists that as neoliberalism was a global phenomenon so too had to be the social movement mobilized to resist it.[204] This recognition had begun to be developed through networks such as PGA: a diverse international network of organizations that was involved in co-ordinating protests in towns and cities around the globe on the occasion of the G8 summit in Birmingham in May 1998[205] and the G8 summit in Cologne in June 1999. Chief amongst these 'anti-globalization' events was the anti-WTO protest in Seattle in November 1999[206] with smaller simultaneous mobilizations in many European countries.[207]

The events in Seattle were followed by a demonstration and the formation of a World Social Forum at the United Nations convention in Geneva.[208] This was

---

201 Excerpt from interview with Michel Rousseau.

202 'De la CGT de España a la Coordinadora de las Marchas Europeas y organizaciones que forman parte de ella' <*marches97@ras.eu.org*> sent on Sat 15 Jul 2000 05:37.

203 'Mobilisations à Nice les 6/7/8 décembre 2000', available at <*www.euromarches. org/francais/00/nicea7.htm*> accessed on 08/01/2001.

204 Information from interview with Patrice Spadoni.

205 Action Populaire Contre la Mondialisation (2001) 'Switzerland: PGA in the belly of the beast', in Abramsky (ed) *op cit.*

206 St Clair, J. (1999) 'Seattle Diary: It's a Gas, Gas, Gas', *New Left Review* 238 pp. 81–96.

207 Working Group against MAI and Globalisation – Turkey (2001) 'November 30th around Europe', in Abramsky (ed) *op cit.*

208 'Les Marches d'Amsterdam à Nice en passant par Millau!', *Marches Européenes/ NEWS (French version)* No.16 Juillet.

followed by a demonstration at the IMF meeting in Prague in September 2000.[209] 'Anti-globalization' was the byword in Millau in October 2000 where ten thousand people demonstrated in defence of Jose Bové of the *Confédération Paysanne* [Federation of Small Farmers] who was standing trial accused of criminally damaging a MacDonalds restaurant.[210] 'Anti-capitalism' was the term used in London where a MacDonalds restaurant was demolished by May Day demonstrators.[211] The European leg of the WWM also mobilized a demonstration in Brussels in October 2000.[212]

The emerging global dimension was also reflected by contact between the European Marches and the marches of the poor and homeless in the Americas[213] and of the homeless that started in Tokyo and passed through seventeen cities before culminating in Okinawa at the time of the G8 summit.[214] The mobilization at the EU summit in Nice was presented as the next date in the 'anti-globalization' as well as the European diary.[215]

Immediately following the 'European Assembly of the Unemployed and Insecure Workers', an international caravan of unemployed and trade union activists and a small group of homeless people left Paris en route for Nice. Drawing on the experience of the Cologne march, participation was much lower than for the previous events.[216] The Caravan passed through Lyon followed by Marseilles where it was decided to carry out a 'free shopping' action in a large supermarket. Several activists filled a shopping trolley with goods and then blocked several aisles by the check-out while a statement was read out outlining why they were refusing to pay. Supporters clapped and blew whistles and gave out leaflets to shoppers and engaged the staff in conversation. The security guards failed to persuade them to leave the premises and the manager entered into negotiations that after two hours resulted in an agreement that allowed the militants to leave with the goods and without payment.[217]

The preferred mode of transport to Nice was by rail and in particular by 'free train'. At 10am on 5 December 2000, two hundred and fifty people gathered on the concourse of the *Gare de Lyon* in Paris. Their aim was to board the 11.14 train to Nice without tickets to highlight their demand for free transport and eventually to take part in the counter-summit events. Their banner read *Contre le sommet de l'Europe*

---

209   Indymedia Prague (2001) 'Open rebellion in Prague', in Abramsky (ed) *op cit.*

210   'Les Marches d'Amsterdam à Nice en passant par Millau!', *Marches Européenes/ NEWS (French version)* Juillet 2000 No.16.

211   'May Day 2000', available at *<www.lobsterparty.org/md_index.html>* accessed on 24/08/2001.

212   'Les Marches Européenes – Chronologie', available at *<www.euromarches.org/chr. htm>* accessed on 17/01/2001.

213   'Emergency: Marcher Arrested', *<kwru-announce@libertynet.org>* sent on Thu 28 Oct 1999 08:44:57.

214   'From Tokyo to Okinawa, 1500 kilometers march of the Homeless', *<marches97-info.eng>* sent on 20 Aug 2000 22:46.

215   'Une Autre Europe Pour Un Autre Monde', *Marches Européenes/NEWS (French version)* No.17 Octobre 2000.

216   Information from notes made during participation in the 'Assembly' on 3 December 2000.

217   Canal Marche (2001) *Le Rendez-vous de Nice* (Paris: Canal Marche).

Libérale, sécuritaire et xenophobe. Toutes et tous à Nice en trains gratuits. Liberté de circulation et d'installation [Against the summit of the neoliberal, xenophobic and law and order Europe. Everyone to Nice in free trains. Freedom of movement and settlement]. Thwarted in their original objective by lines of riot police blocking their passage onto the platform, representatives met with the railway authorities for negotiations that lasted well into the afternoon. On instruction from the transport minister an offer of a 50% discount in line with that granted to trade unionists was made. The demonstrators refused the offer and blockaded the booking office leading to confrontations with the riot police. A stand off ensued in which time Nice railway station was blockaded in solidarity.

Another attempt to board the 22.04 train amidst cries of *Un train gratuit pour les chômeurs* [A free train for the unemployed], was held back by riot police who had taken over the job of the ticket inspectors. The demonstrators responded with *Police partout, justice nulle part* [Police everywhere, justice nowhere]. Skirmishes continued and amidst the confusion many activists (and their dogs) boarded the train. On the train, discussion and debate ranged between union militants from the CGT, students from SUD (Education), and the unemployed from AC!. Many of those that did not board the train turned up at the station the following day when they successfully achieved their objective of travelling to Nice without paying.[218]

A 70,000 strong demonstration for a Social Europe organized by the ETUC took place on 6 December 2000. The large majority of sixty thousand people marched in a contingent that called for the adoption and subsequent improvement of the Charter of Fundamental Rights (see chapter six). A much smaller yet lively contingent followed that grouped ten thousand supporters of the 'Collective for an Alternative Charter', that rejected the proposed Charter outright.

The first section was made up of a series of blocks of national trade unions and trade union federations the largest of which came from the French CGT followed by the CFDT. The Italian CGIL and the Spanish CC.OO were also well represented. Many of the smaller delegations were made up of union functionaries who marched in a subdued manner behind their banners with the plain and simple demand for a Social Europe. The larger sections were made up of militants from the main French unions and these were more lively with chanting and singing and banners declaring: *Nous voulons une Europe des salariés, pas seulement l'Europe du marché* [We want a Europe of wage-earners, not just a Europe of the market].

The second section was led by the French unions FSU and SUD and the CGT-correcteurs followed by activists from an assortment of unions like the Italian COBAS, unemployed associations, left-wing parties, and a large grouping from ATTAC in support of the taxation of capital movements. This block was loud and colourful with much chanting and whistling along with music and singing. A human chain dressed as a snake slithered its way through activists holding banners and giving out leaflets. The banners demanded: 'Another Europe to guarantee real rights', *Pour nos droits, tous nos droits, pour une autre Europe* [For our rights, all our

218   Information from notes taken during participation in free train action on 05/12/00; Canal Marches (2001) *op cit.*; 'Communiqué du Collectif Trains Gratuits', <*ac-forum@ras. eu.org*> sent on December 06, 2000 7:42 pm.

rights, for a different Europe], and *Droit à un emploi garanti pour tous et un révenu decent* [Right to a guaranteed job for all and a decent income]. The demonstrators' perspective on neoliberal globalization was exemplified by a banner declaring *Une autre Europe pour une autre Monde* [A different Europe, for a different World]. Their anti-capitalist outlook was highlighted by a banner reading *Il n'y a pas de Capitalisme à Visage Humain* [There is no capitalism with a human face]. The second block marched to the railway station in an attempt to blockade it in solidarity with the thousand Italian activists travelling on the 'Global Action Express' that had been prevented from entering the country. The demonstrators were met by a cordon of riot police and dispersed by tear gas.[219]

The following day, five thousand people took part in an attempt to blockade the summit called by the Collective for an Alternative Charter. There was a short march at 7 a.m. that was halted by the barricades erected by the police where the majority of militants attempted to carry out the blockade peacefully. The police made liberal use of tear gas to keep them at bay some of which entered the summit building via its ventilators reducing even Prime Minister Jospin and President Chirac to tears. Meanwhile about a hundred protestors smashed the windows of banks and estate agents. Confrontations continued throughout the following two days resulting in thirty five people being arrested and twenty people being injured with flashpoints including the evacuation by the police of the venue of the counter-summit.[220] This was an indication that the authorities were becoming increasingly repressive of the more radical element of the transnational mobilizations which, as can be seen in the Postscript, persisted and even grew in size in the period subsequent to that presented in this chapter.

---

219   Information from notes taken during and after participation in the demonstration in Nice on 06/12/2000; Canal Marches (2001) *op cit.*; 'Conférence Intergouvernementale de Nice', available at <www.france.indymedia.org/> accessed on 11/12/2000; Monnot, C. (2000) 'Syndicalistes et antimondialistes dans la rue pour 'l'Europe des droits sociaux', Le Monde 8 December.

220   Information from notes taken after participation in the blockade of the Nice summit on 07/12/2000; Monnot, C. (2000) 'Le barroud d'honneur des anti-mondialistes', *Le Monde* 9 December.; Canal Marches (2001) *op cit.*; 'Conférence Intergouvernementale de Nice', available at <*www.france.indymedia.org/*> accessed on 11/12/2000.

Chapter 5

A Europe of Citizens

The unemployed are very atomized and individualized. You sit at home and don't have any reason to meet with other people. You get your money with a plastic card rather than collecting it at the office with the other unemployed. Through the marches I wanted the unemployed to show themselves in public, to speak out with dignity and not to consider unemployment as an individual fate, but rather as a result of the system. … For me personally it was a powerful experience that showed that someone could do something and do it well and didn't have to sit silent and passive in the corner. For me it was a confirmation of what I had thought – that it was possible to do something about these things.[1]

We, citizens of all the countries of Europe, unemployed, workers in secure or insecure jobs, pensioners, immigrants, and homeless, have decided to march together to Amsterdam. We are marching together to express our revolt, because the social crisis is not a fatality.[2]

Mobilizing against the 'Dismal Days': From the Despair of Individual Powerlessness to the Hope of a Collective Force

The main focus of this chapter is on showing the contrast between, and the movement from, the powerlessness of individualized 'victims' of neoliberal policies and the existence of a European network based on collective solidarity. While chapter four demonstrated the role of political entrepreneurs in mobilizing the European Marches, this chapter shows how the mobilizations were also the product and producers of strong emotions amongst the participants who experienced the mobilizations as powerful moments of collective solidarity and of personal and collective transformation.

Bourdieu argued that the existence of the unemployed movement in France amounted to a 'social miracle' (p. 89) in that unemployment was the central factor in demobilization as it attacked individual pride and hampered collective action.[3] For Bourdieu, the formation of a movement itself marked a victory as 'it pulls the unemployed, and with them all insecure workers … out of invisibility, isolation, silence, in short, out of non-existence' (p. 89) moreover its existence was 'the most extraordinary encouragement to mobilization, to the rejection of political fatalism' (p. 90).

---

1   Excerpt from interview with Joachim Glund.

2   'The List of Demands following the European *Assises* – Brussels, 22nd and 23rd February 1997', available at <*www-pluto.informatik.uni-oldenburg.de/~also/eusepa65.htm*>, accessed on 07/08/2001.

3   Bourdieu (1998) *op cit.*

The miraculous quality of mobilizing such a movement was magnified when it occurred on the transnational level where the material resources available were even scarcer than at the national level. Therefore, it is important to emphasize how collective action as this level was the product, as well as the producer, of emotions such as anger, joy and empowerment. It also produced a rejuvenated sense of dignity, social standing and moral authority and the creation of relations of camaraderie and friendship as well as a revitalized internationalism. These non-materials resources were central in creating the incentives for, and diminishing the costs of, participation; in creating networks; and in mobilizing discontent which are vital to the formation of collective action.[4]

This chapter also shows how resource poor movements can overcome these limitations on collective action by constituting such resources by the discursive framing of conflictual issues and of the struggle itself which also involves the reconstruction of collective identities.[5] From this perspective, we can see that the European Marches were the product of, and were engaged in, a struggle between two conflicting interpretative frames of unemployment. The neoliberal 'competitiveness' frame promoted by institutional actors such as the European Commission in particular and the 'solidarity' frame advanced by the European Marches.

According to the neoliberal frame, unemployment is explicable through the imperfections of individuals and state policies which hamper competitiveness and thereby growth and employment. The individual lacks the appropriate skills and attitudes required for employment and these are reinforced by 'passive' measures which encourage dependency and stifle individual initiative. The unemployed are regarded as untapped human resources and thereby rendered the objects of selective measures which activate them into employment by promoting their 'employability', that is their ability to compete for work. The unemployed are redefined as 'jobseekers' and are set into competition with each other in the search for work which demobilizes them as a collective actor.

The European Marches developed a counter-frame in which social problems such as unemployment were explicable in terms of the denial of basic human rights to the means to live a dignified existence. This suggests that such problems were the responsibility not of the individual, but of society and in particular were problems produced by governments which pursued policies which denied rights. This frame redefined the unemployed and other socially marginalized groups as *les sans* [those without rights]. It suggested their mobilization as the subjects of new demands for universal rights and their formation as a legitimate social and political actor whose voice must be recognized by social, cultural and political institutions.

In what follows, I concentrate particularly on the experiences and struggles of the unemployed (whose associations were at the heart of the European Marches) to outline the clash between the Europe of 'competitiveness' and the Europe of 'solidarity'. I do so in terms of a struggle against individualization and insecurity, inequality and indignity, and invisibility. These terms arose from the way that the participants represented their own struggles. However, these terms are also

---

4　　Della Porta & Diani (2006) *op cit.*

5　　*ibid.*

comprehensible as arising from *la double peine des chomeurs* [the double difficulties of the unemployed] (pp. 119–132).[6] Their suffering was not simply a matter of a lack of material resources, but was also a question of social devaluation and political disqualification.[7]

These struggles were also a process of production. They produced new personal and collective identities amongst the unemployed as well as new representations of them as an international and internationalist social and political force which was potentially capable of posing a challenge to the internationally institutionalized power structure that they identified as the source of their problems. This in turn served to demonstrate the 'Europe of Citizens' and to engender real hope that its demands could be institutionalized in a 'different Europe'.

The Struggle against Individualization and Insecurity

Part of the initial impetus for the constituent struggles of the European Marches was to counter *'les mauvais jours'* (p. 37)[8] [the dismal days] of unemployment. These dismal days were experienced largely as a miserable, isolated and insecure existence resulting from a lack of material resources to meet basic needs and to take a full part in social and cultural life and also a lack of work and benefits necessary to acquire them. It was against these immediate conditions that the unemployed were mobilizing:

> Listen, the everyday life of an unemployed person is simply really sad. Whoever hasn't got money doesn't go out. She only knows the inside of her flat and the two or three friends that she has and she can't visit them all the time because of the travel money. So you don't have anything that's fun anymore, it's really drinking and watching TV. So it's having something that is not urgh! grey everyday life…. I don't consider unemployment to be a punishment from heaven. Its aim is to depress and to put other workers under pressure. And you half beat the rulers when you don't let yourself get depressed. That's a fundamental thing and why I marched with the drummers in Cologne.[9]

> I got involved in the North East marches because the first time I was unemployed I got really depressed and getting active was doing something instead of just sitting at home all day alone and feeling that you couldn't do anything about it.[10]

> Well I was on an action and one of the police officers asked me why I was doing it and I simply said to him, 'Well I'm afraid of ending up homeless and living out on the street'. I'm on these benefits which are reduced every so often and I thought I don't know what is going to happen and I really didn't, so it was that kind of insecurity.

---

6   Linhart, D. (2005) 'La double peine des chomeurs' in C. Pozzo di Borgo (ed) *Vues de l'europe d'en bas* (Paris, L'Harmattan).

7   For an overview of how unemployment affected the lives of the unemployed in a European context see Sen, A. (1997) 'Inequality, unemployment and contemporary Europe', *International Labour Review*, 136 (2) pp. 155–172.

8   Spadoni & Schmitt (eds) (2000) *op cit.*

9   Excerpt from interview with Barbara Trowe.

10   Excerpt from interview with Andy Robertson.

Is that what made you get involved?

Yes, a mixture of anger and fear, partly anger and the need for self-defence.[11]

I asked a lot of the unemployed marchers why they had come on the march and they replied: to get out of the isolation, to be able to exist.[12]

These personal experiences of unemployment and the struggle against it were confirmed by the experience gained by associations of the unemployed. It was asserted that what were social problems produced through neoliberal policies were widely experienced as a personal fate that left the individual feeling hopeless about changing their situation thereby becoming incapable of mobilizing.[13] Even amongst some of the activists that were heavily engaged in the mobilizations and who expressed a belief that a different society was desirable and possible, there was a sense that the immediate pressures of material insecurity functioned to prioritize demands to alleviate immediately pressing social conditions.[14]

Such pressures resulted in individual strategies of defiance and desperation. Speaking at the 'Parliament' on behalf of the ALSO, a German unemployed centre, Michael explained how a great deal of resistance amongst the unemployed took the form of individuals demanding their rights vis-à-vis the authorities.[15] Claimants in Brighton highlighted the 'recalcitrance' of the unemployed in the face of welfare reform that translated into individual strategies of 'blagging the dole'.[16] Several activists also spoke of endemic avoidance of payment for services such as transport.[17] These individual forms of resistance proved increasingly less effective in the face of conditional and punitive welfare provision and severe measures that criminalized those seeking to avoid payment for services.[18] This pressure drove individuals, including some involved in the mobilizations, to acts reflecting hopelessness such as suicide and desperation such as serious and even deadly assaults on administrative officials.[19]

Although individual responses to unemployment were prevalent, there was also a re-emergence of collective activity that was occurring in localities across the continent and of which the European Marches were a co-ordinated international expression. This collective action was still relatively restricted in size in that whilst France was seen to be at the forefront of unemployed mobilizations, with fifty thousand people taking to the streets for days of action, the activists appeared keen to underline that

---

11   Excerpt from interview with Yvonne Rocomaure.

12   Extract from conversation with Carole Faure in Schmitt & Spadoni (eds) (2000) *op cit.* pp. 112/3 (author's translation).

13   Mawet, C. 'Chômeur pas Chien: Pour sortir les chômeurs du ghetto invisible', undated available at <*www.enter.org/solidarity*> accessed on 06/07/2001

14   Information from interviews with Piet van der Lende and Joachim Glund.

15   Information from notes taken from recording of the 'Parliament' on 30 May 1999.

16   Information from interviews with activists from BABC.

17   Information from informal conversations with several activists.

18   Information from interviews with Piet van der Lende and Yvonne Rocomaure.

19   'Verdener Arbeitsamtchef erstochen', *quer* April 2001; 'Die Mär vom 'Selbstschuldeten Affekt', *quer* Oktober 2001

most actions remained relatively small-scale.[20] In Germany, where fifty thousand people mobilized for the action days[21] this represented only 1% of the five million registered as unemployed.[22] However, while limited in scope, these mobilizations were (as I show later) generally experienced as tremendously encouraging for the participants and were effective in enabling them to represent themselves in the public debate on unemployment.

The key to overcoming individualization in order to construct what was termed 'a movement of rage and revolt'[23] were the unemployed and claimant collectives; some of which were attached to unions while others were independent associations. The Belgian collective *Chômeurs pas Chiens*! [Unemployed not Dogs!] explained how they set about bringing the unemployed out of the 'ghetto of invisibility' and into collective action. They began by petitioning outside the local benefit office and holding meetings in a nearby centre during which the unemployed were able to share their problems and views thereby rejecting the relationship of expert to victim propagated by many advice centres. The Collective also offered support for claimants facing home visits as well as writing and performing a play based on claimant experiences of such visits. They also organized an occupation of the employment offices where the unemployed and claimants were most starkly faced with individualizing administrative practices.[24]

The ALSO provided a similar example of collective organization with advice sessions conducted openly to promote a discussion of common experiences and problems with the administrative agencies and of how to deal with them. The association and fellowship facilitated by the ALSO served to strengthen the resolve to resist the pressure of the competitive individualistic values of the '*Ellenbogengesellschaft*' [literally: Elbow society] and the pressure to accept work at any price. Activists from the ALSO were also concerned with confronting the argument that unemployment was the fault of individuals who lacked skills with the argument that unemployment was a problem of society. This also served to counter feelings of guilt, desperation and hopelessness and encouraged the individual claimant to participate in positive collective responses to social problems. Such actions ranged from street demonstrations through to occupying a bank to highlight wealth and income inequality and occupying the local social security office to protest against benefit restrictions and in support of its main demand for a basic income.[25]

In France, where there were fewer meeting spaces for the unemployed, collective actions such as the occupations also provided an opportunity for discussing personal experiences and situations as well as strategies for dealing with problems such as

20   Information from interviews with Piet van der Lende and Irène Bonnaud
21   KOS (1998) *Info-Rundbrief* Nr. 43 Juni
22   Eironline (1998) 'Nationwide protests as unemployment reaches new record high', available at <*www.eiro.eurofound.ie/*>, February accessed on 31/03/1998
23   Information from notes taking during participation in the conference held in Cologne on 22 January 1999
24   Mawet, C. 'Chômeur pas Chien: Pour sortir les chômeurs du ghetto invisible', undated available at <*www.enter.org/solidarity*> accessed on 06/07/2001
25   Information from interviews with Andi Dallmann, Uwe Durchbach and Willi Lubkes.

accumulating fines for travelling without a ticket. These exchanges promoted a feeling of camaradarie amongst the participants.[26]

The attempt to de-individualize social problems was also a significant feature of the European March to Amsterdam that also enabled the marchers to share their personal experiences of unemployment. As one of the marches passed through Chambery, France the marchers became aware that a local unemployed man was being threatened with an eviction notice dispatched from the same town hall building where a reception in their honour was being held. A town hall official, filmed by the videomarchers (see below), stated that he was not prepared to discuss an individual case in public. However, the marchers refused to accept that homelessness was an individual problem and threatened to camp in front of the town hall in order to demand collectively that he be rehoused. This demand was met and Serge joined the march to Amsterdam.[27]

Collective action also enabled the unemployed to emerge out of the misery and solitude of everyday life and share in an episode of collective existence and solidarity that was on occasions a joyful experience. This served to enhance their feelings of well being and gave them renewed strength to continue with the struggle to meet their immediate needs. As one militant put it:

> There are quite concrete personal interests like the guaranteed income and on the other hand the social movement is a joy in itself, you know. You meet new people and you have really beautiful moments and these keep you going.[28]

An important element of the marches was the opportunity they provided for sharing personal experiences of unemployment, for experiencing a sense of fellowship through sharing elements of everyday life such as food and entertainment, and for collectively tackling common practical and political problems. This sharing of common experiences and common problems helped to establish a sense of camaradarie amongst the marchers and in some cases friendships developed that were cemented through exchange visits and contact by mail between the continental events. One prominent activist emphasized that,

> What was extraordinary about this first march were the networks that were formed out of it. That's to say that the people who crossed over Europe gave their addresses to the people who they came into contact with and since then they have been corresponding amongst themselves.[29]

The inter-personal networks formed through the European Marches also proved to be a mechanism through which continuous exchanges across borders occurred between activists who began to learn more about each other's specific struggles and develop further bonds of solidarity. For example, Yvonne Rocomaure kept in regular contact with activists from the UK, Holland, Denmark and Germany and

---

26   Information from interviews with Yvonne Rocomaure and Irène Bonnaud.
27   Schmitt & Spadoni (eds) (2000) *op cit.*
28   Excerpt from interview with Irène Bonnaud.
29   Excerpt from interview with Patrice Spadoni.

exchanged information about recent actions, debates and also experiences with the administrative authorities as well as discussing more general political ideas. For Gitti Götz, the exchange of e-mails was a frequent event that helped her to break down the barrier of distance and kept her in contact with the situation elsewhere in Europe. Both Yvonne and Gitti took part in informally arranged exchange visits, as did several others of those activists who were interviewed. Yvonne spent several days in Oldenburg and received visitors from there on two occasions. Both herself and the Germans were struck by the different protest cultures existing in France and Germany. She was impressed by the way that the German activists developed their campaigns through analyzing the everyday problems of the unemployed that they encountered and felt that the French movement should make more use of this kind of information. Gitti spent a week in Paris during which time she was able to see many 'small occurrences' that for her proved more effective than written documents in enabling her to appreciate that the political atmosphere there was very different to that in Munich. Although she realized that it would not be possible to replicate directly the actions that she witnessed, she gained some new ideas that she felt could be modified to suit the German situation.[30]

The informal nature of these exchanges meant that the visits involved activists offering hospitality in their own homes, which was reciprocated for the return visit. This contributed to the development of warm personal relationships between them that in some cases developed into friendships that facilitated further exchanges. One activist recalled her experience of meeting others engaged in the movement in France:

> In France in '97 I followed the activists for one week and we became friends. We try to keep in contact with e-mail and we call and fax. If we have projects we are working on then we exchange things. It's very informal and you know it also has to do with friendship. With some people you become friends and then it becomes normal to see them and to call them and to ask them what they are doing? And to say 'we are doing this, why don't you come?'[31]

Through the process of carrying out my research and subsequently I have also had similar experiences of developing friendships with activists from other countries which has involved exchanging hospitality and ongoing exchanges of information about specific actions and discussions about the development of European networks. Therefore, I too have experienced the joy of seeing other activists again at the counter-summit events after an absence of six or twelve months. This explains somewhat why the marches and the counter-summit events were described as like a 'party', a 'festival' or even 'Christmas'.[32]

The marchers refused to organize a march that would project a miserable image of the unemployed and instead they entertained each other with music from the various

---

30   Information from interviews and informal conversations with Yvonne Rocomaure and Gitti Götz.

31   Excerpt from interview with Corinne Barella.

32   Information from interview with several activists.

regions of Europe as well as songs and poems composed during the marches.[33] This also referred to the joyful element of the marches and demonstrations with activists stressing their keenness to demonstrate with the liveliest cortege that had the most singing, chanting and even dancing.[34] The occupations were also an occasion for developing warm personal relationships that contrasted with the individualized and isolated existence of daily life.[35] At times they were also a cultural event in which the participants entertained each other and on occasions a party atmosphere was created. Activists protesting against the introduction of Employment Zones transformed the Bristol Labour Party offices into an 'Enjoyment Zone' and called for 'less labour, more party!'.[36]

To support the demand for a cultural life for all, actions such as occupations of cinemas were carried out with slogans like *Partageons les richesse, pas les misères!* [Share the wealth, not the misery!].[37] On one occasion, during a lengthy occupation of a social security office in Paris, a birthday party was held for one of the militants.[38] Such experiences were an important factor in countering the misery of 'the dismal days' and served to reinforce the bonds of solidarity developed through collective action.

The Struggle against Inequality and Indignity

In chapter six, I will show how the European Marches articulated its demands for social citizenship in terms of the universal right to the resources necessary for a dignified existence. These demands found root in the collective challenges to the inequality and indignity faced by the unemployed in their daily lives as well as in their existing orientation towards achieving social justice. As one unemployed activist involved in organizing the European Marches explained:

> The pressure that is being put on me is so strong that first of all I have to be against this pressure. ... I haven't got a grand theory that I want to achieve, but this is quite general. I want relationships that are based on justice. I'm against people enriching themselves at the expense of others. I cannot accept these differences that lead to some people being destroyed. ... I want to have a roof over my head, and to be productive doing something that I like doing that is not for an alien purpose. Also what is important for me is that I cannot accept such relationships of hierarchy ... that my boss can discipline me and that there are these structures of order and obedience that exist.[39]

Opposition to inequality and indignity took a collective form in the unemployed mobilizations and the European Marches described in the previous chapter. In

---

33   Schmitt & Spadoni (eds) (2000) *op cit.*; Raynal, P, Pouy, J-B, Douyere, Pelletier, C, Goupil, R. (1997) *Marche ou Grève* (Éditions Baleine).

34   Information from interview with Barbara Trowe.

35   Information from interviews with Irène Bonnaud and Nassera Abbed.

36   Information taken from notes taken after action in Bristol on 23 March 2000.

37   Le bande à 35h par jour (1998) *op cit.*

38   Information from interview with Irène Bonnaud.

39   Excerpt from interview with Joachim Glund.

Germany, actions were targeted at financial institutions such as banks and the stock exchange that were engaged in and symbolized the production of wealth and income inequality. In France, the focus was more on places of conspicuous consumption such as chic cafés from which the unemployed were effectively excluded by their unequal access to income. The European marchers also chose to occupy such symbolic locations as the *Château de Versailles* that evoked memories of, and opposition to, massive wealth and income inequality.

Such inequality was addressed by mobilizations in support of the right to an income that was linked to the redistribution of wealth through taxation measures including the Tobin Tax. At the European level, co-ordinated action for such an income linked the level of its payment to the level of wealth produced in society thereby ensuring wealth redistribution. The income would also be available in a form that enabled equal access thereby eliminating discrimination on the grounds of age, sex and national origin.[40]

Mobilization was also directed at gaining the right of access to social provision. In France, collective action targeted utility providers to highlight the social emergency brought about by a lack of resources and demanded collectively the restoration of service provision. One activist explained her thinking behind engaging in such collective action:

> when we meet the director we say: 'look these fifty people don't have electricity anymore and it's winter and they have to live like that and they can't bear it anymore and we have electricity but we also can't bear it anymore. And that's why we are here in your office and we demand that they get back what you have taken away from them'.[41]

Such actions were presented by activists as a requisition of the wealth by citizens.[42] The mobilizations for free transport and free goods also asserted the immediate fulfilment of demands for the resources necessary for a dignified existence.[43] At a more general level, the European Marches opposed the implementation of policies that met the needs of a global economic system that was making the rich even richer and the poor even poorer to the extent to which they were living in conditions that were beneath human dignity.[44]

The mobilizations in France in the winter of 1997/8 were described by a representative of the unemployed association APEIS as a 'common struggle for

---

40   'Résolution adoptée par le Parlement européen des chômeurs et précaires en lutte', available at <*www.euromarches.org/francais/99/cologne.htm*> accessed on 24/08/2001; 'Platform of European Demands', available at <*www.euromarches.org/english/98/0419a. htm*> accessed on 20/08/2001.

41   Excerpt from interview with French activist.

42   Information from notes made from recording of the 'Assembly' on 3 December 2000.

43   Information from interview with Patrice Spadoni.

44   'The List of Demands following in the European *Assises* – Brussels, 22nd and 23rd February 1997', available at <*www-pluto.informatik.uni-oldenburg.de/~also/eusepa65.htm*> accessed on 08/08/2001.

dignity'.[45] This outlook was shared by another militant from Belgium who was part of the group *Chômeurs pas Chiens*:

> We have dignity. It is just that the others do not recognize us. It is that these laws and these practices don't recognize the dignity that is inherent to all human beings. What we demand is not charity, it is justice. It is to be full citizens and not to be discriminated against because we simply do not have a job.[46]

Speaking at the 'Assembly' on behalf of AC!, Eric explained why for him the struggle being waged in France was a fight for dignity:

> The image of the unemployed and insecurely employed is devalued by society. When you are unemployed you are in a Kafkaesque situation. You don't have the chance to live decently. ... The first effect of collective action is to gain some dignity vis-à-vis the authorities which scorn us in our daily life.[47]

This relationship between the claimant and the administrative authorities was emphasized by the *Chômeurs pas Chiens* that asserted that the inhumane regulations experienced by the claimant made them into less than a full citizen in a system characterized as a 'social apartheid'. The effect of facing such a system was to generate feelings of shame amongst the unemployed person and their family.[48] Such a situation gave rise to the group organizing collective action against investigations by social security officials that compromised the dignity of the unemployed. As well as performing a play on this question in the employment offices, the group also carried out an action that turned the tables on those ultimately responsible for these violations of the human rights of the unemployed. They made the Minister of Labour suffer the indignity of being covered in cream cake.[49]

The struggle against indignity was also manifested in relation to the specific questions of unemployment and work. From conversations with a church worker with pastoral duties for the unemployed and activists involved in unemployed centres, it was made clear that the dominant representations of the unemployed promoted feelings of guilt and shame amongst a significant section of the unemployed. This fuelled demands for work at any price that was present in the national mobilizations in the form of placards reading: 'I'll accept any sort of job' or 'These hands want work'.[50] In such a context there was a small element amongst the

---

45   Information from notes taken during participation in the conference held in Cologne on 23 January 1999.

46   Excerpt from Interview with Corinne Barella: in Schmitt & Spadoni (eds) (2000) *op cit.* p. 108 (author's translation).

47   Excerpt from a talk by 'Eric' representing AC! at the 'Parliament' on 3 December 2000.

48   Mawet, C. 'Chômeur pas Chien: Pour sortir les chômeurs du ghetto invisible', undated text available at <*www.enter.org/solidarity*> accessed on 06/07/2001.

49   'Belgium's Minister of Labour Cream-caked and Plastered' *Marches Européenes/ NEWS (English version)* No.13 April 1999.

50   Information from interviews with anonymous activist, Willi Lubkes & Uwe Durchbach.

national mobilizations epitomized by the 'Happy Unemployed' (p. 12) that focused on opposing this discourse by becoming 'crusaders for idleness' (p. 12) under the slogan of 'Workshy of the world unite: you have nothing to lose but your shame' (p. 12).[51]

However, the main attitude voiced by those activists I interviewed and at the events I attended was neither a clamour for work, nor its complete rejection. It was rather a rejection of work that compromised the dignity of the worker alongside demands for the right to work at decent pay levels and conditions in socially necessary jobs that promoted a sense of dignity. As one unemployed activist explained:

> Well I feel from time to time that I'd quite like to have some money again, but I won't accept any sort of job at any price because of that. Once I worked in a shoe factory for five marks an hour on a production line and I asked myself, 'what sort of shit job is that, you've got no time, little money, bad working conditions and are exploited as cheap labour'. … But when you want to create work it is important to look at what type of work you want to create and not simply to stress work at any price. We don't reject work, but people should not be forced into poverty work.[52]

The various attitudes to work were developing in a situation in which the unemployed were increasingly being compelled to make a choice between low paid insecure employment or 'Workfare' style jobs. It was asserted by one activist speaking at one of the meetings that, in the face of such a choice of work that compromised the worker's dignity, there was a better third option of remaining unemployed:

> If this is the only kind of work that they can offer us then we are better off unemployed and living off our benefits.[53]

However, this form of resistance was fast becoming an impossibility:

> It is not possible to live with dignity. You are offered a few hours work for even as little as a hundred and twenty (Belgian) francs per hour and you can't refuse it because then they stop your benefit. It's a modern form of slavery. What it is important to learn is how to say no to all of this shit that they are offering us.[54]

Hostility to the indignity of forced employment in low paid and insecure jobs was evident in campaigns of collective action. In the UK, for example, welfare reforms involving compulsory work training gave rise to the slogan amongst its opponents of 'I'm not a shirker. I won't be a slave'.[55] Actions involved claimants occupying job centres during which time they scoured the notice boards for cards offering

---

51   Staunton, D. (1998) 'Happy jobless laugh off the German work ethic', *The Guardian*, 29 July.

52   Excerpt from interview with Willi Lubkes.

53   Extract from contribution to the plenary session at the *'International Colloque'* taken from recording made on 10 June 2000.

54   Extract from contribution to the plenary session of the 'Assembly' taken from recording made on 3 December 2000.

55   Information from notes taken after job centre picket in Bristol on 10 December 1999.

employment at low pay rates that were either torn up[56] or marked with a stamp stating 'crap job'.[57]

The Struggle against Invisibility

The mobilizations enabled the unemployed to emerge from their privatized, invisible existence through highly symbolic and direct forms of action which made them visible in the public sphere and allowed them to intervene in the political debate over unemployment. This also involved an element of cultural production which enabled forms of self-representation which also challenged the dominant representations of the unemployed by cultural and political institutions.

Associations such as the *Tute Bianche* highlighted the lack of participation of marginalized groups in the public sphere by mobilizing around the term 'Invisibles'. They were involved in opposing the imprisonment of illegal migrants that made this most socially marginalized group disappear from public view. They prioritized high profile actions such as travelling on trains without paying not only to assert the right to free movement but also by so doing to make the participants visible and thereby assert their existence as citizens.[58] Unemployed activist, Joachim Glund, described the mobilization in Amsterdam as 'the crowning of his engagement' in that it showed that those who were seen as 'socially dead', that had neither an effective lobby nor material power, were capable of organizing effective political activity. This success was experienced as both a moment of personal and political confirmation.[59]

Yvonne Rocomaure described how engaging in collective action transformed the unemployed from being a passive invisible figure in a report into an active protagonist made visible to themselves, to others like them and to powerful institutions. Moreover, French militants particularly emphasized the efficacy of direct action in enabling the unemployed to attempt to intervene in the political debate from which they were excluded:

> These actions are fantastic. You are taking the initiative and you are doing something about something. It's like when we wanted to meet Madame Aubrey who is the French Employment Minister. We decided to invade a conference of job centre managers that she was speaking at. We met Aubrey coming in and she said our actions were fascist. But we said that we were simply a number of unemployed people who were trying to meet with the people who make decisions without consulting us. These actions give you as the unemployed a feeling of doing something instead of just submitting to the system time and time again and being confronted by a kind of blind alley, being blocked etceteras. You do have, with a bit of initiative, the chance to confront them.[60]

---

56   Canal Marche (1997b) *op cit.*
57   Information from notes taken after job centre picket in Bristol on 10 December 1999.
58   Movimento delle Tute Bianche Padova (1999) *op cit.*
59   Information from interview with Joachim Glund.
60   Excerpt from interview with French militant.

This element of confronting the decision-makers directly that were responsible for the adoption and dissemination of neoliberal policies was also evident in actions organized to coincide with the EU summits. As one activist recalled,

> It was the weekend of the Euromarch and Tony Blair was due to speak to the European leaders and promote his idea of the 'New Deal' and welfare reform and flexible labour practices and hold it up to all the other European leaders as a model for where they should go. So we did an occupation of the Welsh Labour Party offices in Cardiff. Suddenly it seemed like all these high powered Labour Party Officials were running around like blue-arsed flies trying to persuade us to leave. And you know what, after a while when you hear all these people saying that this is the wrong way of going about things, you realize that it is exactly the right way to go about things.[61]

Farid, a prominent figure in the European Marches, described how for him the main suffering generated by being unemployed was not to be recognized by society ['*de n'être pas reconnu pas la société*'] (p. 112). But he refused to accept that he was excluded and demanded his recognition as a full citizen.[62] This social and indeed political recognition was a major achievement of the European Marches, as one marcher stated:

> There, by marching, we had a social position, an existence, and that was fundamental. … That was above all because we finally found the right to a voice and to be listened to and even: our voice was asked for, solicited by the press, by the political structures.[63]

This extract also indicates that the public debate on social issues was largely conducted through a media that also rendered the unemployed invisible objects. Moreover, when represented, it was argued that T.V. programmes tended to present the unemployed in a pathetic and miserable light to be followed by the opinions of 'experts' that focused on the need to reduce labour costs.[64] Activists emphasized how such representation reinforced the discourse of the passive unemployed requiring 'activation' and spoke of increasingly frequent media campaigns that highlighted the supposed unwillingness of the unemployed to work.[65] The *Tute Bianche* directly challenged such reporting by organizing an action in a T.V. studio in Rome from where a live debate over unemployment was being broadcast. A group of activists got into the building and onto the stage, and managed to transmit their own demands regarding unemployment. This action was repeated a fortnight later in Padova and the activists used the opportunity to condemn the media's treatment of the issues of unemployment and insecurity as well as to publicize a day of action.[66]

---

61   Excerpt from interview with 'Activist 2' of BABC.
62   Schmitt & Spadoni (eds) (2000) *op cit.* p. 112.
63   Extract from conversation with Carole Faure in Schmitt & Spadoni (eds) (2000) *op cit.* pp. 112/3 (Author's translation).
64   Schmitt & Spadoni (eds) (2000) *op cit.*
65   Information from interviews with Piet van der Lende and Andi Dallmann.
66   Movimento delle Tute Bianche Padova (1999) *op cit.*

As part of the fifth day of action in Germany, called under the theme of *Schluss mit Scham und falscher Bescheidenheit* [End shame and false modesty],[67] a group from Dortmund carried out an action that was provoked by media pressure to accept low paid work:

> The best action was when we cooked and ate twenty kilos of asparagus in the city centre.
>
> What was that about and why did you choose asparagus?
>
> That was because the farmers got worked up because they said that the unemployed should harvest asparagus, so forced work for the unemployed. And the farmers said we were lazy and so on. And there were actually newspapers commenting that we were too lazy to bend over. ... Someone went on T.V. and told how they managed to stay for a week at one place, then three days at another and finally at the third they left on the first day. The programme had a go at him and said they couldn't understand why he would rather get money from the state than work. But he had had no time to rest after seven days work and he tried on three separate occasions. He really wanted to work and must have had good reason for stopping and then to be publicly put down. The action was excellent. We spent so much time peeling and cooking the asparagus and it was delicious.[68]

The invisibility of the unemployed in the media was also challenged through deploying spectacular actions carried out in high profile locations such as storming the Stock Exchange and occupying the *Château de Versailles*. Such spectacular actions were, on occasions, highly successful in enabling the unemployed to generate and intervene in the public debate about unemployment and welfare reform. Unemployed activists in the North-East of England occupied a job centre to highlight the way that the Jobseekers Allowance (JSA) regulations were denying benefits to the unemployed and this action received high profile media coverage. One of the activists involved commented:

> One minute you're an unemployed nobody and the next minute you are the lead item on Channel Four News and everyone is wanting to know what you are doing and what you are thinking.[69]

The marchers in southern Spain also indicated that the struggle for visibility was an important element of the European Marches by singing:

> Although nothing comes out in the press, nor on the tele. You'll see us passing in the streets, struggling for what is ours. 10,000 times they silence us, 10,000 times we'll speak.[70]

---

67   KOS (1998) *Info-Rundbrief Nr.43* Juni.

68   Excerpt from interview with Barbara Trowe.

69   Excerpt from interview with activist.

70   Extract from song on the march of Almeria in Schmitt & Spadoni (eds) (2000) *op cit.* p. 61 (Author's translation).

It has been emphasized that ensuring media coverage played an important part in the effectiveness of the European Marches.[71] Initiatives such as the *Canal Marche* video project indicated that as well as struggling against invisibility there was also a struggle for self-representation. A dozen marchers were supplied with a video camera with the aim of giving a voice to those who were excluded from giving their opinion about their situation and about European integration. Most of the videomarchers had never held a camera before, but after a short period of training they combined taking an active part in the march with recording the events occurring en route as well as the personal situation, outlook, and experiences of the marchers. On occasions such as an argument over filming in front of a factory in Roubaix, France, the videomarches themselves became embroiled in the struggle. Over a hundred hours of film were recorded and then edited into four films[72] that were distributed amongst activists and broadcast on French television.[73] Further film was shot during the march to Cologne and the Caravan and mobilizations in Nice out of which two further films were produced.[74]

The struggle for visibility and self-representation was also waged through employing artistic and theatrical modes of expression. Works of art such as *'la plus grande chausette du monde'* [The Longest Sock in the World] (p. 88–9), knitted by *'Euromarcher'* Didier, symbolized the disappearance of textile jobs with the numerous stitches representing the huge numbers of unemployed people in Europe. For him producing the sock was a matter of challenging the image of the lazy unemployed.[75] On the Cologne demonstration, a man dressed as the Pope was carried by four workers and blessed everyone he passed with the 'Holy Water of the EURO' in order to highlight the subordination of social Europe to monetary Europe.[76] The collective *Chômeurs pas Chiens!* wrote and performed a play to highlight the way that home inspections transgressed the human rights of the unemployed and social security claimants. The play went on a tour of Belgian cities and through these performances the issue became a matter of national interest that was debated in Parliament. One activist commented that although there were only relatively few of them, the coverage they received made it feel like there were suddenly thousands of people in the same situation who were demanding their rights.[77]

Individual and Collective Transformation

As well as enabling an intervention into the public debate on social issues, the mobilizations were also experienced as moments of individual and collective

---

71   Chabanet (2002) *op cit.*

72   Canal Marche (1997a) *op cit.*; Canal Marche (1997b) *op cit.*; Canal Marche (1997c) *op cit.*; Canal Marche (1997d) *Carnets de Route* No.3 (Paris: Canal Marche).

73   Schmitt & Spadoni (eds) (2000) *op cit.*

74   Canal Marche (2000) *op cit.*; Canal Marche (2001) *op cit.*

75   Schmitt & Spadoni (eds) (2000) *op cit.*

76   Information from notes taken during participation in the demonstration in Cologne on 29 May 1999.

77   Information from interview with Corinne Barella.

transformation. For some of those involved in them the experience of the marches profoundly changed their attitude to their situation. Scarlett, for example, had been unemployed for three years before getting involved in the unemployed movement and three weeks later took part in the march to Amsterdam. Her attitude to being unemployed reflected how the experience of the marches had led her to challenge the dominant discourse of culpability and passivity:

> All of my attempts (to find work) have led into dead ends. I say 'dead ends' because I don't want to use the word 'failure'. ... I don't want either pity or compassion, only to be recognized and respected.[78]

Collective action amounted to a different form of activation to the neoliberal framework and enabled the participants to utilize and develop their skills and to co-operate to meet their own collectively defined ends. The longer-term occupations in particular required detailed planning, the organization of resources, the use of new communication technologies, and negotiation with the media, officials, and the police. They also involved participants in a collective decision-making process that contrasted with their usual daily subordination.[79] This collective activity not only differed markedly from the kind of work being offered in 'Workfare' schemes and low paid employment, but was also described as a form of work that provided a sense of dignity.[80]

As well as undertaking collective practical and political tasks the marchers also utilized and developed their capacities in a way that contrasted with the discourse that the unemployed lacked skills and enterprise. Many of the 'Euromarchers' were inspired to learn new languages or to improve their existing command of a foreign language[81] and the lack of funding meant that the absence of professional translation required the activists themselves to provide the bulk of the translation at the continental events.[82] Alongside the handcrafted banners, the marchers made works of art, took photographs, and wrote diaries and poetry. A group of video-marchers documented the daily life of the marches and these were turned into films (see previous section).[83] A group of women marchers also made a book out of the comments and experiences of women struggling against unemployment, job insecurity and exclusion that they recorded en route.[84]

Engaging in collective action such as the European Marches had a destabilizing effect on some of the marchers that left behind familiar surroundings and old habits

---

78   Excerpt from conversation with Scarlett in Schmitt & Spadoni (eds) (2000) *op cit.* p. 38 (author's translation).

79   Information from interview with Laurent Guilloteau.

80   Information from interview with Willi Lubkes.

81   Information from interviews with Denise Wood and Nassera Abbed.

82   Information from notes taken during participation in the 'Parliament' and the 'Assembly'.

83   Schmitt & Spadoni (eds) (2000) *op cit.*

84   'European March diary', available at <*www.snore.org/archief1997*> accessed 30/09/1999.

and attitudes and were exposed to new ideas and new ways of life.[85] Many of the unemployed marchers had not travelled outside of their own town for many years and rarely, if ever, abroad and they experienced the marches as a moment of intense politicization that opened them up to different experiences and outlooks.[86]

Although the European Co-ordinating Committee ensured an international participation on each leg of the march to Amsterdam, it was largely left to the marchers to develop a way of life that was a real expression of the internationalist and inclusive ideals that they held. While there was a conscious attempt to practice a new form of living in which each person was of equal value, had an equal say and an equal right to material goods,[87] these principles were severely tested en route due to the problems of prejudiced attitudes and inadequate resources.

The marchers were drawn from different immediate social situations and there was evidence of prejudice and division, but also of a change of attitudes amongst the unemployed and workers towards the homeless marchers and amongst the homeless themselves.[88] Denise Wood explained how both regionalist and nationalist prejudices were expressed in the early stages of the march to Amsterdam, but also how these were actively confronted and debated. She explained how the hours of marching were an opportunity to 'swap realities' with people from different regions and countries and how this resulted in a growing *esprit de corps* and also how she learnt a lot herself through the almost continuous debates and arguments.[89]

Fritz Walter described how on the final leg of the march to Amsterdam a lack of accommodation threatened to compromise the bold declaration of internationalist principles seen at the afternoon rally. He described how the marchers refused an individualist scramble for beds or allocation by national contingent, but rather allotted spaces according to need with the longer-term marchers having priority over the day marchers.[90] This event indicates that the international events such as the demonstrations, meetings, international camp as well as the marches were experienced as powerful examples of a lived internationalism. Although slogans such as 'Unemployed of the World Unite', 'The Workers United Will Never be Defeated' and 'Long Live International Solidarity' were prominent on the mobilizations, these were actually put to the test in that all of the three main European demonstrations were heavily policed. Each of these events was to some degree experienced as a common international stand against such repression with the demonstrators attempting to stop the harassment of the free train protestors in Amsterdam, halt the attempt to split the Cologne demonstration and obstruct the dispersal of the blockade in Nice.

Joachim Glund recalled how the sense of internationalism on the marches was developed at both an interpersonal and political level. He recalled the emotion of his meeting with a Dutch unemployed man who shared many of his own experiences,

---

85   Schmitt & Spadoni (eds) (2000) *op cit.*

86   Information from interview with Patrice Spadoni; Raynal (1997) *op cit.*

87   Schmitt & Spadoni (eds) (2000) *op cit.*

88   *Ibid*; information from informal conversation with Chrystelle Blanc-Lanaute.

89   Information from interview with Denise Wood.

90   Walter, F. (1997) 'Bettgeflüster', in EuroMarsch-Komitee (Duisburg) *Euromarsch in Duisburg* Unpublished document.

situations and problems and how this contrasted with the rather abstract idea of internationalism found in theoretical texts. He also recalled the powerful experience of marching through the Brandenburg Gate alongside unemployed people from other European countries and how this contrasted with the national socialist marches of the inter-war period.[91]

The cultural element of the protest events was also a concrete expression of how the regional and national diversity of participants was appreciated through, for example, sharing food and music. Again this was an uneven process with the Cologne marchers complaining about the poor quality food they received on arrival,[92] but this was matched by other expressions of appreciation of different food not usually available at home.[93] Activists also spoke warmly of the international camp where they stayed between the EU and G8 summits in Cologne as a 'celebration of life'.[94] The camp was a site of shared cultural and political experiences for activists coming from such diverse backgrounds as Brazil, Namibia, Russia and from across the member states of the EU. Each evening various groups cooked dishes that were made available at either a nominal cost or, as acquaintances were made, people invited each other for a meal. The discussion and debate around the campfires took place in a variety of languages and ranged well into the night. The facilities were extremely rudimentary but were shared by all and gave rise to the shared language of humour and as the campsite was situated on the outskirts of Cologne some of the activists travelled together on the metro refusing to buy a ticket.[95]

The joyful quality of this 'lived' internationalism was evident in the spontaneous singing at events such as the 'Assembly'. Comments such as 'the borders no longer existed in my head'[96] or 'Europe all of a sudden feels very small'[97] were indications of how such experiences promoted an internationalist outlook amongst the participants. However, this was not a uniform or blanket process as there were open expressions of prejudice even at events such as the 'Parliament'. After an argument about the facilities and reporting on the opening day, a young French woman shouted out that the policing in Cologne showed that the Germans were still 'fascists'.[98] However, this was immediately challenged by other participants and the general conclusion was that the European Marches refusal of globalization was on no account a withdrawal into nationalism or xenophobia, but a lived expression of internationalism that expressed a view of a tolerant and anti-racist world.[99]

---

91   Information from interview with Joachim Glund.

92   Information from notes taken from recording of the 'Parliament' on 31 May 1999.

93   Information from informal conversation with Antonino Campenni on 4 December 2000; information from notes taken after informational conversations with unknown activists on Cologne demonstration on 29 May 1999.

94   Information from interview with Denise Wood.

95   Information from informal conversations with activists on the fringes of the 'Parliament' on 01 June 1999.

96   Information from interview with Gitti Götz.

97   Information from informal conversation with Antonino Campenni on 3 December 2000.

98   Information from notes taken from recording of the 'Parliament' on 30 May 1999.

99   Schmitt & Spadoni (eds) (2000) *op cit.*

For established militants it was striking how quickly some of the marchers came out of their 'hole' and developed a sense of confidence in themselves and in the possibility of changing the social and political situation.[100] Some of these marchers to Amsterdam developed new skills of organization and played an important leadership role in the nationally based unemployed mobilizations of the following winter.[101] In this sense some of the marchers had undergone a transformation from the isolated, passive unemployed of 'the dismal days' and had become an active militant involved in a movement.

As well as creating new militants, the mobilizations were also an inspiration to longer-term activists. Joachim Glund recounted the sense of disillusionment that he felt as many of his generation of activists became shining entrepreneurial examples of the market economy. For him the marches served to reinforce his belief that a different society was possible whereas before it had appeared as if such a conviction was as irrational as suggesting that water flowed upstream.[102] For some longer-term activists the marches also served as an inspiration for them to continue to engage in collective organization:

> For me everything about Amsterdam was very inspiring and I think that without the European Marches I wouldn't be in the unemployed movement anymore.[103]

Such feelings of inspiration were also generated by the way that some of the collective actions went beyond being experienced as a method of self-defence[104] or having the purpose of highlighting issues.[105] They were also experienced as moments during which the usual relations of power were overturned and new forms of social relations were directly practised.[106] Whereas market forces appeared to the individual market participant as overpowering and omnipotent forces, they were suddenly swept away in the face of collective action. For the participants this was experienced as a moment of joyful liberation and of collective power:

> We organized an action to promote free transport and we made a recording of a song with lyrics like 'they'll get nothing from me, the train is too expensive' and played it on an enormous ghettoblaster. We had sandwich boards with 'the New A-Class' and 'faredodging is self-defence'. We got on, played the song and handed out leaflets and then got off at the next stop. After two hours we got caught by the inspector and he read out his regulations and we kept playing this music really loudly (laughter) and then over his radio came the message, that as long as we were peaceful and didn't sell anything, then we could carry on. That was brilliant, but afterwards I couldn't listen to that song anymore! (laughter). ... Really to see the inspector come and walk by because we were untouchable,

---

100 Information from interview with Michel Rousseau.
101 Information from interview with Patrice Spadoni.
102 Information from interview with Joachim Glund.
103 Excerpt from interview with Piet van der Lende.
104 Information from interview with Andi Dallmann.
105 Information from interview with Irène Bonnaud.
106 Information from interview with Laurent Guilloteau.

because we were in the unemployed movement, was really brilliant, it was the best. It meant the overcoming of powerlessness.[107]

This experience of the power of collective action was also present at the continental level with the activists involved in the marches and mobilizations gaining a sense of being part of a force with the power to challenge the priorities of social and political institutions. The sense of being part of an international network and movement also reflected back onto the national and local mobilizations in a way that served to strengthen them:

> When we are in France and we do actions, the administrative people try to make us think that we are doing it alone and so we are crazy, and that everything we do amounts to nothing, so why continue to do it? And through the European Marches we see that we are not alone and we also see that we are not so crazy because we all think the same things and all fight against the same things. So afterwards we are happy that we are not reduced to a region or a place and that we are not just European, but global too. So that brings us confidence, that brings us the network, moving all together, Germans, English, Belgians and Italians. So that brings us the power, it reverses the power with the numbers.[108]

The establishment of such a collective force served to generate amongst activists a renewed sense of hope that a different world was possible. As one militant claimed,

> The actions, the marches, have been a source of hope; they have enabled us to state that it is possible to change things, they have made us aware that we are a real force, ... that a different world is possible.[109]

It is to the development of an agenda for the content of this 'different Europe' and of the structures through which it was formulated that I now turn in chapter six.

---

107 Excerpt from interview with German activist.

108 Excerpt from interview with Nassera Abbed.

109 Excerpt from 'Mon engagement contre le chômage', Charles Piaget in Schmitt & Spadoni (eds) (2000) *op cit.* p.124 (author's translation).

Chapter 6

A Different Europe

> They have been constructing Europe for about fifty years. The movement in Europe: the unions, the associations, the Left parties, are not united, but they are suspicious of everything that comes out of Europe, for them it's like the devil. We haven't constructed a Europe that we want, a Social Europe that is fair, equal and democratic.[1]

This extract from an interview with a prominent participant in the European Marches highlights how it was an alliance of SMOs all of which were opposed to the neoliberal version of 'Europe' being advanced through the institutions of the EU which was producing an 'Unsocial Europe',[2] The European Marches also began to develop ideas and demands for an alternative variant which it proclaimed under the banner of a 'Different Europe'. This indicated a move from a focus on the specific issues of unemployment, job insecurity and exclusion to a more general concern with a whole array of social rights at the European level. This process was facilitated by the EU's expanding social agenda in the wake of the introduction of an Employment Chapter in the Treaty of Amsterdam and the proposal to include a Charter of Fundamental Rights in the Treaty of Nice.

The content of a 'Different Europe' began to emerge through a process of exchanges between participants in the organizations that were engaged in the resistance to the social consequences of neoliberal policies outlined in previous chapters. These exchanges were enabled mainly through a series of 'coalition forums' (pp. 243–4)[3] alongside the publication of a newspaper titled 'European Marches News', a website, and books. The forums included the larger *Assises* at which the European Marches were launched and the smaller 'European Parliament of the Unemployed and Insecure Workers in the Struggle' (the 'Parliament') and the 'European Assembly of the Unemployed and Insecure Workers in the Struggle' (the 'Assembly'). These forums included plenary and workshop sessions at which exemplary struggles from across the continent were showcased and in which debates took place over the declarations for the European Marches including the main platform of demands.

This chapter shows how producing an alternative agenda for a 'Different Europe' was not simply a smooth process of consensus forming which is seen to characterize the decision-making in the GJM. It also developed by way of conflict and contest over the main points of opposition and the main elements of the alternative agenda. This was seen most clearly in relation to the controversy surrounding the demand for

---

1   Excerpt from interview with Michel Rousseau.
2   Gray (2004) *op cit.*
3   Bandy & Smith (2005) *op cit.*

a return to full employment that led to a decline in support from some quarters for the European Marches in the wake of the summit in Amsterdam. Moreover, the counter-agenda changed in relation to the shifting agenda of the EU which itself partially incorporated elements of the earlier agenda such as the call for full employment. In this sense, the 'social movement from below' (p. 5) which began to develop its own agenda for a 'Different Europe' did so in direct relation to the 'social movement from above' (p. 2) which was advancing its liberalization project through EU institutions.[4] Therefore, the various social policy alternatives: 'welfare', 'neoliberal', 'new paternalist' (p. 91) which seemed to be emerging[5] were the products of a clash of social movements which were contesting their formation. I attempt to show this by relating the debates in the European Marches over the common points of criticism and the elements of a 'Different Europe' to the particular policy contexts which existed in the periods leading up to the EU summits in Amsterdam, Cologne, and Nice.

In the final section of the chapter, I discuss the tensions that existed in the European Marches based around two main strategies. The first strategy regarded the European Marches as a vehicle for mobilizing pressure to assist in gaining immediate material improvements based on its core demands. The other strategy was to use these demands as a basis for constructing a broader social movement which could advance a longer-term project of social change.[6] I focus mainly on the second strategy and present how the European Marches related its social concerns and its proposed solutions to those of the other European and global networks of resistance to neoliberal policies. This can be regarded as a process of 'frame extension' (p. 82)[7] whereby the European Marches extended its demands for social justice achieved through universal rights to income, work and services. However, I show again how the development of links between the SMOs in these networks was not an automatic process and was subject to some resistance. However, from the perspective that social movements are always in the process of being constructed, the European Marches appears to have played a role in moving the demands of the emergent European social movement away from defensive 'militant particularism' (p. 5) and in the direction of more universal and utopian goals.[8]

The Policy Context for the Amsterdam Campaign

The immediate policy context for the European Marches to Amsterdam was the failure by European nation states to tackle record levels of unemployment and

---

4   Nilsen, A. G. & Cox, L. (2005) 'At the heart of society burns the fire of social movements: What would a Marxist theory of social movements look like?', Paper presented to the Tenth International Conference on *Alternative Futures and Popular Protest* 30 March–1 April Manchester Metropolitan University.

5   MacGregor, S. (1999) 'Welfare, Neo-Liberalism and New Paternalism: Three Ways for Social Policy in Late Capitalist Societies', *Capital & Class* 67 pp.91–118.

6   Again see Chabanet (2002) *op cit.* for a discussion of strategic and discursive differences within the European Marches.

7   Della Porta & Diani (2006) *op cit.*

8   Nilsen & Cox (2005) *op cit.*

poverty that had been exacerbated by budgetary pressures exerted by the convergence criteria to qualify for EMU. Leading players in the EU, such as France, Germany and Italy, introduced severe austerity measures that, in the German case, amounted to the largest state spending cuts ever recorded. This resulted in the reduction of public spending by seventy billion *Deutschmarks* that impacted mostly on the social sector.[9] The adverse social consequences of EMU were considered so severe that the European Parliament released a report outlining its negative effects on employment and public services.[10] However, the Dublin Summit in December 1996 endorsed the arrangements for a 'Growth and Stability Pact' to ensure fiscal rectitude before and after the inception of the 'EURO' by levying penalties on member states running an excessive budget deficit.[11]

The adverse social conditions arising from EMU were set within the broader context of a European social dimension that had progressed little in the forty years since the Treaty of Rome stated its aim of the upwards harmonization of social rights. The attempt led by Jacques Delors, ex-President of the Commission, to develop a legally binding 'Social Charter' failed when opposition to it from the British Government succeeded in relegating it to being merely an appendix of the Treaty of Maastricht.[12] The attempt led by Jacques Santer, ex-President of the Commission, to construct a 'European Employment Pact' was scuppered by the failure of national social pacts in Germany and Belgium.[13] Nevertheless, there was continued pressure from some member states for an Employment Chapter to be included in the Treaty of Amsterdam.[14]

The Amsterdam Campaign

The initial appeals for the European Marches were agreed at small meetings of activists in Turin[15] and Florence[16] in the spring and summer of 1996 (for participating organizations see chapter 4). These appeals focused on the social consequences of EMU and took the first steps to filling the empty space of 'social Europe' with some common demands. This reflected the concern amongst some of the initial proponents

---

9   Teague, P. (1998) 'Monetary Union and Social Europe', *Journal of European Social Policy,* 8(2) pp. 117–137.

10   European Parliament (1994) *The Social Consequences of Monetary Union*, Final Report DG IV E-I.

11   For details on the Growth and Stability Pact see Roney, A. (1998) *EC/EU Fact Book* (London:Kogan Page) pp. 128–9

12   Falkner, G. (1998) *EU Social Policy in the 1990s. Towards a corporatist policy community* (London:Routledge).

13   Pochet, P. & Fajertag, G. (1997) *op cit.*

14   Goetschy, J. (1999) 'The European Employment Strategy: Genesis and Development', *European Journal of Industrial Relations*, 5(2) pp. 117–137.

15   'Euromarches - Appel européen de Turin pour une initiative de grande ampleur contre le chômage', available at <*www.euromarches.org/francais/96/turina1.htm*> accessed on 17/01/2001.

16   'Appeal from Florence', available at <*www.euromarches.org/english/96/floa1.htm*> accessed on 20/08/2001.

of the European Marches about the dangers for forming a broad alliance of addressing the EMU issue too directly. It was feared by some militants that adopting a specific position on EMU or specific demands such as an unemployment rate of 2–3% for entry into the 'EURO' could provoke disunity and so jeopardize a successful campaign.[17]

This concern was grounded in the existence of two main tendencies within the campaign. The majority argued for a strategy of campaigning around the social consequences of EMU and a set of basic common demands relating to unemployment and poverty whilst a minority argued for a clearly political campaign against EMU and even the EU as a whole. Angela Klein, a prominent figure in the European Marches in Germany, remembered how this debate worked its way through in the lead up to the marches:

> We had the discussion about whether to have a common position on the EU. In Germany, groups said that we couldn't simply say that we are against unemployment, but we must also say that we are against the EU. We had a real debate as others said that we have a lot of criticisms of the EU, but if we start to say that we are against it then half of our supporters will leave the room. And the militant groups wanted us to have a campaign against the EURO, but we said 'no'. Anyone can run such a campaign, but as the European Marches 'no'. That is a campaign against unemployment and we have our demands about that. There were people who weren't against the EURO even though they were against the convergence criteria. You can say that that was contradictory and it may well have been, but that was the situation and how people thought and it was agreed that we wouldn't oppose it. We simply said that here is a scandal, there are twenty million unemployed and fifty million poor people living in the EU and we are going to show you that by marching to you from every country in Europe.[18]

A similar debate occurred in the UK[19] and consequently, in spite of highlighting the breakdown of the welfare state and increasing unemployment, both associated with the EMU related austerity measures, the initial appeals included no mention of EMU. Rather, these appeals criticized the EU's emphasis on institutional reform at the expense of action to combat what was regarded as the pressing new social question of unemployment standing at 20 million and poverty affecting 50 million people. Restoring full employment was targeted as the major priority to be achieved by reducing the working week without loss of pay, linked to job creation in the areas of health, education, and environmental protection. These demands for tackling the central problem of unemployment were accompanied by the call for social rights for all, nationals and migrants alike, and the demand for a living wage. There was also a call for a redistribution of wealth to be achieved through taxation on capital transfers.[20]

---

17   'Pour des marches européenes contre le chômage au printemps 97' available at <*www.euromarches.org/francais/96/premier.htm*> accessed on 17/01/2001.

18   Excerpt from interview with Angela Klein.

19   Information from notes taken after participation in the UK European Marches Steering Committee on 5 September 1998.

20   'Euromarches – Appel européen de Turin pour une initiative de grande ampleur contre le chômage', available at <*www.euromarches.org/francais/96/turina1.htm*> accessed

Avoiding a political position of opposition to the Single Currency in favour of opposition to its social consequences and support for demands to alleviate them, seemed to enable a broader alliance to be formed. However, no consensus could be reached for the declaration issued at the *Assises*, held to launch the European Marches which took place in Brussels over the weekend of 22–23 February 1997 and attracted over six hundred people from seventeen countries. The European Marches remained an umbrella for a range of individuals and organizations to express their different particular grievances against the neoliberal EU and through which to present their particular demands for an alternative 'social Europe'. While the seemingly dominant voice was calling for a return to full employment, this was not without criticism.

The mainstay of the participants at the *Assises* were directly experiencing the problems of unemployment, job insecurity, and exclusion.[21] In line with the aims established at the European Co-ordinating Committee meetings, there was an emphasis on hearing the personal experiences of those most affected by the social consequences of restructuring and a number of unemployed, homeless, and illegal migrants described their situations.[22] The event was also a platform for representatives of a panorama of struggles from across Europe including the striking UK dockers from Liverpool and Belgian steelworkers from the Clabecq forge that was threatened with closure.[23] Other sessions on the economic policies being implemented across EU member states enabled representatives of the various associations to highlight the particular consequences of neoliberal restructuring. Irish unemployed associations underlined the problem of long-term unemployment and Spanish associations and unions highlighted the proliferation of short-term contracts.[24] The draft of a declaration to be issued in support of the marches articulated how these various problems had a common cause:

> The construction of the European Union, welded to neoliberal ideas, has had disastrous consequences for workers, in particular those in insecure jobs and the unemployed throughout the world. For this reason confronted by such an economic system there is an urgent need for convergence and solidarity.[25]

Despite general agreement about the need for a common European struggle, there was some disagreement about what the goal of this struggle should be. The draft declaration included an array of demands including a shorter working week and job

---

on 17/01/2001; 'Appeal from Florence', available at <*www.euromarches.org/english/96/floal.htm*> accessed on 20/08/2001.

21   Canal Marche (1997c) *Réunion de Bruxelles 22–23 Février 1997 Panorama des luttes européenes* (Paris: Canal Marches).

22   Information from minutes of European Coordinating Committee meeting held on 30/11/1996, available at <*www.euromarches.org/english/96/brup1.htm*> accessed on 20/08/2001.

23   Canal Marche (1997c) *op cit.*

24   *ibid.*

25   Excerpt from 'The List of Demands following in the European *Assises* – Brussels, 22nd and 23rd February 1997', available at <*www-pluto.informatik.uni-oldenburg.de/~also/eusepa65.htm*> accessed on 08/08/2001.

Struggling for a Social Europe

creation measures alongside a call for universal rights and wealth redistribution.[26] While some participants were in support, others like those representing the Spanish CGT, concluded that these demands did not amount to a significant enough departure from the proposals of mainstream trade unionism and argued for the inclusion in the declaration of statements demonstrating a much clearer opposition to the Maastricht Treaty and even the EU as a whole.[27]

There were also workshops on the questions of the shorter working week and full employment, but the prominence of such demands came in for criticism by activists from some of the unemployed associations. These associations were arguing that the immediate priority for the unemployed was for more income rather than more work and that this should be reflected in the demands adopted for the marches.[28] It was also asserted by some unemployed activists that the goal of full employment left certain fundamental issues about the question of work unchallenged. For example one unemployed activist stated that,

> In these marches, certain people are demanding full employment. I think that it is first of all a matter of posing the choice of the society that it would make. How do we want to work, to produce, for whom and with whom?[29]

That there was an ongoing debate about this issue was significant in that the marches began as the final preparations were being made for the 'Full Employment Convention'. This was convened by Ken Coates and Anne van Lancker of the PES and Frieder Otto Wolf and Luigi Vinci of the NGL/GUL and attracted nine hundred participants drawn from every EU country and comprised official representatives and grass roots activists from unemployed associations and trade unions as well churches and political organizations.

The Appeal for the Convention focused on opposition to monetarist policies such as the EMU convergence criteria and argued for an economic strategy harmonized at the EU level based on investment programmes centred on job creation and funded from corporate profits. This, it was argued, would lead to an ecologically sustainable recovery that would form the basis for a new kind of full employment involving the redistribution of paid and unpaid work and a reduction in the working week without loss of pay. Such public policies would amount to a 'new deal' between those living in poverty and the wealthy and be based on the mobilization and shared interests of 'broad popular alliances' (p.9).[30] This appeal gained the support of many hundreds of

---

26   *ibid.*

27   Information from minutes of European Coordinating Committee meeting held on 30/11/1996, available at <*www.euromarches.org/english/96/brup1.htm*> accessed on 20/08/2001.

28   Information from interviews with Willi Lubkes and Piet van der Lende.

29   Excerpt from interview with Philippe Gentilli: ADC: Lausanne in Schmitt & Spadoni op cit p. 126 (author's translation).

30   Coates, K. (ed) (1998) 'Full Employment – A European Appeal', *The Spokesman* 64

signatories amongst mainly MEPs and MPs, but also ranging from trade union and church leaders to NGO representatives, and writers, artists and academics.[31]

The Convention was actually held in May 1997 and gained financial backing from the PES and the NGL/GUL. It was greeted by Jacques Delors, ex-President of the Commission, and was opened in the European Parliament by its President. The Convention had four workshops on 'Full Employment and the European Institutional Agenda; New Models for Full Employment; Alternative Perspectives for Society and the Environment; and Exclusion, Insecurity, Participation and Equal Rights'. These workshops were co-ordinated by MEPs and representatives of supporting organizations such the ILO, the Platform of Social NGOs, the INOU and the TUC that gave information papers to begin each session. The submission by the TUC highlighted the unacceptability of the 'Project Work' scheme, introduced by the Conservative Government in the UK, due to the compulsory participation of the unemployed.

The Convention issued a declaration that demanded that the IGC in Amsterdam reject neoliberal policies based on an acceptance of high levels of unemployment and on austerity programmes resulting from the EMU convergence criteria. It also demanded the adoption of a legally binding employment chapter and argued for it to take priority over the 'Growth and Stability Pact'. This should lead to a new economic policy involving the use of EU funds to guarantee 'a new social contract for full employment' (p. 162) achieved through working time reduction and job creation in the Public and Third Sectors. The Convention expressed its support for the European Marches and a contingent of 'Euromarchers' met with MEPs from the 'Full Employment Convention Group'.[32]

The Convention was one of more than a thousand public meetings that were held in towns and cities along the routes of the marches.[33] These meetings were an opportunity for a whole range of opinions and ideas to be voiced about the concrete social problems of unemployment and poverty and the more abstract questions of European integration and EMU. The city government in Eindhoven, Holland gave over the city hall to a meeting on 'EMU and its social consequences' at which the speakers included a critical economist and a Renault striker.[34] In Gisres and Chateaulin in France, public debates focused more on the local problems of unemployment and social exclusion.[35]

The European Marches produced its own publicity to support the campaign including a book titled *Europe: Modes D'Emploi*[36] [Europe: Ways of Working] with articles expressing the viewpoints of associations, NGOs, trade unionists, and

31   *Full Employment: A European Appeal* Promotional Leaflet published by 'Full Employment Appeal, Bertrand Russell House, Gamble Street, Nottingham, NG7 4ET, England; Information from interview with Ken Coates.

32   Coates (ed) (1998) *op cit.*

33   Aguiton & Cremieux (1997) *op cit.*

34   'Eindhoven: Preparations for receiving the March in full swing', available at <*www.snore.org/archief/1997*> accessed on 30/09/1999.

35   'Carnets des Marches Européenes', available at <*www.euromarches.org/francais/97/carnet.htm*> accessed on 17/01/2001.

36   Marches Européenes (1997) *Europe modes D'emploi*, (Paris: Editions Syllepse).

academics and a more popular journal, titled *à Amsterdam*, that was sold by the 'Euromarchers'.[37] An overview of the contents illustrates how the main focus was on highlighting the disastrous social consequences of the EU's neoliberal agenda and the pressing need for a social dimension. Amongst the articles written by academics, Pedro Montes evaluated the Single Currency as a stage in the construction of a neoliberal European economic space favouring capital through the competitive pressures to reduce salaries and social provision.[38] Michel Husson also emphasized the neoliberal perspective of the Commission and the Ecofin committee and linked rising unemployment and job insecurity with labour market deregulation.[39] Laurent Vogel argued that deregulation, the Single Currency, and the lack of a social dimension were leading to a crisis of legitimacy that was strongest amongst those whose citizenship rights were being denied.[40] Articles written by representatives of unemployed associations such as the MNCP and APEIS highlighted how the misery that resulted from neoliberal policies was a spur to action[41] and Eliane Vogel-Polsky[42] and Hosny Abd el Rehim[43] called for the affirmation of equal rights for women and migrant workers.

The alternative to neoliberal policies focused on filling the empty social dimension with demands for substantive social rights with the main emphasis on calling for a return to full employment. In contributions on behalf of NGOs, Kairos Europe argued for a fair single currency, common employment and social policies, and a legally binding social charter.[44] Kairos joined the ENU[45] and the Convention for Full Employment[46] in demanding a return to full employment. Articles by trade unionists from the German IG Metall[47] and the Spanish CGT[48] called for measures to oppose mass unemployment and job insecurity and in particular the reduction of the working week. Representatives of the association DAL highlighted deregulation

---

37   Marches Européenes *'à Amsterdam'*, Paris: Marches Européenes.

38   Montes, P. (1997) 'Union européenne et modèle néolibéral', in Marches Européenes *op cit.*

39   Husson, M. (1997) 'Chômage et précarité en Europe', in Marches Européenes *op cit.*

40   Vogel, L. (1997) 'Conference Intergouvernementale et politique sociale. Réflexions sur un échec annoncé', in Marches Européenes *op cit.*

41   'Guerre au chômage, guerre à la misère: Questions à Philippe Villechalane', *à Amsterdam*, No.7, Mardi 6 Mai 1997.

42   Vogel-Polsky, E. (1997) 'Femmes, citoyenneté européene et Traité de Maastricht', in Marches Européenes *op cit.*

43   Abd el Rehim, H. (1997) 'Les immigrés: des travailleurs désarmés', in Marches Européenes *op cit.*

44   Kairos Europe (1997) 'Pour une union monétaire juste', in Marches Européenes *op cit.*

45   European Network of Unemployed (1997) 'Le plein emploi avant la monnaie', in Marches Européenes *op cit.*

46   Coates, K. (1997) 'Appel européen pour le plein emploi', in Marches Européenes *op cit.*

47   Dierkes, H. (1997) 'La crise du modèle allemand', in Marches Européenes *op cit.*

48   'Le patronat veut plus de précarité pour toujours plus de bénéfices. Questions à José-Maria Olaizola', *'à Amsterdam'* no.6 22 Avril 1997.

of housing provision and demanded a European directive to enforce the right to housing.[49]

While the European Council was meeting in Amsterdam to agree the inclusion of an employment chapter in the Treaty of Amsterdam, a counter-summit event was held that attracted hundreds of participants from a diversity of unions, associations and political organizations. The final declaration identified full employment amongst its central goals which was to be achieved through a reduction in the working week.[50]

The Policy Context for the Cologne Campaign

The Treaty of Amsterdam paved the way for significant moves towards the co-ordination of member states' employment and social policies by a soft policymaking approach[51] in which the European Commission played an important agenda setting and co-ordinating role. The outcome of this approach was a harmonization of policy objectives rather than a harmonization of policies or a single policy at the EU level. The European Commission had set the agenda for reform in the early 1990s by publishing White Papers on 'Growth, Competitiveness and Employment'[52] and on 'Social Policy'.[53] Commentators remarked that these documents focused on dealing with unemployment through reorienting government intervention towards producing labour market flexibility. The outcome of this supply side approach would be generalized job and income insecurity.[54] These changes were regarded as evidence of how existing social rights were being disbanded.[55]

The Treaty of Amsterdam adopted a high level of employment and social protection as aims of the Community, but this was accompanied by a high degree of competitiveness. Article 109 stated that member states and the Community shall develop 'a coordinated strategy for employment and particularly for promoting a skilled, trained, and adaptable workforce and labour markets responsive to economic change' (p. 32).[56] Commentators noted that although the aim of the Treaty was 'to

49   Arnold, P. & Marancy, S. (1997) 'Le logement et l'Europe', in Marches Européenes *op cit.*

50   *'Alternative Summit Declaration: More steps to go Towards a different Europe'* Copy of Printed Declaration Amsterdam 1997.

51   De la Porte, C. (2000) 'Is there an Emerging European Consensus on Social Protection?', in E. Gabaglio & R. Hoffman (eds) *European Trade Union Yearbook 1999*, (Brussels:ETUI).

52   European Commission (1993) *Growth, Competitiveness, Employment: The Challenges and Ways Forward into the 21st Century – White Paper*, Brussels COM (93) 700.

53   European Commission (1994) *European Social Policy – A Way Forward for the Union – A White Paper*, Brussels COM (94) 333.

54   Mullard, M. (1997) 'Introduction' in M. Mullard & S. Lee (eds) *The Politics of Social Policy in Europe*, Cheltenham: Edward Elgar.

55   Kuper, B-O. (1994) 'The Green and White Papers of the European Union: the apparent goal of reduced social benefits', *Journal of European Social Policy*, 4 (2) pp. 129–137.

56   'The Treaty of Amsterdam' available at *http://www.eurotreaties.com/amsterdamtext. html* accessed on 10/09/06.

bring about a new equilibrium between monetary union and employment' (p. 608), the reality was that the goal of a stable currency was still paramount.[57]

Following the Amsterdam Treaty, the European Commission moved swiftly to develop a five year European Employment Strategy[58] that was adopted at the 'Jobs Summit' in Luxembourg in November 1997.[59] An interim assessment was carried out prior to the Lisbon summit in March 2000 where the strategy formed the basis of the reassertion of full employment as the central policy goal.[60]

The strategy's general aim was to increase employment rates to those comparable to the USA. By 2010, the overall employment rate should have risen from 61% to 70% and that of women from 51% to 60% with the service sector as the main area of employment growth.[61] The strategy involved two elements: encouraging the expansion of overall employment by growth focussed macroeconomic policies and by introducing structural reforms of labour markets and welfare systems. The BEPG urged member states to introduce policies aimed at reforming the labour market, taxation, social security and welfare systems.[62] Structural reforms were agreed at the Cardiff summit in June 1998[63] whilst talk of an employment pact in Vienna in December 1998[64] was translated into a weak agreement in Cologne in June 1999 including the establishment of a European macroeconomic dialogue.[65]

The centrepiece of the Employment Strategy was the European co-ordination of employment policies according to the principles of 'employability', 'adaptability', 'entrepreneurship', and 'equal opportunities' (pp. 12–13) around which member states compiled National Action Plans (NAPs).[66] The Commission issued Employment Reports in which it evaluated member state performances, highlighting good practice and promoting its dissemination. In 2000, the Commission issued

---

57   Goetschy, J. & Pochet, P. (1997) 'The Treaty of Amsterdam: a new approach to employment and social affairs?' *Transfer*, 3(3) pp. 607–620.

58   European Commission (1999) *The European Employment Strategy – Investing in People, investing in more and better jobs* Luxembourg: Office for Official Publications of the European Communities.

59   European Commission (1997) 'The European Employment Summit', available at <*www.europa.eu.int/comm/employment_social*> accessed on 11/01/2001.

60   European Commission (2000) *Employment in Europe 2000* available at <www. europa.eu.int/comm/dgs/employment> accessed on 01/11/2001.

61   *ibid.*

62   European Commission (1998) *The broad guidelines of the economic policies of the Member States and of the Community* Brussels COM (98) 454.

63   Eironline (1998) 'Cardiff summit debates next steps in employment strategy' available at <*www.eiro.eurofound.ie/1998/06/features/eu9806109f.html*> accessed on 08/08/2001.

64   Eironline (1998) 'Vienna summit reaffirms employment as priority' available at <*www.eiro.eurofound.ie/1998/12/inbrief/eu9812141n.html*> accessed on 08/08/2001.

65   Eironline (1999) 'Expectations and outcomes of the Cologne European Council' available at <*www.eiro.eurofound.ie/1999/06/inbrief/eu9906180.html*> accessed on 08/08/2001.

66   European Commission (1999) *op cit.*

fifty two recommendations in areas of unsatisfactory progress.[67] Most progress was made in implementing employability measures[68] and policies recognized as good practice were the UK's 'New Deal for young people', Denmark's initiatives aimed at unemployed youth and Belgium's job creation programme for the long-term unemployed that also focused on the provision of training and counselling.[69]

The Cologne Campaign

The period between the Amsterdam and Cologne summits saw from some quarters a reduction in the support for the European Marches. This was due to its opposition to the Employment Strategy which was presented as a mechanism for advancing labour market and welfare restructuring that was detrimental to the interests of workers and the unemployed. This analysis failed to impress some of the previous political backers of the European Marches to Amsterdam as well as its trade union opponents.

Herman Schmid, a newly elected MEP from the NGL/GUL, saw the positive elements of active welfare policies and argued that measures to promote full employment could break the confines of the 'Growth and Stability Pact'. The key was for a strong labour movement to ensure that full employment was not achieved through casualization.[70] Peter Coldrick, an official of the ETUC, was a more enthusiastic supporter of employability measures that he argued were promoting 'positive flexibility'. He asserted that such measures were helping to put the European economy back on the right track with the result of rising employment. He concluded that current 'Third Way' thinking was in tune with what the ETUC had been arguing for years and could ultimately lead to the return of full employment.[71]

Anne van Lancker MEP, from the PES, was a supporter of the European Marches to Amsterdam and had been heavily involved in the work of the Convention for Full Employment and became the moderator of the parliamentary Social Policy Committee. She argued that the implementation of active welfare policies provided a good opportunity to develop high quality training measures. However, she did not rule out compulsory participation in such schemes, even though she admitted that this had led her into an argument with the unemployed movement in Belgium. She was an opponent of proposals for a 'Citizen's Income' and felt that the future debate lay in the definition of full employment with the answer lying in the development of good quality jobs and especially service employment in the Third Sector. Consequently she preferred to continue the work of the Convention.[72]

---

67   European Commission (2000) *Employment Recommendations* Brussels COM (99) 5161.

68   European Commission (2000) *Joint Employment Report_* available at <*www. europa.eu.int/comm/dgs/employment*> accessed on 11/01/2001.

69   European Commission (1999) *Employment Guilelines 2000* Brussels COM (99) 441.

70   Information from interview with Herman Schmid MEP.

71   Information from interview with Peter Coldrick.

72   Information from interview with Anne van Lancker MEP.

The second 'European Full Employment Convention' was held at the European Parliament on 4–5 February 1999 with the opening statement given by Ken Coates MEP from the PES. There were four workshops including matters such as future employment trends; the redistribution of work; social rights and social exclusion; and employment creation. The final declaration, that was adopted by the plenary, moderated by Frieder Otto Wolf MEP from the NGL/GUL called for a 'global New Deal' and a 'new model of European social development' (p. 9). This would form the basis for tackling social problems such as mass unemployment and social exclusion through achieving a level of growth that was economically and ecologically sustainable. The declaration also highlighted specific measures in the employment and social fields such as the creation of jobs in the Third Sector. This would contribute to achieving the specific objective of a 10% rise in job creation in order to reduce existing unemployment rates by 50% within five years leading ultimately to the establishment of full employment. Such a programme would be underpinned by a strengthened social and civil dialogue involving both the unions and NGOs in a 'deepening of social partnership' (p. 9).[73]

Prominent supporters of the European Marches such as Marie-Paule Connan, whilst supportive of the first Convention, thought that the second Convention had resulted in a disappointing compromise owing to the involvement of MEPs from across the political spectrum.[74] However, her most severe criticism was reserved for the Employment Chapter:

> After Amsterdam everyone like the unions said, 'it's marvellous, they've created an Employment Chapter' and everyone said 'bravo, bravo'. But the problem was that nobody had read this Employment Chapter. So we started to read it and realized that this text was a terrible trap because it said that all of the employment policies would be compatible with all of the main economic orientations. … Up to Cologne we worked to show all this and to make links between the employment policy and the main economic policy guidelines like the Stability Pact.[75]

Marie-Paule and other prominent figures in the European Marches such as Michel Rousseau and Angela Klein set about developing a critical analysis of the EU's Employment Strategy locating it within its overall policy context. Ideas and information about EU employment policies were exchanged at the European Co-ordinating Committee meetings and declarations and press releases were produced. Documents outlining the origin and significance of the coordinated employment policies were circulated and speeches were made at conferences of activists, at the 'Parliament' and later at the 'Assembly'. Articles were also published in the European Marches journal and later made available on the European Marches website. It is

---

73   European Full Employment Convention (1999) *Full Employment in Europe* (Nottingham: Spokesman).

74   Information from interview with Marie-Paule Connan.

75   Excerpt from interview with Marie-Paule Connan.

possible to give an overview of the analysis that was circulated by summarizing the ideas contained in these articles and speeches. [76]

The analysis highlighted the undemocratic way in which employment and labour market policies were formulated and their neoliberal character. The Commission was regarded as being like a European Government that was working behind the scenes to encourage member states to implement employer friendly policies. This was regarded as a shift away from the initial goal of the EU to harmonize policies so as to ensure equality towards a co-ordination of policies around the neoliberal principle of competitiveness. The European Central Bank was regarded as having a large influence over economic policymaking which also dominated the direction of employment policy. The overall aim of the employment strategy was to emulate the American model which was characterized by high employment rates and a dual labour market. This would require the expansion of a sector of low paid insecure employment which was to be achieved by cutting pay rates of lower skilled workers and enforced by reducing the levels of unemployment and social benefits. To support this analysis reference was made to the EU's own documents and the following passage from the Commission's communication, 'Growth and Employment within the framework of EMU Stability' was often quoted:

> Widen the wage scale at the base: To obtain the desired results ... supposes a reduction of about 20–30% of the wage costs of the lower qualified activities, as was the case, for example, in the United States between 1970 and 1980. Moreover, in order to be effective, such a measure would necessitate, in Europe, an equivalent reduction of unemployment benefits and of social benefits, in order to eliminate what is called the 'poverty trap' (p. 20).[77]

The leading role played by the Commission in developing a new individualizing discourse around unemployment was highlighted. Documents produced by the Commission emphasized how unemployment was the product of individual failings rather than state inaction in that the unemployed lack the necessary adaptability and

---

76   'Les politiques d'emploi dans l'Union européene', available at   <*www. euromarches.org/francais/00/eu1.htm*> accessed on 01/07/2001; 'The Neo-Liberal Wind of Europe Blows over Lisbon' available at <*www.euromarches.org/english/00/inliss.htm*> accessed on 08/08/2000; 'Sommet de Lisbonne: L'Europe sociale, c'est pas NET', available at <*www.euromarches.org/francais/lissmpc.htm*> accessed on 17/01/2001; 'Sommet Social de Lisbonne', available at <*www.euromarches.org/francais/lisbpr1.htm*> accessed on 17/01/2001; 'No to the Dismantling of Social Protection Systems', *Marches Européenes: Groupe d'Initiative pour la Belgique*, Photocopied Document, Undated; 'Le Sommet européen de Cologne: ça ne sent pas bon pour les chômeurs et les précaires', *Marches Européenes*, Photocopied Document, Undated; 'Vienne: la valse des chomeurs' *Marches Européenes/ NEWS (French version)* No.8 Décembre 1998; 'Que sera le 'Pacte pour l'emploi?' *Marches Européenes/NEWS (French version)* No.9 Février 1999; 'Ce qu'ils ont décidé à Cologne nous laisse un an avant la régression sociale massive', *Marches Européenes/NEWS (French version)* No.12 Juin 1999; Information from notes taken from recordings of the 'Parliament' on 30/05/1999 and of the 'Assembly' on 02/12/2000.

77   Commission européenne (1998) 'Croissance et emploi dans le cadre de stabilitie de l'UE', *Communication de la Commission*. Bruxelles, le 25.02.98 COM 103 final.

enterprise to be employable. This new discourse was the underpinning for a new approach to employment and social policies which focused on activating the passive unemployed. This translated into the reform of unemployment benefit systems under the guise of employability which reduced benefit levels and enforced participation in training programmes which resembled the workfare schemes that were widespread in the USA. The outcome of these reforms was to compel as many of the unemployed as possible back into the lower echelons of the labour market and at reduced levels of pay. The general results were that even as unemployment was falling, poverty was on the increase and a new group of working poor was rapidly coming into existence. Whereas in the past, poverty had largely been the product of unemployment, under the new conditions governing the labour market and welfare system, it was low paid employment that was the primary cause of poverty.[78]

These criticisms were confirmed by the everyday experiences of the grass roots activists from the unemployed associations that formed the mainstay of the European Marches. These associations did not participate in the civil dialogue promoted by the Commission, but assembled independently in the forums mentioned at the start of this chapter. These forums were an occasion for activists to share their experiences and analyses developed at the frontline of resistance to the neoliberal policies implemented within nation states. For these activists, employability measures had also come to be associated with benefit cuts and controls that resulted in a compulsion to work and intensified labour market competition ultimately leading to lower levels of wages and poorer conditions.

Speaking to the opening plenary of the conference held in Cologne, Marika, representing APEIS, argued that employability policies were turning the labour market into a jungle resulting in endemic low pay and dangerous working conditions. She described how welfare reforms deprived the unemployed of benefits so driving them further into poverty and black market work.[79] Speaking at the 'Parliament', a representative of BABC, gave his group's analysis of the UK government's 'New Deal' programme:

> The New Labour government is trying to force as many people as possible into the labour market. …Enhanced employability across previously 'excluded' sectors of the labour market is a huge attack. Increased competition will drive down wages and conditions. That is the iron law of the labour market. We have seen this process begin in Brighton … The employed person who would have ordinarily applied for the post is not considered, but instead finds herself facing stiffer competition for similar posts.[80]

He argued that the 'New Deal' was a continuation of the shift towards Workfare programmes that had begun with 'Project Work'. He outlined the successful campaign that had been waged against it in Brighton highlighting how unemployed activists had organized alongside grass roots trade unionists working in benefit offices to

---

78   See footnote 76 above.

79   Information from notes taken during participation in the conference held in Cologne on 23 January 1999.

80   Excerpt from contribution to the 'Parliament' by a representative of BABC taken from *Cologne 99 op cit.*

engage in a series of strikes and militant direct actions that targeted agencies running the Project. His talk generated a good deal of enthusiasm amongst activists in the audience representing unemployed associations as it was an example of how it was possible to resist the 'Workfare' style schemes that they judged were being promoted and introduced across the EU.[81] This perception was particularly acute amongst activists who had been most involved in the cross-border links between the nationally based unemployed movements. One such activist, involved in organizing the 'Parliament', commented:

> It's not true that we haven't got a social policy in Europe. We've certainly got a social policy, but it's more against the unemployed and against the workers. When you see the measures that Tony Blair has started to take, at the beginning everyone in France said 'well they want to follow the USA, that's nothing to do with us, that's a British matter'. Now you see that the French government has really the same set of policies. And in '98 when I went to Germany, I still had the image that, well in Germany there's a really strong social insurance system. But now you can see with the new projects from Schröder that he is pursuing exactly the same policies. And now there's a general movement in Europe to get rid of social rights and that leads to cuts in income support and unemployment benefit. And these 'Workfare' programmes are not only spreading out in Great Britain, but in the whole of Europe.[82]

This viewpoint was articulated in the 'Brussels Declaration' issued by the *Assises* held in Brussels in April 1998 that was attended by more than six hundred participants many of whom had taken part in the national unemployed mobilizations. The final declaration affirmed that those present were:

> Against all measures of forced work, that under the cover of 'return to work' and 'employability' want to impose jobs with unacceptable conditions on the unemployed.[83]

In the period up to the summit meeting in Cologne, the publicity material produced by the European Marches continued to highlight the role being played by the EU in the restructuring of labour markets and welfare systems. An article in the journal showed how the Commission had identified as good practice the new employability measures being introduced in the UK, Denmark and Belgium and how the aim was to spread such schemes across the continent.[84] The most well attended workshop at the conference held in Cologne was on the topic of the EU's employment policy and this discussion contributed to the final declaration making an even clearer condemnation of the EU's employability agenda:

> The so-called Employment policies dreamed up by the Commission and the Council of Europe are clearly designed to develop work flexibility, 'adaptability', 'employability'

---

81   Information from notes taken from recording of the 'Parliament' on 31 May 1999.

82   Excerpt from interview with Irène Bonnaud.

83   'Platform of European Demands', available at <*www.euromarches.org/english/98/04/0419a.htm*> accessed on 20/08/2001.

84   'Bonnes pratiques, mauvaises triques', *Marches Européenes/NEWS (French Version)* No.8 Décembre 1998.

and to impose on wage earners, whether in a job or on vocational training or unemployed, worsening working conditions and lower wages for the greater profit of employers.[85]

Another workshop on welfare reform was held as part of the Cologne counter-summit event in June 1999. I was present at this workshop and was asked to outline the situation in the UK and especially the 'New Deal' programme. In the discussion that followed, German activists in particular noted the similarities to elements of the policies being implemented by the new social democratic government. There was much discussion about the increasing conditionality of benefits across the continent and 'Workfare' style schemes were identified as the ultimate outcome of the reform process initiated by the Commission and carried out by member states.[86] Several of the contributions at the 'Parliament' underlined how *le Workfare* or *das Workfare* was the epitome of the EU's aims and with this in mind a workshop proposal for a European day of action in opposition to 'Workfare' was agreed by the final plenary session.[87]

The outcome of these criticisms of the Employment Strategy was that the European Marches rejected entirely the Lisbon strategy of full employment through employability and therefore decided to disassociate itself from the demand for full employment. The explanation given was that it was precisely through the rhetoric of a return to full employment that the EU's strategy of low paid job creation through pay reduction and welfare reform was to be made acceptable.[88]

The decision to abandon the demand for full employment was not uncontested and in the final plenary session of the conference in Cologne, a representative of the ENU, an organization that supported the goal of full employment, argued strongly for its inclusion in the appeal for the demonstration in Cologne. Patrice Spadoni, who was involved in drafting the appeal text, answered that many of the organizations present would not agree to support it under any circumstances. Consequently, according to the process of consensus decision-making, full employment would remain omitted, but this did not exclude specific organizations from making this demand on the demonstration.[89]

As I highlighted in chapter four, the main slogans on the demonstration in Cologne were arguing against forced labour and low paid work and not for full employment. The main argument presented at the press conference after the demonstration in Cologne was that the European Marches were opposed to the EU

---

85   'Cologne International Appeal European Demonstration, 29 May 1999: Against Unemployment, Job Insecurity, Exclusions and Racism. For a Europe and a World of Solidarity and of Liberty', available at *<www.euromarches.org/english/99/appeal.htm>* accessed on 20/08/2001.

86   Information from notes taken after participation in the 'Cologne Alternative Summit' on 30 May 1999.

87   Information from notes taken from recording of the 'Parliament' on 1 June 1999.

88   Information from interviews with Gerhard Klas and Willi Lubkes.

89   Information from notes taken during participation in the conference held in Cologne on 24 January 1999.

cure for unemployment of 'Work at any price'.[90] In the lead up to the summit in Porto, at which the EU reasserted its policy goal of full employment, the European Marches Co-ordinating Committee issued a press statement condemning the policies through which it was to be achieved:

> The announcement of full employment threatens to be an overfull employment of insecure jobs and the loss of fundamental guarantees won in their time by social struggles. A second labour market has been insidiously organized by sub-statutes, of forced part-time work, by policies of 'insertion', by activation of social spending from that declared passive. Governments are subsidizing firms that are creating jobs at very low wages.[91]

While rejecting the strategy for full employment through employability, the European Marches were also developing a set of demands for social citizenship rights that began to be articulated at the first *Assises* and culminated in the declaration of a 'Charter of Demands' at the 'Assembly'. This counter agenda was underpinned by a discourse that asserted the universal right to a dignified life and the resources necessary to realize it.[92] There were three main elements to this counter agenda for a 'social Europe': the right to an unconditional income; the right to work realized through job creation and work redistribution resulting from a shorter working week; and the right to social provision including free access to essential services.[93] These elements were developed through the process of exchanges between the individuals and organizations involved in the European Marches.

Speaking on behalf of AC! at the 'Parliament', Laurent Guilloteau argued that there were two tendencies in the development of European social policy: towards Workfare or an unconditional income.[94] While there was a good deal of support for demanding an unconditional income amongst the unemployed associations, there remained the difficult task of Europeanizing a demand that hitherto had only been expressed at the national level. The slogan *un emploi est un droit, un revenu est un dû* [a job is my right, an income is my due] epitomized how the demand for an unconditional income was expressed strongly in the French unemployed mobilizations described in chapter four. There was also significant support for it amongst unemployed and claimant associations in Germany[95] and a joint declaration of French and German associations issued on the occasion of the demonstration in Paris in January 1998 called for an unconditional income and European level

---

90   Information from notes taken from recording of the European Marches Network press conference on 2 June 1999.

91   'Appel de la Coordination des Marches Européenes': Contre la précarité en Europe: luttons pour imposer des revenus garantis et des droits sociaux. 27-28/5/2000' available at <*www.euromarches.org/francais/00/0528a/htm*> accessed on 20/08/2001.

92   Information from interview with Angela Klein.

93   'The European Marches Charter of Demands For European Basic Social Rights', available at <*www.euromarches.org/english/00/charta.htm*> accessed on 20/08/2001.

94   Information from notes taken from recording of the 'Parliament' on 30 May 1999.

95   Rein, H. (1997) 'Wir kämpfen um das, was wir brauchen', *Forschungsjournal NSB* 10 (2) pp. 70–5.

social rights.[96] Associations in Spain[97] and Italy[98] were also demanding the right to an income and political parties such as the Italian RC, the French Green Party, and the German PDS also supported this demand.[99] This relatively widespread support came through strongly at the *Assises* held in April 1998 at which it was adopted as the first of a set of demands for harmonized European social rights:

> We demand that everyone should have the right to a guaranteed income according to the wealth produced by society.[100]

Although the European Marches adopted the right to an unconditional income as its foremost demand, it was by no means clear that it had the same meaning for all its participants. There were differences in the specific demands made by the various organizations and there were still participants from both Northern and Southern Europe that remained sceptical about its applicability across the continent. These issues became apparent during a workshop on the question of the unconditional income that was held at the conference in Cologne and attracted approximately seventy participants.

The workshop was led by German unemployed activist, Willi Lubkes, who presented an overview of the development of the demand for *Existenzgeld* [basic income] that had begun back in the early 1980s. He placed particular emphasis on how demanding an unconditional right to an income countered current policies that were tightening benefit entitlements and promoting low paid employment. He also outlined how the demand had become increasingly prominent during the unemployed mobilizations of the previous year and how the links established between the German and French mobilizations had fuelled the call for a European Network for Income.

The discussion that followed indicated the array of positions and perspectives that existed amongst the participants. A precise formula for calculating a European income was advanced by Belgian participants. According to an Italian contributor a basic income was part of a new set of citizenship rights commensurate with the new post-Fordist social order, whereas a British trade unionist dismissed demands for a minimum income as a diversion from the central issue of demanding a European minimum wage.

---

96   'Unemployment movement French and German delegations: Joint Declaration', available at *<www-pluto.informatik.uni-oldenburg.de/~also/eusep219.htm>* accessed on 07/08/2001.

97   'Revenu le grand debat', *Marches Européenes/NEWS (French Version)* No.9 Février 1999.

98   Movimento delle Tute Bianche Padova (1999) *op cit.*

99   'Contributions des coordinations nationales des Marches européenes contre le chômage, la précarité et les exclusions' *Marches Européenes* Unpublished photocopied document, undated.

100   'Platform of European Demands', available at *<www.euromarches.org/english/98/0419a.htm>* accessed on 20/08/2001.

Despite these differing perspectives a consensus position was apparently reached around a number of basic principles that were reported back to the plenary session.[101] The income must secure basic needs and must be independent of work and of work history. It must be available to all including young people and migrants and individualized so as to apply to women and men regardless of personal situation. The income should be linked to access to services including housing, culture, and transport and should be financed by a redistribution of wealth through taxation including the Tobin Tax on capital movement.[102]

For some activists, the experience of such events confirmed the differences in terminology still existing across borders and therefore the need for a more regular and detailed exchange of ideas to clarify the concepts underpinning the demand.[103] Representatives from AC! proposed that these matters should be addressed by promoting ongoing communication through establishing a European Network for Income.[104] Although the exchanges through this network were rather intermittent, background texts were made available in paper and electronic format and some progress was made on clarifying the terms used and their conceptual underpinning.[105]

Producing a common text and a common rate for a European income were the stated aims of the first session of the 'Parliament'.[106] However, the speakers from French, German and Spanish associations mainly reasserted the arguments in favour of a European unconditional income as a mechanism for opposing the EU's drive towards employability and Workfare. The discussion that followed moved away from the question of the income, but it remained an issue for later sessions with a workshop held on this question arguing that the existing demand remained too vague and that a specific figure should be adopted. Various proposals were made ranging from five hundred to a thousand Euro's per month.[107] However, it was felt by some that the rather chaotic plenary debates hindered a full discussion of the issue and by the third day there was judged to be an insufficient attendance to adopt such a specific demand.[108] The continued lack of a clear demand for the level of the

---

101   Information from notes taken during participation in the conference held in Cologne on 23 January 1999.

102   'Revenu: le grand débat', *Marches Européenes/NEWS (French version)* No.9 Février.

103   Information from interviews with Willi Lubkes, Laurent Guilloteau and Patrice Spadoni.

104   Commission Revenu AC! (1998) *'Towards A European Network for Income'* Paris: AC!

105   Information from interview with Laurent Guilloteau; access to background documents on the unconditional income emanating from France, Germany and Italy available at <*http://perso.wanadoo.fr/marxiens/politic/revenus/index.htm*> (French language) accessed on 20/09/2001.

106   Photocopied agenda document for the 'Parliament'.

107   Information from notes taken from recording of the 'Parliament' on 31 May 1999.

108   Information from notes taken from recording of the 'Parliament' on 1 June 1999; Information from interviews with Uwe Durchbach and Willi Lubkes.

European income was considered by some activists to be a hindrance to organizing a campaign that could resonate amongst European citizens:

> I am concerned that at the 'Parliament' there was a discussion of the income but it was no farther forward. I would be very much in favour of putting a figure. So you say a thousand Euro, two thousand Euro or five hundred Euro. It now makes it so difficult because it is totally abstract.[109]

The second element of the common platform of demands was established as the right to work and this was linked to demands for a shorter working week and job creation. While calling for the right to work did not lead to controversy, the supporting demands provoked debate. A meeting of European trade unionists in March 1998 in Paris issued a discussion text: its first demand was for a European Directive to enforce legislatively a reduction in working time with an objective of reaching a thirty five hour week across Europe by 2002.[110] In this vein, a representative from the Spanish CGT spoke at the 'Parliament' to outline his union's campaign for legislation to introduce a thirty five hour week leading to a redistribution of work. However, a Dutch trade unionist explained through a talk on the 'Polder Model', on which he argued that much EU employment policy was based, how legislation for a shorter working week had been implemented in a way that was against the interests of workers and the unemployed.

Launched in 1982 under the slogan of 'Profit means Jobs', he reported that by the 1990s the working week had been reduced from forty to thirty six hours. During this period official unemployment figures fell from 7% to 5% while part-time and temporary working increased dramatically. General wage levels rose by 1%, but the minimum wage fell dramatically, unemployment benefit levels went down and the numbers living in poverty doubled. He argued that there were also large increases in disability benefit claims as many workers were forced out of work by increased workloads and production speed-ups as highlighted by a doubling of complaints by workers. In the same period, labour productivity leapt massively resulting in profit levels rising by 200%. His general message was that reduced working hours had been an incentive to employers to rationalize production resulting in work intensification rather than work redistribution and in job insecurity rather than job creation.[111]

A similar concern was voiced at the 'Parliament' by Estelle from AC! who argued that recent legislation for a thirty five hour week in France did not appear to be resulting in significant employment creation, but was rather leading to work 'intensification' and 'flexibilization' as working hours were spread through the year. The 35 hour week was also being linked to salary freezes with the result of redistributing poverty rather than work. She asserted that demands for job creation must be for 'decent proper jobs with a decent proper wage and working conditions'.[112] The experience of French militants that such legislation could be a 'false friend' for

---

109   Excerpt from interview with Ailko van der Veen.

110   'Urgent change needed in Europe! No EURO without a Social Europe!' available at <*www.labournet.net/1998/may/euroe.html*> accessed on 18/11/1999.

111   Information from notes taken from recording of the 'Parliament' on 31 May 1999.

112   *ibid.*

the unemployed and workers was transmitted across borders to countries such as Italy and Spain in which there were popular campaigns in support of the shorter working week. Patrice Spadoni spoke on behalf of AC! at a mass meeting in Madrid and his message was that if legislation came without grass roots mobilization it would merely be a mechanism for a further flexibilization and degradation of work and unlikely to result in the creation of socially useful jobs.[113]

The question of job creation was a matter of debate at both the 'Parliament' and the 'Assembly'. Hubert, representing the MNCP, argued that in a situation where business did not generate sufficient employment, the Third Sector could be encouraged to provide work to meet human needs no longer met by the state.[114] Paolo, however, speaking on behalf of his union Sin Cobas, argued that such forms of employment were a mechanism for deregulating state employment and services resulting in job insecurity and undermining public services. He asserted that the struggle of the LSU was for permanent and regularly paid public sector jobs and quality public services.[115] In the light of such concerns, the 'Charter of Demands' stated that the demand for a reduction in working hours must be without loss of salary and without flexibility or annualization of hours. The resulting job creation in socially, culturally and ecologically necessary employment had also to be at guaranteed salaries and terms and conditions.[116]

The third element of the 'Charter of Demands', alongside the right to income and the right to work, was the right to social provision including free access to essential services. The array of social rights included housing, health-care, education and culture, transport, communication and utilities.[117] The adoption of these demands not only reflected the concerns of some of the trade unions and unemployed associations, but also arose from the participation in the assemblies of activists involved in campaigns amongst young people, pensioners and students and from issue based campaigns including housing, health and education. At the conference in Cologne there was a workshop of 'youth' that issued its own specific demands including the right to free access to education, culture, public transport and health care and opposition to the privatization of education.[118] A workshop of trade unionists at the same event also issued an appeal that included opposition to the dismantlement of public services as well as the strengthening of social protection including equal

---

113   Information from interview with Patrice Spadoni.

114   Information from recording of the 'Parliament' on 31 May 1999.

115   Information from notes made from recording of the 'Assembly' on 3 December 2000; information from interview with Paolo Iafrete; *'Le Travail Atipique en Italie vers la fin des Années 90'*, S.in.COBAS Undated leaflet.

116   'Platform of European Demands', available at <*www.euromarches.org/english/98/0419a.htm*> accessed on 20/08/2001.

117   'The European Marches Charter of Demands For European Basic Social Rights', available at <*www.euromarches.org/english/00/charta.htm*> accessed on 20/08/2001.

118   Information from notes taken during participant observation at the *Assises* held in Cologne on 23 January 1999; Marches Européenes/News (*French version*) No. 9 Février 1999.

access to rights.[119] This was an indication of an understanding amongst these trade unionists that in order to defend successfully the gains represented by the welfare state it was necessary to defend the rights of workers in the public services, but also to link the trade union struggle with other social forces to demand free quality public services.[120]

The Policy Context for the Nice Campaign

Following the development of co-ordinated employment policies, the Commission utilized the same framework for co-ordinating European social protection systems. It did so according to the maxim of 'social policy as a productive factor' (p. 5) thereby contributing to the goal of full employment.[121] The Commission had already established the new principles of social protection including 'to make work pay' (p. 13)[122] and had highlighted the need to transform unemployment insurance into a form compatible with employability as well as asserting that current benefit levels were not motivating the unemployed to seek work.[123] Commentators concluded that a main aim of social protection reform was to increase motivation by linking benefit receipt to active jobseeking and attendance on activation schemes.[124] The principles established at the European level were subsequently translated into substantive welfare reforms at the national level. Significant examples were the introduction of the *Plan d'aide au retour à l'emploi*[125] [Help to Return to Work Plan] in France and the *Job Aqtiv Gesetz* [literally Active Job Law] in Germany.[126]

The new social policy agenda, due to run from 2001–6, called for 'the modernisation and improvement of the European social model' (p. 7) in order to tackle the growing problem of a lack of social cohesion. The answer was to develop the social policy agenda around the principle of quality leading to 'more and better employment' (p. 7) thereby identifying full employment as the key to achieving social inclusion. The quality agenda would not require additional public spending, but rather its redirection towards active social policies. Social policy harmonization

119   '*Appel Syndical Pour Manifester Le 29 Mai 1999 à Cologne*' available at <*www. euromarches.org/francais/99/appelsyn.htm*> accessed on 20/08/2001.

120   Information from interviews with Paolo Iafrete and Antonino Campenni.

121   European Commission (2000) *Social Policy Agenda*, Brussels COM (2000) 379 Final.

122   European Commission (1999) *A Concerted Strategy for Modernising Social Protection* Brussels COM (99) 347.

123   Commission européenne (1998) 'Croissance et emploi dans le cadre de stabilitie de l'UEM', *Communication de la Commission,* Bruxelles, le 25.02.98 COM103 final.

124   Pochet, P., Barbier, C., De Decker, C., Kabatusuila, F., Vernay, C. & Vanhercke, B. (1999) 'Digest: Employment', *Journal of European Social Policy* 9(2) pp. 175–177.

125   Eironline (2000) 'Negotiations open on unemployment insurance' available at <*www.eiro.eurofound.ie/2000/04/Inbrief/FR0004514N.html*> accessed on 17/12/2001.

126   Eironline (2001) 'Government proposes reform of labour market policy' available at <*www.eiro.eurofound.ie/2001/11/feature/DE111203F.html*> accessed on 17/12/2001.

was rejected in favour of policy coordination through the OMC.[127] The Commission issued a communication outlining its strategy for achieving social inclusion shortly before the Lisbon Summit and this was subsequently adopted at the Nice Summit. This was subject to the same process of open co-ordination as the employment strategy, but without the same sanctions of guidelines and recommendations. The Commission was also criticized strongly by the Social Policy Committee for the lack of balance between economic and social policies and for not giving due consideration to tackling social exclusion.[128]

The decision to launch a process of formulating a Charter of Fundamental Rights was taken by the EU Council in Cologne in June 1999. Impetus was provided by expert reports that called for existing rights to be clarified in one document and by concerns amongst the European polity and executive that the high profile declaration of the Charter could serve to enhance the Union's moral and political legitimacy. The Tampere Council appointed a 'Convention' to draft the Charter that met throughout the first half of 2000; during which time it held public hearings at which submissions were given by representatives of member states and candidate countries and by the social partners and other civil society organizations. A draft Charter was published in July 2000 and amendments were then proposed before the final draft was adopted in October 2000 by the Biarritz Council. This final draft was then approved by the European Parliament and Commission, before it was signed at the Nice Summit in December 2000.

The Charter can be considered in terms of its substance and status. The Charter contained six chapters: Dignity, Freedoms, Equality, Solidarity, Citizens' Rights and Justice. Most of the Charter restated the rights that already existed in international treaties. But the chapter on solidarity was more controversial and provoked intense opposition from the British and Spanish governments as well as from the UNICE that lobbied fiercely around it. As a consequence, the final document hardly made reference to rights in the economic and social fields.[129] The Cologne Council left the question of whether the Charter would be incorporated into the EU treaty open. This matter was debated hotly throughout the consultation process with leading politicians such as German Foreign Minister, Joschka Fischer, making high profile

---

127   European Commission (2000) *Social Policy Agenda*, Brussels, COM (2000) 379 Final.

128   Ferrera, M., Matsaganis, M. & Saccchi, S. (2002) 'Open coordination against poverty: the new EU 'social inclusion process', *Journal of European Social Policy* 12 (3) pp. 227-239.

129   Degryse, C. (2000) 'Electronic newsletter on the Intergovernmental Conference' Number 2 available at <*www.ose.be*> accessed on 20/07/2001; Barbier, C. (2001) 'Electronic newsletter on the Intergovernmental Conference' Number 6 available at <*www.ose.be*> accessed on 20/07/2001; Council of Europe (2000) *Charter of Fundamental Rights of the European Union: Explanations relating to the complete text of the Charter*, (Luxembourg: Office for Official Publications of the European Communities); European Commission (1999) *Affirming fundamental rights in the European Union. Time to act* (Luxembourg: Office for Official Publications of the European Communities).

speeches that reasserted the case for a Federal Europe.[130] After an expectation that it would form a 'solemn declaration', the Charter was merely signed in Nice by representatives of the Council, Parliament, and Commission.[131]

The Nice Campaign

As had been the case with the coordinated employment policies, prominent participants in the European Marches developed a critical analysis of the co-ordination of social protection systems and social inclusion measures. Speaking to the 'Assembly', Angela Klein argued that social democratic governments across the EU were presiding over a change in the form of social security systems. Whilst unemployment had fallen, the numbers living in poverty had risen from fifty seven million in 1997 to sixty five million in 2000 and this was consistent with a rise in the numbers of working poor. The EU had indeed made tackling poverty a priority, but it was simultaneously implementing labour market and social protection reforms that were pushing increasing numbers of people into work at poverty pay levels and depriving many people of any income whatsoever. In response to this situation she reasserted the demand for an unconditional European income that would halt wage and social dumping and would guarantee a minimum standard of living to people in work, out of work, and in retirement.[132]

Klein's analysis was reinforced by the experiences of grass roots activists and especially those involved in unemployed and claimant associations. Reporting back as the moderator of the 'Assembly' workshop titled 'The Experience of the Unemployed', Philippe, from the MNCP, summarized how European governments were putting in place a coercive benefits system that placed the unemployed under permanent surveillance and constant pressure to accept any job at any price. The workshop confirmed that the most effective response was to campaign for an unconditional European income. This analysis was supported by contributions from the floor in the plenary sessions that explained how benefit cuts were operating in various countries to coerce the unemployed into work. It was argued that an unconditional income was required as a mechanism to halt benefit cuts and to defend the unemployed against forced work. It was also argued by a participant from the East of Germany that governments should 'activate job creation not activate the unemployed'.[133]

In this context of the reform of social protection systems and in the light of the concerns raised during the 'Parliament', in the period following Cologne there was an emphasis placed on developing a more specific demand for the unconditional

130   Fischer, J. (2000) *Vom Staatenverbund zur Föderation* (speech at the Humboldt University on 12 May 2000) cited in Habermas, J. (2001a) 'A Constitution for Europe?', *New Left Review* 11 pp. 5–26.

131   Barbier (2001) *op cit.*

132   Information from notes taken from recording of the 'Assembly' on 2 December 2000.

133   Information from notes taken from recording of the 'Assembly' on 3 December 2000.

income. However, a summary of the 'Parliament' highlighted how proposals for a specific figure, such as a thousand Euro's, was treated with scepticism by activists from Southern Europe.[134] In a situation in which average pay rates ranged from 4.75–25.40 Euro per hour and minimum wage levels from 334–1141 Euro per month, adopting an average figure would be unrealistically high for Southern European countries and represent a cut for Northern European states.[135]

The task of overcoming this problem was taken forward by a small working group that put forward its findings and proposals to the European Co-ordinating Committee meetings. This deliberation process resulted in the decision to adopt a formula for calculating the unconditional income that it was judged could encompass the variety of conceptions and demands of those involved in the European Marches and also be applicable right across the continent. The decision taken was to demand a European income set at 50% of Gross Domestic Product (GDP) per head of the population plus the right to housing costs.[136]

This Europeanized demand would translate into an increased standard of living for the unemployed and poor across the continent. For example, it would raise the minimum income in Portugal from 125 to 407 Euro's, in the UK from 338 to 1000 Euro's and in Denmark from 930 to 1218 Euro's.[137] Using GDP as a common benchmark was considered particularly apt as it was the EURO zone's main indicator and was especially used in relation to restricting budget deficits within the 'Growth and Stability Pact'. An unconditional income set at this level would, it was argued, act as a de facto minimum benefit, minimum wage, and minimum pension and would act as a barrier to what was identified as a 'spiral of poverty' (p. 1).[138]

This link with pensions reflected how the European Marches had developed contact with FERPA, an ETUC affiliate, with its President, Georges Debunne, speaking at the *International Colloque*, held in Brussels in June 2000. This meeting was organized by the European Marches to publicize the demand for an unconditional European income. Debunne expressed his evaluation that while the demand for an income remained imprecise it remained useful to assert a principle such as the inclusion of the right to an income in the Charter. However, he argued that in the immediate situation it was not possible to live off principles and therefore it was necessary to fix a specific demand. Speaking on behalf of the European Marches, Christophe Aguiton, asserted that the objective was to elaborate such a common demand that would be supported by the unemployed, insecure workers and the excluded from across the entirety of the EU. This was reinforced by representatives

---

134   'Parlemente des chômeuses, chômeurs et précaires'. La Marche Permanente', *Marches Européenes/NEWS (French version)* No.12 Juin 1999.

135   'Minimums sociaux en Europe', available at <*www.euromarches.org/francais/euro.htm*> accessed on 01/07/2001.

136   'Quel revenu garanti individuel dans le zone euro?', *Marches Européenes*, Unpublished photocopied document, Undated.

137   'Minimums sociaux en Europe', available at <*www.euromarches.org/francais/euro.htm*> accessed on 01/07/2001.

138   'Appel de la Coordination des Marches Européenes: Contre la précarité en Europe: luttons pour imposer des revenus garantis et des droits sociaux. 27-28/5/2000', available at <*www.euromarches.org/francais/00/0528a.htm*> accessed on 01/07/2001.

of the German claimant group BAG-SHI who explained that in Germany there was support for the income amongst associations representing the unemployed, claimants and homeless. They also argued that a basic income must also be available to non-nationals. However, they claimed that the demand for an unconditional income was not supported widely amongst the unions.

This situation was reflected on the platform with no speaker on behalf of the unions: a point that was recognized on the floor by an activist who inquired 'Where are the unions'? This was followed by a response from a trade unionist from the floor who spoke in favour of the unconditional income as a defence against the proliferation of low paid work.[139] This indicated that the guaranteed income was considered as compatible with the demand for a European minimum wage that was at the head of a joint 'Platform of Demands' issued by unions such as the French SUD Education, the Spanish CGT, and the Italian COBAS.[140]

The call for quantifiable minimum standards of social protection for the unemployed was also made at an international conference of unemployed trade unionists held in Bielefeld, Germany from 5–8 October 2000. It assembled 70 unemployed activists together with trade unionists from Germany, Austria, Belgium and Holland. The conference also demanded that local, national and European institutions create socially useful and environmentally friendly jobs with stable and regular contracts. It also called on the ETUC to admit the unemployed into its organizational structures on an equal footing and for it to act more offensively and forcefully on the questions of unemployment and exclusion.[141]

As the Nice summit approached, the European Marches became increasingly preoccupied with the Charter. Prominent activists, such as Patrice Spadoni, recognized the enduring differences of perspective in the European Marches on the question of European integration, but emphasized that the strategy of opposing the neoliberal policies emanating from the Commission had been largely successful in forging unity amongst the various participating organizations.[142] Similarly to the debate over EMU, opposition to the Charter was not mainly on the basis that it could be the forerunner of a European constitution, but due to its inadequate content that only guaranteed minimal rights for EU citizens.[143]

Prominent activists once again took on the task of developing an analysis of the Charter that was disseminated through the European Marches Network. As a future constitution the Charter would take precedence over national laws and could consequently be an instrument by which higher levels of social rights contained in national constitutions could be replaced by a lower European level. The idea of first establishing a European constitution and then adding improved social rights to it was

---

139   Information from notes made from recording of the *International Colloque* 'A social minimum in Europe for all' on 10/06/2000.

140   'Suggested Platform for Alternative European Trade Unionism: The European March against Precariousness on May 29 in Cologne' Leaflet, Undated.

141   'Pour une Europe sociale – sans chômage, pauvreté ni exclusion', available at <*www.euromarches.org/francais/bielefl.htm*> accessed on 17/01/2001.

142   Information from interview with Patrice Spadoni.

143   Information from notes made from a recording of the 'Assembly' on 3 December 2000.

viewed as seeing things the wrong way around. An improved constitution could only be achieved by a strong social movement. The idea of a constitution was rather to be seen as a way of legitimating the move towards a 'Super Europe' (p. 5) under the control of the core states of Germany, France, Great Britain and Italy.[144]

Speaking at the 'Assembly', Patrice Spadoni compared the Charter to one of the cakes seen in old gangster movies. It appeared inviting, but inside lurked a bomb that threatened to explode and destroy social rights acquired over years of struggle. Behind the smoke of the fine words of liberty and solidarity, there was no fire. In terms of content, the Charter amounted to a statement of rights that did not even reach the level of existing declarations like the European Convention of Human Rights (1951) and the United Nations Declaration of Human Rights (1948). The rights guaranteed by the Social Chapter were not included and the Charter focused on guaranteeing the rights of citizens to freedoms in relation to the state rather than on recognizing that citizens had rights to make substantive claims upon the state.

The right to work appeared in the section on liberty, but not in that on solidarity. European citizens were free to look for work, but had no guarantee of finding work. The Charter did not recognize the right to benefits and rather than establishing the right to an income and housing, it merely recognized the right to social and housing assistance. In cases of extreme poverty this could be translated into the provision of goods in kind rather than cash benefits.

It was also argued that it was unsatisfactory to demand simply the retention of existing national level social rights. In a situation in which the EU was globalizing markets for capital and goods whilst maintaining subsidiarity in social matters, the antidote was to create substantive European level social rights.[145] Several of these criticisms were echoed by organizations that supported the European Marches such as the French union federation G10 that argued that the Charter was derived from a neoliberal logic and that it marked a setback in the rights of EU citizens.[146]

A detailed analysis of the draft Charter including the particular ways in which it amounted to a curtailment of existing rights was compiled and made available to the participants at the 'Assembly':[147] a session of which was devoted to a debate on the Charter. The debate touched on the dangers and opportunities of the Charter becoming a basis for a European constitution and there were calls for referenda before it could take precedence over national constitutions. It was emphasized that the Charter recognized social rights in terms of 'political objectives' rather than as

---

144 'Geteiltes Europa: Grundrechtcharta und Regierungskonferenz in Nizza', available at <*www.euromarches.org/deutsch/00/eu5.htm*> accessed on 07/08/2001.

145 Information from notes made from a recording of the 'Assembly' on 3 December 2000. 'EU-Grundrechtcharta: Politische Ziele nicht erwünscht', available at <*www.euromarches.org/deutsch*> accessed on 07/08/2001. 'Alerte! L'Union européene réécrit nos droits', available at <*www.euromarches.org/francais/00/alerte0.htm*> accessed on 07/08/2001. 'Grundrechtcharta der EU – ein undemokratisches Verfahren', available at <*www.labournet.de/diskussion/eu/index.html*> accessed on 07/08/2001.

146 'Une charte au rabais', *Solidaires Le journal de l'union syndicale G 10* no.6 November 2000.

147 'Projet pour l'Assemblée des chômeurs et des précaires en lutte' *Marches Européenes* Unpublished photocopied document, undated.

legally enforceable rights. There was also concern about the social consequences of enlargement in the context of eroding social rights. There was a difference of opinion over the position towards the campaign for approving and improving the Charter organized by the ETUC and Social NGOs. Some speakers argued that it was pragmatic to support it while the majority argued that it was necessary to oppose the Charter outright.[148] The outcome of the debate was made clear in a press statement:

> The European Assembly of the Unemployed ... demands that the Heads of State do not integrate the Charter of Fundamental Rights in the Treaty because social rights will not be guaranteed in this Charter and in particular the right to work, the right to unemployment benefits, the right to a minimum income, the right to a pension, the right to housing, and equal treatment for women.[149]

The 'Assembly' also endorsed the 'Charter of Demands for European Basic Social Rights' that was structured around the rights to income, to work and access to social provision that were the main pillars of the European Marches' counter agenda for a 'social Europe'.[150]

A Europe (and World) of Universal Rights and Social Justice

> We wish that our struggles against unemployment meet other social movements of solidarity and struggle in Europe and in the world in order to extend and guarantee all rights, equality of men and women, freedom of movement and Peace on Earth.[151]

This extract from the appeal for the demonstration in Cologne indicates that the European Marches attempted to link its particular struggle to the wider set of international networks so as to form a broader social movement. This was a conscious strategy that was articulated by prominent activists. Angela Klein articulated how she considered the European Marches as a mechanism through which the diversity of social movements could leave the specific corners from which they were fighting their enemy in isolation and communicate with other movements. Through this process a broad social movement against the main 'social plagues' of unemployment, racism, war and environmental destruction could be formed. What was specific about the European Marches though was that it did not start from an abstract unity imposed by a preset political programme, but developed unity through linking the specific

---

148   Information from notes made from a recording of the 'Assembly' on 3 December 2000.

149   'Communiqué de Presse du 4 décembre 2000', available at <*www.euromarches. org/francais/00/assemb4.htm*> accessed on 01/07/2001.

150   'The European Marches Charter of Demands For European Basic Social Rights' available at <*www.euromarches.org/english.charta.htm*> accessed on 20/08/2001.

151   'Cologne International Appeal European Demonstration, 29 May 1999: Against Unemployment, Job Insecurity, Exclusions and Racism. For a Europe and a World of Solidarity and of Liberty' available at <*www.euromarches.org/english/99/appeal.htm*> accessed on 20/08/2001.

demands of each movement engaged in struggle. Through a process of concrete discussion these demands could become practically and conceptually linked thereby promoting common mobilization in support of them.[152]

This strategy could be seen in operation during the Cologne campaign that saw the various networks begin to express a common opposition to a neoliberal Europe. Moreover, as I showed above in relation to the demand for the right to free services, the common platform did begin to resonate amongst a wider network of organizations. This resonance was facilitated by the articulation of these demands in terms of universal rights to a dignified existence: a perspective that emanated from the struggle against inequality and indignity waged by *les sans* that was outlined in chapter four.

This discourse was circulated at meetings such as the *International Colloque* for 'A social minimum in Europe for all' organized by the European Marches. Speaking on behalf of the League for Human Rights, Dan van Raemdonck argued that the dignity of human life had to be respected in all of its constituent areas: economic, political, social, and cultural. For full citizenship to be achieved it required more than an individual right to protection from the state, it required the recognition of collective rights to have common needs met.[153]

The demands for basic social rights also resonated with the concerns of women in the WWM who were highlighting opposition to poverty. The individual right to a decent income was presented as a measure that would counteract the growth of poverty pay that was particularly prevalent amongst women workers.[154] The unconditional right to the income would also counteract the indignities arising from coercive benefit regulations. The 'Charter of Demands' also highlighted equal rights for men and women, but specifically in relation to access to social citizenship rights.[155] The payment of the unconditional income to all regardless of age would also combat the discrimination faced by young people with regards to benefit entitlement and curb the extension of low pay amongst this group.[156]

The demand for the right to live in dignity also found expression beyond the struggles of the unemployed and became a major concern of the 'Caravan for the Rights of Refugees and Migrants' that participated in the Cologne events.[157] At the national level there were developing links between unemployed and migrants' associations in France, Germany and Belgium.[158] This was reflected at the European Co-ordinating Committee meeting in September 1998 at which participants from

---

152 Information from interview with Angela Klein.

153 Information from notes taken from recording of the *International Colloque* 'A social minimum in Europe for all' on 10 June 2000.

154 'Marches mondiale des femmes', *Marches Européenes/NEWS (French version)* Avril 1999 No.10.

155 'The European Marches Charter of Demands For European Basic Social Rights' available at <*www.euromarches.org/english.charta.htm*> accessed on 20/08/2001.

156 'Les jeunes pour la manifestation des Marches européenes du 29 mai 1999 à Cologne', *Marches Européenes/NEWS (French version)* No.9 Février 1999.

157 Information from notes taken during participation in the 'Alternative World Economic Summit' on 18 June 1999.

158 Information from interviews with Patrice Spadoni and Corinne Barella.

these countries spoke out in favour of linking the issues of unemployment and racism. This proposal was also supported by a representative of *Ya Basta*, and it was agreed to draft an appeal for the Cologne campaign in the name of the 'European Marches against Unemployment, Job Insecurity, Social Exclusion, and Racism'.[159]

There was a strong representation of migrant and anti-racist associations at the conference in Cologne at which decisions were taken to extend the appeal for the demonstration to include opposition to the Schengen agreement and to adopt as one of the four major demands:

> For a Europe without frontiers, a Europe of solidarity towards people from the South as well as the East, without racism, exclusions or deportations, with equal rights and guarantees for all its inhabitants whatever their origins.[160]

Although the appeal included demands relating to both unemployment and migration, the European Marches was also concerned to confront racism and migration as social questions thereby linking them more closely with its central issues.[161] To this end, a session of the 'Parliament' was titled 'Immigration, job insecurity, and unemployment'.

The session began with a Peruvian migrant describing how many of the migrants living in Germany were unemployed and did not have the right to benefits or the right to work and therefore lived in extreme poverty. Moreover, illegal migrants could not gain access to social provision. This was accompanied by information about the Caravan and a call for support for a picket of a deportation camp at which female refugees were held. Eric, speaking from the floor, emphasized that the situation of migrants was just like the unemployed in that they were denied the right to live a decent and dignified existence. Antonio stated that holding illegal migrants in detention camps was a denial of their rights and that money should be taken from the security and military budgets to pay for an unconditional income available to all regardless of origin.[162] While the European Marches made some progress with its strategy of linking its social demands to the concerns of anti-racist networks, there was less discernible success in relation to the issues of peace, ecology and development.

Although the war in the Balkans was not on the agenda of the 'Parliament', it was raised by a number of contributors who wanted to contrast the development of a militarized Europe with the lack of a 'social Europe'.[163] Several representatives of unemployed associations took part in a meeting at the 'European Alternative Summit' that issued a common declaration against the war that expressed its support

---

159   'Meeting Coordination of EM Secretariats 26/27 September 1998', *European Marches* Photocopied Document, Undated.

160   'Cologne International Appeal European Demonstration, 29 May 1999: Against Unemployment, Job Insecurity, Exclusions and Racism. For a Europe and a World of Solidarity and of Liberty' available at <*www.euromarches.org/english/99/appeal.htm*> accessed on 20/08/2001.

161   Information from interview with Gerhard Klas.

162   Information from notes taken from a recording of the 'Parliament' on 1 June 1999.

163   *ibid.*

for the 'rights of all peoples living in the Balkans'.[164] However, evaluation meetings in France and Germany concluded that while linking social issues to the question of war was welcomed by many activists, it was also met with scepticism and resistance by a number of unemployed activists and representatives of their organizations.[165] For such activists, the agenda should remain narrowly focussed around the core issues. By extending the marches to issues of racism and war the European Marches had shown a 'red face' that frightened off more moderate supporters and in particular the trade union leaders who could deliver the mass mobilization necessary to enforce the demands for a 'social Europe'.[166]

The demand for the creation of employment that was ecologically useful indicated a concern to link social and environmental issues. However, unemployed activists encountered a problem at the Amsterdam counter-summit meeting when raising the issue of the environment in relation to unemployment. This was met with a negative response by established ecological organizations that preferred that the focus remain on the single issue of environmental destruction.[167] A broader outlook was taken by the Indian farmers of the Inter-Continental Caravan that linked actions against genetically modified crops with an opposition to economic globalization.[168] The conference in Cologne called for a 'globalization of struggles' to support a worldwide redistribution of wealth and committed itself to link the mobilization at the EU summit to that opposing G8 summit later the same month.[169] The question of globalization was prominent at the 'Alternative World Economic Summit' held in Cologne parallel to the G8 summit.

This event assembled representatives from a broad range of organizations from across the globe that held discussions in forums on work, migration and the economy. In contrast to the discussion amongst the grass roots activists at the 'Parliament' over concretizing the demands for the right to work and to an unconditional income, the questions of work and money at the G8 counter-summit were more abstractly formulated. The forum on work discussed such questions as 'Beyond Wage Labour?' and the 'Ethos, Utopia, and Ideology of Work' in the metropole and the periphery and that on the economy addressed 'Re-regulating the World Economy' and 'Breaking the Power of the Financial Markets'. There were thirty three speakers and moderators in these sessions of which the majority were journalists, academics and NGO representatives, with a single representative from an unemployed centre and

---

164   'Common Declaration of the international workgroup 'War in Kosovo' at the 'Alternative European Summit'*, The international workgroup 'War in Kosovo', Cologne May 30 1999 Photocopied Document.

165   Information from notes taken during participation in the German co-ordinating committee meeting in Cologne on 20 June 1999

166   Information from interview with anonymous activist.

167   Information from interview with Piet van der Lende.

168   'Transcontinental Caravan', available at   <*www.gn.apc.org/june18/caravan*> accessed on 13/05/1999.

169   'Cologne International Appeal European Demonstration, 29 May 1999: Against Unemployment, Job Insecurity, Exclusions and Racism. For a Europe and a World of Solidarity and of Liberty' available at <*www.euromarches.org/english/99/appeal.htm*> accessed on 20/08/2001.

no trade unionist.[170] However, a speaker from the newly formed ATTAC network did argue for an unconditional income financed through such measures as the Tobin Tax.[171]

Another aspect of the strategy advanced by certain prominent activists in the European Marches was to link the immediate concrete social situation and struggles and the demands to which they gave rise to a longer-term project of developing a different society. This perspective was articulated by Thies Gleiss, speaking on behalf of the European Marches at the counter-summit in Cologne. He argued that the main task was to build a movement of all those affected by the attacks on the welfare state and to link this movement to a project of social transformation.[172] This view was also expressed amongst some of the activists who were interviewed who stated that while it was correct for the movement to concentrate on the immediate struggle over the content of a 'social Europe', an attempt should be made to link this immediate struggle to a project of longer-term social change:

> When you see how rights that the worker's movement struggled centuries for are being destroyed, it is quite right and necessary to say 'that's enough'. But we can't afford to just fight for these small steps and forget the big aims and visa versa we can't just focus on the utopia. In the here and now it is this common struggle against welfare cuts that is bringing people together. But we must work on and join our alternative perspectives to these daily struggles and we must make it clearer what this society, which I call socialist, will be like otherwise it will always be a question of trying to stop things getting worse.[173]

However, it is also worthwhile to recognize that the overriding outlook of a number of the activists interviewed was that the European Marches was first of all engaged in formulating a defensive strategy to counter the immediate problems of material inequality and insecurity brought on by the neoliberal offensive. In this vein another activist stated that:

> The goal of the European Marches must be that we can exist. I don't know about a revolution that is a long way away, but a strong social movement is necessary today. And when it doesn't develop, the right-wing politicians and the bureaucrats will continue with their policies.[174]

This perspective was highly evident in that the meetings concentrated on developing common demands around which it was possible to organize common mobilizations rather than on abstract discussions about an alternative society. However, the

---

170   Information from notes taken during participant observation of the 'Alternative World Economic Summit' on 17/06/1999 & 18/06/1999; Agenda for the 'Alternativer Weltwirtschaftsgipfel', *Hg. Bündnis Köln '99*.

171   Information from notes taken during participation in the 'Alternative World Economic Summit' on 17 June 1999.

172   Information from notes taken during participation in the 'EU Alternative summit' meeting in Cologne on 2 June 1999.

173   Excerpt from interview with Uwe Durchbach.

174   Excerpt from interview with Piet van der Lende.

aspiration of linking the immediate struggles and demands to a project of social change was expressed in the call for the mobilization in Cologne.

> The struggle against unemployment, job insecurity and social exclusion has highlighted the terrible social injustices of a capitalist society where an extreme minority dominates all aspects of life for the sake of the profit motive … We want to convey, via our struggles and our demands, a message of hope and of new perspectives: the Abolition of unemployment, plans for a society based on liberty and social justice, for a Europe and a World where politics and economics are at the service of men and women.[175]

The perspective that the immediate struggles contained the seeds of social change was expressed at the 'Assembly' by Patrice Spadoni. He argued that the specific quality of the unemployed associations was that while they were mobilizing a challenge around the immediate issues of material insecurity, the demands that they were raising also posed more radical questions about the nature of the existing society. By struggling against the compulsion to work that was being imposed by Workfare schemes, the associations had begun to pose the question of what was socially useful human activity and by demanding the right to an unconditional income, they were posing the question of wealth distribution.[176] Uwe Durchbach reinforced this point by arguing that the question of working to meet concrete human needs and not for an abstract idea of economic growth had largely disappeared from the German labour movement. By rejecting the demand for full employment in favour of claiming an unconditional right to an income and work redistribution the unemployed associations were reintroducing this question.[177]

For some activists engaged in the unemployed mobilizations the demand for an unconditional income was the key to linking the defence of material living conditions to the desire for social transformation:

> The guaranteed income has become more and more important in the unemployed movement. But not only because it effects the everyday life of the unemployed, the level of income support, but it is also a kind of demand that can be utopian in some way - perhaps in the direction of a liberation from capitalist wage labour. For us this demand has this utopian seed in it and that has not been the case with the social movements of the last twenty years.[178]

This and other radical claims for the unconditional income were made in documents produced by several of the unemployed and claimant associations involved in the European Network for Income. AC!'s Commission on Income stated that the unconditional income was an offensive measure for tackling the new methods of capitalist exploitation that accompanied new forms of production. The demand went beyond the limited interests of the unemployed to include migrants, people with

---

175   Excerpt from 'Platform of European Demands' available at <*www.euromarches. org/english/98/04/0419a.htm*> accessed on 20/08/2001.

176   Information from notes made from a recording of the 'Assembly' on 2 December 2000.

177   Information from interview with Uwe Durchbach.

178   Excerpt from interview with Irène Bonnaud.

AIDS, women, prisoners, homeless, students and all those affected by job insecurity. The guaranteed income would also be a vital catalyst of fundamental social change in that it would be paid as a citizenship right and would valorize activities which were not valued by a capitalist society.[179]

The German claimants group, BAG-SHI, argued that the unconditional income would challenge capitalist logic by ending the compulsion to work.[180] The German unemployed association, BAG-E, identified four utopian characteristics of the unconditional income: it enabled each citizen to have a claim on the wealth produced by society; it broke the link between income and work; it challenged the dominant conception of work; and it criticized the sexual division of labour.[181]

The immediate emphasis on constructing a set of common European demands meant that debates over the utopian character of the unconditional income were held largely on the fringes of meetings or at events at which there was more of an emphasis on discussion than on organizing mobilization. During the workshop on the unconditional income at the conference in Cologne there was a debate, mainly conducted by the Italian participants, over the suggestion that the income was one of many citizenship rights being demanded by the new social subjects arising from resistance to the Post-Fordist social order. Opponents of this view asserted that there now existed more workers than ever and that the workplace remained the key location from which to mount a challenge to capitalist exploitation.[182]

This debate was also waged at the conference organized by FeLS held in Berlin in March 1999 at which the potential for the unconditional income to be an anti-capitalist demand was debated.[183] The debate posed the question of the anti-capitalist character of the demand for a guaranteed income emanating from groups external to the labour process. One side supported the radicality of these social actors whilst the other side argued for combining the guaranteed income with the central demand for work redistribution coming from employed workers that were inside the labour process.[184]

Support for developing a set of complementary demands around which to mobilize was also expressed by a representative of the *Confederazione Cobas* speaking at the 'Assembly'. He explained that by starting from the various demands for universal substantive rights to meet common needs it was possible to develop solidarity between the unemployed, insecure workers, the now not so stable workers

179   AC! Commission Revenu (1999a) *European network for a Guaranteed Income*, Leaflet; AC! Commission Revenu (1999b) 'Revenu garanti pour tous avec ou sans emploi, trois arguments' *Vacarmes* 9.

180   BAG-SHI (2000) *Existenzgeld für alle* (Neu-Ulm: AG Spak).

181   BAG-E (1996) *Existenzgeld. 10 Positionen gegen falsche Bescheidenheit und das Schweigen der Ausgegrenzten* (Frankfurt:BAG-Erwerblose).

182   Information from notes taken during participation in the conference held in Cologne on 23 January 1999.

183   'Konferenz: Für Existenzgeld und eine radikale Arbeitszeitverkürzung. Zur Kritik der Lohnarbeitsgesellschaft 18. März – 21. März 1999, Berlin, organisiert von FelS available at <*www.nadir.org/nadir/initiativ/fels/archiv/existenz/aufruf.html*> accessed on 17/01/2001.

184   'Mit Aussteigermodellen gegen die Weltwirtschaftskrise? Zur Existenzgelddebatte'. *Sozialistische Zeitung* 18 March 1999.

as well as migrants and other marginalized groups. He argued that this was a project to put the working class back together and to aim for social and political transformation.[185] However, this strategy of mobilizing around demands for social rights met with severe criticism from a tendency that argued that it was a 'reformist' attempt to rescue social democracy from the clutches of 'Third Way' politicians such as Blair, Schröder, and Jospin. Such activists felt that the main purpose of events like the European Marches was not to co-ordinate demands, but to meet other militant unemployed and workers' groups from across Europe in order to co-ordinate resistance to both specific EU policies and to the EU itself.[186] In the Cologne campaign this outlook was articulated in terms of an opposition to the call for a 'social Europe' and in favour of the immediate 'destruction of the capitalist work prison'.[187]

In this light, behind the set of common demands for social citizenship rights there appeared to be some fundamental differences amongst the activists about how social transformation was to be achieved. At the meeting titled *Sozial Frage oder Klassenkampf?* [Social Question or Class Struggle?], that was held at the EU counter-summit in Cologne, there was a debate over whether existing state institutions could be utilized to bring about social change. One activist commented that the overriding impression was one of a new generation of activists addressing the same old questions.[188]

---

185   Information from notes taken from a recording of the 'Assembly' on 4 December 2000.

186   Information from interviews with activists from BABC.

187   'Gegen das 'soziale Europa!' Kein Frieden mit dem Kapitalismus! Stoppt den imperialistischen Krieg!' Leaflet distributed on the Cologne demonstration on 29/05/1999.

188   Information from notes taken during participation in the Cologne Alternative Summit meeting on 2 June 1999.

Chapter 7

The European Marches, Social Europe, and the Limits of the New Reformism

Introduction

In this chapter I return to the work of seven of the eight authors from the 'New social democratic Left' that I outlined in chapter two. I outline and make specific criticisms of the work of Giddens, Touraine, Beck, Offe, Gorz, Castells, and Habermas which was published in the period after the emergence of the European social movement. I label the work of these writers as the 'new reformism' which describes how it was an attempt to overcome the continued 'impasse' of social democracy[1] in the face of the purportedly 'new' conditions of neoliberal globalization.

This attempt to develop a 'new reformism' marked a continuation of the earlier ideas of the death of the 'old' class politics. Organized labour as the agent of social change has been replaced by 'new' social actors with the focus now shifted onto 'excluded' groups such as the unemployed or insecurely employed, and migrant workers. It was also based on a continuation of the idea that there has been a fundamental break in socio-structural conditions which has now been extended to include the purported shift from the national to the transnational terrain which is the level at which the 'new' capitalism must now apparently be regulated.

As well as setting out this analysis of the main writers from the 'new reformism' I also identify their proposals for the renewal of the welfare state and its institutionalization beyond the nation state. In this respect, most of these authors have produced explicit proposals for the development of a 'social Europe' as a 'new' civilizing social democratic project in the age of neoliberal globalization.

At this point, I turn to the work of Pierre Bourdieu who, as I showed in chapter one, was amongst the most enthusiastic supporters of the anti-neoliberal mobilizations and who was one of the main prominent proponents of a renewed labour movement as the main agent of a 'social Europe'. I argue that while Bourdieu's work[2] did direct attention at the need to transform trade unionism, he also accepted some of the assumptions of the 'new reformism'. This was also the case for Peter Waterman who developed an argument for a 'new' trade unionism based on the theoretical insights of the writers from the 'New social democratic Left'.

---

1   Panitch (1986) 'The Impasse of Social Democratic Politics' in Miliband et al *op cit.*

2   Bourdieu (1998) *op cit.*; (2003) *op cit.*

After having demonstrated how the ideas of the 'new reformism' have been influential in the argument for renewing labour as a new social movement, I then show how they have also been advanced to explain and support a new social democratic politics. I then turn my attention to the way that the limitations of the policies of social democratic parties in office and of the 'new reformism' in animating the resistance to neoliberalism have opened up a space for the development of more radical political alternatives in the GJM.

I outline and criticize the work of Tony Negri who, like the late Alberto Melucci, was interested particularly in the autonomous social centres developed in Italy which have undergone a resurgence of mobilization through organisations like the *Tute Bianche* and *Ya Basta*. I highlight how Negri's work shared the main assumptions of the 'new reformism' and therefore, while presenting itself as a theoretical underpinning for a new revolutionary movement, actually amounted to a radical version of the 'new reformism'.

I then consider the argument for the development of a socialist alternative. I set out the work of André Brie MEP and political scientist who argued for a democratic socialist version of 'social Europe'. I then present the revolutionary socialist alternative, in particular through outlining relevant work by Trotskyist writers such as Ernest Mandel and Alex Callinicos whose work has influenced socialist participation in the European Marches and the broader GJM. I conclude by comparing and contrasting the kind of social movement conceived of by the thinking of the 'new reformism' and the socialist alternative by way of Touraine's framework for analyzing the formation of a coherent social movement.

Giddens

Anthony Giddens built on his earlier work[3] to argue for the renewal of social democracy as the 'Third Way' which rejected both old style statist social democracy and the idea that the only feasible alternative was neoliberalism's celebration of the market. He presented this project as a 'new progressivism' (p. 2) which followed through the political implications of the 'new times' thesis advanced by post-Marxist thinkers in the late 1980s and early 1990s.[4] In this sense, he accepted the processes of globalization and the development of the information society as incomplete but unstoppable revolutions which have produced the new realities which have structured the development of political alternatives. The 'Third Way', therefore, was presented as a modernizing project where 'modernization ... means reforming institutions to meet the demands of a globalizing information order' (p. 32). This analysis rendered the Keynesian Welfare State (KWS) outmoded and, moreover, lacking in political support due to the disappearance of social democracy's traditional working class constituency.

The disappearance of the economic, social and political foundations of the old welfare state required its renewal based on a new social contract between state and

---

3   Especially Giddens (1994) *op cit.*
4   Giddens, A. (2000) *The Third Way and its Critics* (Cambridge: Polity).

citizens based on the maxim of 'no rights without responsibilities' (p. 52). The 'Third Way' project was to modernize the welfare state around the new life political principles of 'autonomy', 'active health', lifelong 'education', 'well being' and 'initiative' (p. 128).[5] This required a shift away from the state distributing financial benefits towards it investing in human capital. This involved state intervention focused mainly on the labour market which translated into active measures to improve the social capabilities of those individuals and social groups excluded from labour market participation. Such measures targeted spending away from the provision of financial benefits towards training courses which improved skills, and counselling sessions which boosted morale.

Giddens' analysis rationalized the retreat of social democracy as the only realistic response for the supporters of social justice in the face of globalization. However, this analysis tended to naturalize processes, for example, his representation of financial markets as an institutionalised risk environment risked rendering them 'transhistorical features of human existence' (p. 84).[6] The corollary of this analysis was to represent governments (and citizens) as relatively powerless in the face of omnipotent global financial markets. Therefore, any utopian elements of a renewed social democratic project such as redistribution of income and wealth were restricted by the realistic limits set by such institutions. When governments were faced by the demands of citizens for rights to have needs met and by the demands of the financial markets for monetary stability, Giddens' analysis suggested that they would be compelled to accede to the latter. The conclusion to be drawn was that 'far from renewing social democracy, the 'Third Way' amounts to an attempt to mobilize the political capital of the reformist left in support of a project that abandons substantial reforms altogether and instead embraces neoliberalism' (p. 123).[7]

The fact that the European Marches' demands for specific reforms such as the guaranteed income and job creation measures would breach the terms of the 'Growth and Stability Pact' suggests that its political capital was not recuperable within the 'Third Way'. This was even more the case for its complete opposition to measures which amounted to forced labour which was influenced by experiences of the 'New Deal'. Any mention of this programme was omitted entirely from Giddens' work, but formed the main welfare policy reform emanating from the New Labour government under the explicit influence of the 'Third Way'.

The demands formulated by the European Marches were articulated through a discourse of rights to have needs met independently of work. This contrasted starkly with the 'Third Way' discourse of 'no rights without responsibilities' which translated into a moral duty to participate in the labour market as the means of meeting needs. While the European Marches demanded that the state guarantee its citizens the right to work, the 'Third Way' spoke the language of the state providing citizens with opportunities to gain access to the labour market. While the European Marches evoked the idea of a citizen's mobilization demanding that the state act to fulfil its

5   Giddens (1998) *op cit.*

6   Callinicos, A. (1999) 'Social Theory put to the Test of Politics: Pierre Bourdieu and Anthony Giddens' *New Left Review* 236 pp. 77–102.

7   Callinicos, A. (2001) *Against the Third Way* (Cambridge: Polity).

obligation to deliver universal rights, the 'Third Way' suggested the state mobilizing its citizens as independent labourers thereby fulfilling their obligation to work. This latter representation was connected to the redefinition of equality as inclusion in society which entailed personal as well as state responsibility for action.

This emphasis on individual initiative is indicative of Giddens' assertion that state action should promote rather than stifle individual autonomy so as to enable self-actualization. However, the measures emanating from the 'Third Way' project focused on the development of human beings as human capital by providing training and counselling to improve the quality of labour-power. These measures encouraged forms of identification based on the competitive market such as 'jobseeker' which eroded further collective solidarity based on an identification of common human needs. It is unsurprising therefore that there was no apparent collective agent identified by Giddens that associated to popularize the measures prompted by 'Third Way' thinking. All that was present was a minority of excluded individuals seeking out government assistance to help them to help themselves back into work. Indeed, in the UK, unemployed workers' centres have now become far less numerous than training centres for the unemployed. If government training programmes have largely mobilized the unemployed into low paid work in the UK thereby demobilizing collective opposition, in France intellectuals wishing to promote the renewal of social democracy have responded to the resurgence of collective action.

Touraine

Alain Touraine was explicit in his attempt to claim elements of the resistance to the social consequences of restructuring as the emergent new social agent that could show society the way 'beyond neoliberalism'.[8] However, this new collective actor did not emanate from the NSMs identified by Touraine in the 1980s. This was because the central social conflict has moved away from the issues arising from the application of knowledge and now revolves around the social effects of capitalist modernization: unemployment, inequality and exclusion. Touraine explained this changing focus by stating that, although a new 'mode of production' (p. 8) (information/post-industrial society) has emerged, there has also been a change in the 'mode of modernization' (p.9). These changes has been from socialism understood as a 'state administered economy' to capitalism defined as a 'market economy' (p. 9).

For Touraine, it has been this return of capitalism and in particular the dominance of finance, rather than the illusory enemy of globalization, that has resulted in the 'dualization of society' (p. 25) and its attendant social problems. In this context, the state has not been powerless to act, but should have developed new social policies which could civilize the new capitalism. These policies have to be developed through a constructive engagement with the new social actors which have been advancing demands for rights which have addressed the social problems of unemployment, inequality and exclusion.

---

8   Touraine (2001) *op cit.*

Like its historical precedent of the labour movement, the new social actor must emerge from its victimhood and its defensive struggles to become conscious of itself, not as a disparate set of interests and identities, but as a unified actor. It too, by making positive demands for rights, is an agent not of revolution, but of democracy. However, unlike labour, the new social actors do not form the basis for a political party. Therefore the task has not been to involve the resistance in the construction of a new political force to the left of the plural left, but rather to align the new social protests with existing political forces and institutions. This would enable the demands for rights to be translated into a new citizenship regime which would socially integrate the excluded and civilize the new capitalism.

Based on this analysis, Touraine asserted that the movement of the *sans-papiers* was the most advanced in developing as a distinct social actor. The movements of the homeless and the unemployed have been much weaker and their transformation from victims to actors has been stifled by the overbearing influence of ideological and political forces which have been manipulating them into being part of a populist project. Therefore, Touraine called for the realignment of these movements away from the 'ultra left' and towards the formation of a democratic 'social left' (pp. 74–88).

This new 'New Left' could have developed closer links with the plural left government to realize its demands for rights in a new social policy which could combine the modernization of the economy with the achievement of social justice. Touraine propounded his own version of this new social policy which he labelled as a 'two and a half way' (p. 92). This approach rejected the 'Third Way' as a 'form of neoliberalism' (p. 91) which did not make the social integration of the excluded its main objective. This aim was to be achieved by policies focused on increasing growth and employment. This would mean the introduction of active employment and social policies which protected labour while being compatible with the new reality of flexible labour markets. Such policies would reorient the state away from subsidizing the jobs and welfare of privileged categories and towards training measures thereby enabling job creation and the formation of an appropriately skilled workforce. Such measures would produce both 'McJobs' in the service sector and 'Microsoft jobs' (p. 95) in the high tech sector.

It is interesting to note that having rejected any 'core' sectors of the working class as the agent of the new social settlement, Touraine's search for an alternative agent led him to alight on the excluded . In this sense, his analysis mirrored that of some writers from the 'New Right' who identified the unemployed, migrants and other dispossessed sectors as an 'underclass' that was a threat to social order.[9] Touraine, as a writer from the 'New social democratic Left', argued against concerns about 'dangerous classes' and a return to the values of 'public order, authority and security' (p. 31).[10] Instead he seemed to identify the socially excluded as the harbingers of the newly formulated values, solidarities and rights which would form the basis of a new social settlement. Touraine, therefore, seemed to have proclaimed that it was time to

---

9   Murray, C. (1990) *The Emerging British Underclass* (London: IEA); (1994) *Underclass the Crisis Deepens* (London: IEA).

10   Touraine (2001) *op cit.*

stop worrying and to learn to love the poor as a new agent of social integration and social order.

While attributing agency to those who have been marginalized by neoliberal restructuring, Touraine was mistaken in privileging them as the central actor capable of advancing an alternative to neoliberalism. This perspective deprived movements of the marginalized of a powerful ally in organized labour and placed severe limits on the alternative project. For Touraine, the 'dualization of society' (p. 25) has been producing two distinct social groups with different interests: a class of secure workers (the included) and a non-class of insecure workers and the unemployed (the excluded). The included have job security which has still been guaranteed largely by the state which has been dependent partially on the support of organized labour. The 'excluded' have faced job insecurity: an issue which has not been addressed by the state.

The strategic possibility of developing an alliance with organized labour has been rendered impossible by Touraine's analysis which has deemed unions as organizations representing solely the narrow instrumental class interests of the included. However, the dual society is only composed of two distinct social groups when classes are viewed as categories. When classes are viewed as deriving from the social relation of capital, it is possible to identify the included and excluded as sections of the working class both of which are subject to measures which serve to facilitate their exploitation. From this perspective, the European Marches project suggested the development of a set of demands which countered this process by recomposing the working class around demands for rights to have needs met independently of labour market participation. Touraine's analysis, meanwhile, actually served to facilitate welfare state restructuring by dividing the opposition and by advancing a project which recomposed the working class around labour market participation while producing a new segmentation of the working class around differential levels of skill.

It is also noteworthy that the project advanced by Touraine resembled that being articulated by the European Commission in that its emphasis was on modernizing the so called 'European Social Model' by introducing active employment policies as a means of achieving higher levels of growth and employment. These measures actually found very little resonance in French public opinion in general or in its movements of the marginalized in particular. This marked a failure to popularize the idea of labour market and welfare state restructuring by presenting them as necessary modernization processes which actually served to produce social justice. However, this does not discount the role that Touraine played as a conduit for the dissemination of this policy discourse in French society and its proposed adoption by policymakers as well as by some unions and associations. Nevertheless, rather than allying themselves to the modernizing project, the movements of the marginalized active in France, alongside a section of the unions, largely adopted an oppositional stance to active employment policies based on a different policy discourse. It was this oppositional discourse which was legitimated and circulated through participation in the European Marches and which contributed to the rejection of the European Constitutional Treaty in the referendum in 2005.

Beck

In 'The Brave New World of Work',[11] Beck based his version of the 'new reformism' on his analysis of the radicalization of modernity which has produced a shift from a first modernity characterized by relative closure, security and certainty to a second, open, insecure and risk filled modernity (pp. 17–35). His general purpose was to oppose the generalization into Europe of the neoliberal version of free market capitalism epitomized by the United States with a renewed social democratic version of socially embedded capitalism based on a new social contract. This translated into a project of modernizing the 'European Social Model' to meet the new challenges posed by the end of the 'old' work society of early modernity and the establishment of a 'new' regime of risk in the second late modernity. His concrete proposal for a 'Europe of civil labour' (p. 134) amounted to a rescue of global capitalism from itself through the establishment of a new material basis for a democratic transnational social order.

Beck argued that all of the main scenarios for the future of work, both optimistic and pessimistic, under the conditions imposed by the second modernity (information technology, globalization, ecological crisis and individualization) (p. 37), were based on the illusory framework of the persistence of a society based on full employment. For Beck, the idea of full employment was an anachronism belonging to the old 'Fordist regime' (pp. 68–9) which was well on the way to being replaced by a new 'risk regime' (pp. 69–72). Beck identified five dimensions of this new regime: 'globalization, ecologization, digitalization, individualization, and politicization of work' (p. 72) each of which has produced new risks for capital and labour alike. However, in an analysis that replicated the work of Castells, capital and labour have developed highly unequal access to the 'new transnational power game' (p. 29) as capital has become global, mobile and co-ordinated while labour has remained local, fixed and individualized. Under the conditions of the risk regime, working people have experienced unprecedented levels of dependence and vulnerability and work increasingly in a destandardized, flexible system of employment where insecurity is the norm.

Beck presented two possible responses for Europe under the new conditions imposed by the risk regime: the neoliberal model of development or a social and political alternative. The neoliberal model would lead to a 'Brazilianization' (pp. 92–109) of society with a pluralized social structure based on a labour market segmented into four categories: 'money and knowledge elites', highly skilled precarious workers, low and unskilled 'working poor' (p. 106), and the 'socially excluded' (pp. 106–7). Not only would neoliberal development lead to social polarization and disintegration it would also result in the destruction of democracy. Taking the USA as his example, Beck showed how increasing pressures to work have resulted in the destruction of social capital which was the basis of an active citizenship.

Beck's alternative was to link the destruction of work society with the creation of a social dimension to Europe. Whereas paid work was the foundation for citizenship in early modernity, in late modernity it should be enabled through access to 'civil

---

11   Beck, U. (2000) *The Brave New World of Work* (Cambridge: Polity).

labour' (pp. 126–31). Civil labour (citizen's work) would be freely chosen and self-fulfulling work for the benefit of other people. It would be paid for by 'civic money' (p. 126) granted at a level at least equal to minimum welfare or by non-material rewards such as free childcare or pension credits. Civic money would ideally be raised through foundations not taxation and civic labour enabled by 'public welfare entrepreneurship' (p. 129) not directed by state officialdom.

Beck argued that 'a citizens' Europe will only emerge in a Europe of civil labour' which was how 'European democracy ... wins its soul' (p. 134). The EU would be the site for democratic renewal as the transnational has now become the only effective level of social and political regulation. Moreover, the EU has been the most open of the transnational institutions to developing a sphere of 'cosmopolitan democracy' (p. 175). The evidence was that it has offered 'special opportunities' (p. 135) for citizens' groups to engage with ministers and officials to advance progressive policies. Therefore, the agent of this new social contract could be found amidst the younger, better educated whose values have led them into self-fulfilling moral engagement and into participating in the transnational organizations, networks, and forums which Beck characterized as a 'transnational civil society' (p. 125).

Some of the criticisms levelled at Gorz (see below) are also attributable to Beck: in particular the notion of generalized labour market insecurity and the encouragement of 'new' kinds of enterprise and work in civil society. In relation to labour market developments, Beck was refuted by his own evidence which showed a reduction of standard employment relations in Germany between 1970–95 from 84% to 68%: which still left a substantial majority untouched by job insecurity. Moreover, while fixed-term contract work remained stable, part-time work doubled and was overwhelmingly undertaken by women.[12] These developments suggest an extension of standardized employment to women rather than the demise of the 'Fordist' model.[13] The notion that European labour markets are becoming 'Brazilianized' and that there is no future for a stably employed sector was a huge overstatement which was not substantiable. Beck's thinking that job insecurity has been generalized appeared wishful and, like Gorz, distracted attention away from the limits to, and possible contradictions of, labour market restructuring as well as precluding a resurgence of workplace militancy.

While introduced as an antidote to 'Workfare', Beck's proposal for civil labour would worsen the material conditions of the unemployed by introducing payments in kind for voluntary work and would also replace the legal compulsion wielded by state officials with a moral compulsion wielded by welfare entrepreneurs. While establishing an apparent choice between formal and informal employment, civil labour would actually offer the 'excluded' a choice between relative poverty and civility and relative affluence and incivility. It is unsurprising that I could find no organizational supporters for it amongst unemployed or migrant associations. Beck's presentation of civil labour as a mechanism for creating an active civil society was

---

12   *Ibid*: p. 94 & p. 105.
13   I made this observation while reading Beck's work, but wish to acknowledge that it is also one made in a review of his book by Cerni, P. (2005) in *Review of Radical Political Economics* 37 (3) pp. 390–2.

one which actively depoliticized civil society and neutralized it as a locus of political change. Indeed, he explained how engaging citizens in civil labour would serve to defuse protest by focusing attention on alternative activities and would deflect attention away from making demands on the state.

The flipside of civil labour would be civil enterprise. This would mean the further dismantling of the welfare state and could also mean a creeping privatization of welfare under the guise of socially responsible corporate funding. Beck was unashamedly open about how civil labour would create low cost jobs and establish a low wage sector thereby expanding the very category of 'working poor' that he wished to eliminate. This is suggestive of how, for Beck, it seemed that in order to become less like American society, it would be necessary to become more like it and that in order to have less liberalization, it would be necessary to have more liberalization. Like Giddens, who also regarded contemporary capitalism as a risk society, the content of Beck's 'social Europe' also characterized him as a social liberal.[14] From this perspective, Beck's work, along with that of Giddens and Touraine, amounted to little more than an ideological justification for the liberalization policies pursued by social democratic parties in government in Germany, the UK and France respectively.

A final criticism of Beck is based on his observation that the EU has been a particularly favourable arena for developing a cosmopolitan democracy due to its openness to citizens' groups. However, the apparent openness of the EU to citizens' organizations has largely been an attempt to tackle its lack of legitimacy through incorporating civil society organizations and networks into a consensual process of deliberative democracy. In relation to the development of a 'social Europe', this has mainly taken the form of the social dialogue involving trade unions and more recently the civil dialogue involving NGOs. The latter process has been funded by the Commission to involve NGOs in consultation over social policy developments. However, this has been consultation conducted within the overall constraints of the Broad Economic Policy Guidelines (BEPG) which have set a liberalization agenda for the development of employment and social policy.

Despite some mild criticism voiced by NGO representatives, in general terms, the development of a so called European civil society has been an almost exclusively top-down process which has attempted to stifle dissent and to utilize the symbolic power of organizations representing the poor to bolster the ailing legitimacy of employment and social policy developments. It has been designed not to enhance democratic participation, but to transmit the message of modernization through the experts employed by organizations that have been dependent largely on the EU for funding. In contrast, the European Marches remained largely autonomous of EU institutions and its ideology of consensus through dialogue and favoured a more conflictual approach to politics which took the form of extra-institutional protests.

---

14   The term 'social liberalism' (p. 54) was used by Bourdieu (2003) *op cit.* to describe the policies enacted by New Labour and it has also been used in relation to the 'plural left' government in France by Bachet, D. & Durand, J-P. (2001) 'Social-Liberalism in France', *Capital & Class*, 75 pp. 135–148.

Offe

Offe's contribution to the 'new reformism' will be outlined through an examination of two articles the first of which focused on the prospects for the welfare state in Germany in the context of the processes of unification, European integration and globalization (p. 20).[15] For Offe, these processes had resulted in a fundamental destabilization of the political and economic foundations of the 'institutional architecture' (p. 11) of the German welfare state. The opening up of the German economy had led to mass unemployment and to the abandonment of any prospect of full employment as Keynesian demand management was rendered redundant. Unemployment was much worsened by unification which also put a heavy financial strain upon state finances, while these were also subject to the EMU convergence criteria. 'Negative' European integration encouraged a 'politics of regulatory disengagement' (p. 25) and the prospect for transnational regulation was weakened by the national embeddedness of collective actors who themselves were facing 'rampant disorganization' due to processes of 'splintering' and 'fragmentation' (p. 27). These factors resulted in a new political consensus for 'remodelling the welfare state' (p. 26) based on a discourse that had shifted from a rights based entitlement to welfare to its contribution to economic performance.

Offe's contribution to this debate was to argue for a new form of rights based welfare. He highlighted how any new regime had to tackle two forms of precariousness which threaten social integration. 'Precariousness of productive activity' referred to the insecurity of labour market participation and 'precariousness of distributive status' (p. 28) referred to insecurity of access to income and basic services. This left two options for the basis of a new welfare regime: a restoration of the link between work and income or its severance and replacement by a new bond between citizenship and income.

Offe favoured the latter approach due to his assessment that restoring full employment was only possible by economically and morally unacceptable measures. He argued that the new task of a welfare regime should be to make 'non-employment tolerable' (p. 30). To this end, Offe argued against policies that subsidized low paid work and in favour of a universal basic income that was to be introduced gradually. This meant the recognition of new valid exemptions from the labour market such as activity in the voluntary, personal care and associational sectors as well as a 'sabbatical account' (pp. 31–2).

Turning his attention to the European level, Offe then asked whether the social model of European capitalism could survive the pressure placed on it by globalization in the form of Europeanization.[16] For Offe, what was distinctive about, and ensured the relative success of, the 'Continental European' model of capitalism vis-à-vis the 'Anglo-Saxon' (p. 442) model was that it embedded markets in a wider status order. This model was under attack by 'aggressive market liberals' (p. 455) that argued

---

15   Offe, C. (2000) 'The German Welfare State: Principles, Performance And Prospects After Unification' *Thesis Eleven* 63 pp. 11–37.

16   Offe, C. (2003) 'The European Model of 'Social' Capitalism: Can It Survive European Integration?', *The Journal of Political Philosophy* 11 (4) pp. 437–69.

that increasing employment to repair the roof of the welfare state construction was only possible through demolishing some of its floors that protected workers and citizens. It was also assailed by 'militant rightist populists' (p. 455) that sought to replace worker protection and its associated high spending and taxation with more basic provision targeted at those most in need and designed to bolster the family. The third actor in this triangular political contest over the future of the welfare state were the 'reluctant social democrats' (p. 455) that proposed a return to full employment and growth through modernizing social protection systems so as to boost economic performance.

At the EU level, the first and second projects would mean 'negative integration' and 'positive disintegration', (p. 456) while the third would require 'a positive integration of a 'social' Europe' (p. 457). The inter-governmental character of the EU seemed to preclude the final course of action and its advancement through the Open Method of Co-ordination (OMC) also seemed doomed to failure as its voluntaristic character made it easily resistable at the national level. Offe concluded that 'social Europe' could only develop if the European Court and Commission could be forced to act, but saw such a development as 'counterfactual' (p. 468).

Rather than focus on some of the more obvious criticisms of Offe's work which I have already outlined and will develop further in relation to other writers, it is worthwhile remarking on how it expressed a kind of realistic pessimism in the 'new reformism' that contrasted with the overblown optimism expressed by Beck and the hopeful utopianism of Gorz. Offe revealed quite starkly and honestly what kind of minimalist reforms a pragmatic alternative to neoliberalism might achieve based on the disappearance of a 'Left' political alternative and apparently fragmented and demobilized social actors.

Offe made no proposals for new taxation measures to fund social protection and income redistribution. The sabbatical account appeared to be self-funding from workers' contributions and offered little more than periodic extended holidays from intensified work. The basic income offered the unemployed no prospect of a return to employment. It rather existed to boost their morale by offering to pay for non-work activities. Faced with this alternative, the social liberal alternative of training programmes and the prospect of a return to work, if only most likely in low paid insecure employment, might seem like an acceptable risk to run. Any measures to create employment and to guarantee protection against poverty pay were notable by their absence.

The meagre character of this dubious alternative to neoliberalism was overlaid by Offe's inability to identify any credible social and political agency to deliver it. According to Offe's analysis, the 'new' hoped for European Left had yet to appear. However, it was unclear whether this was because it did not yet exist (even in an embryonic form) or because Offe was unwilling to look any further than the kind of NSMs and new political parties that he envisaged. The mobilizations at the EU level and in member states suggested that the fragmentation of social actors was starting to be overcome and that there existed the beginnings of the remobilization of organized labour.

Moreover, while the Greens in Germany were becoming 'reluctant' social democrats in office, the new mobilizations seemed to express discontent with social democratic parties that in Germany led to the formation of a new political party on the Left.[17] This suggests that a process of political polarization has been occurring. This has been between those willing to take office and introduce liberalizing measures and those implacably opposed to any participation in their introduction and in favour of developing policies with an anti-capitalist flavour and dynamic. From this perspective, the European Marches may have suggested the emergence of a fourth political force and a fourth political option for the future of the welfare state in Europe.

Gorz

In 'Reclaiming Work: Beyond the Wage-Based Society',[18] Gorz developed his previous analysis to argue that capitalism has gone beyond the crisis of its Fordist stage of development. Capitalism has entered a new post-Fordist phase in which knowledge is the main form of capital and intellect its accompanying form of labour-power. This changing structure has had significant implications for the new agent of social change which I will outline shortly. It is significant to note, meanwhile, that Gorz also identified how information technology has facilitated economic globalization which undermined the power of the nation state and movements mobilizing within national societies.

However, Gorz argued against the idea that globalization was irresistible and resulted inevitably in rising unemployment and job insecurity as well as welfare cuts. This was an alibi for governments submitting willingly to the power of the financial markets and wishing to redistribute wealth in favour of the wealthy. To counter such thinking and such policies he called for 'resistance to transnational capital' which he asserted 'can only be transnational itself'. Its product would be a 'different globalization, based on worldwide solidarity and vision' (p. 16). This vision was realizable through a different Europe which would break from the Anglo-Saxon model to produce an alternative model of development that was ecologically and socially sustainable.

Gorz contended that the application of information technology in the post-Fordist labour process has ended the class antagonism between capital and labour in the factory and has shifted the location of conflict to the wider society. While the core of 'elite' (p. 45) workers has been tied into the work ethic, a new periphery of insecurely employed and unemployed workers has developed who have rejected the work ethic and have embraced new life projects based on freely chosen activities outside of work. Therefore, the 'old' central protagonist of the 'old' Fordist order – the 'mass worker' (p. 50) – has been replaced by a 'new' leading actor of the 'new' post-Fordist order – the insecure worker.

The 'insecure worker' (p. 53) has taken the form of the 'jobber'(p. 50) who has chosen to work in temporary jobs so as to meet basic needs and to maximize free time for non-work activities. In Gorz's words, 'the new protagonists are those people

---

17   This party was called *Arbeit und soziale Gerechtigkeit – Die Wahlalternative* [Labour and Social Justice – the Electoral Alternative].

18   Gorz (1999) *op cit.*

who, instead of passively putting up with the insecurity and discontinuity of most jobs, try to use these as a springboard for their self-affirmation and for a richer, freer, more solidary life' (pp. 60–1). The political corollary of this analysis was for Gorz to reject demands for the right to work in the sense of a right to citizenship. Instead, he favoured demands for citizenship rights to be detached from work so as to facilitate a shift beyond capitalism understood as a society based on the wage-form.

To achieve this end, Gorz proposed what he regarded as an anti-capitalist agenda of reforms with a revolutionary content. This agenda included the unconditional 'guarantee of a basic income' (p. 81) understood not as an element of a new system of social protection, but to enable the right to refuse undignified work and to allow a free choice of unwaged activities. It also included the 'redistribution of work' (p. 93) so as to develop new forms of flexible working which enable the worker to choose when to work and also to maximize the time available for freely chosen activities. These activities would be developed through new urban policies and support for co-operative initiatives such as 'Local Exchange Trading Systems' (pp. 102–8). While these activities would exist in a largely autonomous and expanding non-market, non-state sphere, there would be a continued co-ordinating role for the state and a continued economic role for the market.

It is clearly apparent that Gorz's analysis resonated strongly with some elements in the European Marches which could be seen in the content of its platform of demands which focused on the unconditional right to an income and the redistribution of work and income. It was also evident in the characterization of the right to an income as a utopian demand which could result in liberation from wage labour. Despite this clear influence, the resistance expressed transnationally through the European Marches cannot, and should not, be claimed unproblematically for this version of the 'new reformism'. This is not least the case because of deficiencies in Gorz's argument and limitations in his strategy.

Gorz seemed to regard the technical revolution as an unstoppable and even welcome process which has been proceeding hitherto along the wrong path. What was required, according to Gorz, was for the mobilization of a social movement which 'rejects the irrational capitalist management of technological rationalization' (p. 145) which has been enslaving humanity.[19] This social movement could humanize the process by placing it on a self-managed basis thereby liberating humanity to engage in the pursuit of a multiplicity of self-defined ends.[20]

This argument is open to the charge of technological determinism and of seeking to make a false separation (and connection) between the logic of technology and the logic of capital. The application of information technology into the labour process has been driven by the logic of capital accumulation. Far from resulting in the attenuation of class conflict, the 'end of work' and to new 'paths to paradise', it has been deployed as a weapon in an attack on existing forms of working class organization. This attack

---

19   *Ibid*.

20   This depiction and criticism of Gorz's analysis is one that could also be directed broadly at the work of Touraine and Castells as the other sociologists writing from the post-industrial perspective.

has amounted to an attempt to intensify work and thereby overcome the barriers to profitability and usher in a new phase of sustained accumulation.

This means that the transition to a post-Fordist order has not been a smooth or inevitable process which has opened up new possibilities for demands which humanize the new capitalism. It has rather been a contested process of capitalist restructuring which has given rise to various elements of resistance each of which has produced defensive demands. Indeed, it might be the strength of this resistance which has contributed to the limited success of post-Fordist strategies. However, Gorz's analysis has not contributed to the development of this resistance, but has misdirected it into utterly utopian projects of social change.

Firstly, Gorz's depiction of post-Fordism as a new phase of development led him to identity and petrify divisions in the working class based on an idealized consciousness towards work. This works neither empirically nor logically. Work adherence amongst the working class has neither been a delusional state to be grown out of, nor an historical phase to be surpassed. It has rather been an inevitable consequence of the contradictory position of wage labourers within the labour process which has produced a contradictory relationship and consciousness towards work.[21] Therefore, to posit demands which relate to the rejection of work is to appeal to anti-capitalist aspirations amongst the working class whilst failing to root them in everyday resistance to exploitation.

This led, secondly, to the identification of core workers as a privileged strata which identified itself through work and so consented to its exploitation. This outlook presented defeats in battle as signifying the end of the war and therefore cannot recognize worker's resistance to work intensification as the basis for a defensive demand for a shorter working week. However, as some participants in the European Marches highlighted, this demand, imposed from the outside as the means for redistributing work, could actually result in increased work flexibility and thereby increase the rate of exploitation. This demonstrated a tendency in Gorz's work to produce artificial demands for 'revolutionary reforms' which emerged from his ideological predisposition as opposed to the daily realities of class struggle.

Moreover, thirdly, Gorz's analysis rendered demands for paid work evident amongst the overwhelming majority of the unemployed as reactionary and indeed as evidence of something akin to false consciousness. This was mistaken and unduly pessimistic. It also failed to recognize the way that the guaranteed income could resonate with the everyday experiences of the unemployed and insecurely employed as a defence against deteriorating wages and working conditions. Gorz's outlook also suggested that it was mistaken for temporary workers to organize themselves at work to demand stable employment and solidarity with more securely employed workers was ruled out of the question. Indeed, the liberation of the insecurely employed workers outside of work was based on the apparently acceptable exploitation of the securely employed workers. This thinking was based upon the apparent impossibility of developing collective projects based on working class solidarity due to the state

---

21   Dauvé, G. (undated) 'To work or not to work? Is that the question?', available at <*http://www.libcom.org/library/to-work-or-not-to-work-dauve*> accessed on 28/07/2006.

of 'generalized insecurity' (p. 52) which was the basis of new individual projects advanced by individualized actors.

It is vital to distinguish here between generalized insecurity as an objective state and as a subjective sense. The deployment of flexibility/insecurity as a capitalist strategy has had limited success as most workers still face relative employment stability and new employment relations have a contradictory effect on workers and offer new opportunities for resistance. The generalized sense of insecurity therefore described not a fundamental objective shift in employment relations, but rather a contingent crisis of working class consciousness, organization, and leadership.[22] From this perspective, it is not the working class that has disappeared, but the labour movement.[23] This means in the sense of its organizational existence as a collective expression of an oppositional consciousness that links everyday collective resistance to an anti-capitalist project. Gorz accepted, and indeed celebrated, the atomization, demoralization, and retreatism produced by defeat as the basis of a new project. Like those unemployed who based their new lifestyles on welfare payments, he turned what appeared as a necessity into a virtue.[24] However, this outlook reinforced the crisis of class politics rather than resolving it. It posited a false unity around an ideological rejection of work rather than developing a practical unity around resistance to exploitation which served to sever anti-capitalist politics from its material foundations and to recuperate it within the bounds of wage-labour.

Gorz's analysis placed him towards the radical end of the 'new reformism' in that he spoke the language of anti-capitalism and rejected the variants of the 'Third Way' which sought to restore competitiveness by mobilizing labour as human capital. However, a fourth criticism of Gorz is that his project was a utopian one which was based on the illusion that the ethical basis of the new social movement could deliver humanity from the dictates of the technocrats to produce a caring capitalism. In relation to the European Marches, it seemed to suggest that the rights of the 'excluded' to work, income and access to social provision could be realized through the development of the 'socially useful third sector' (p. 100). This would involve the creation of jobs in areas such as environmental, cultural or social provision that have not been covered by the market or the state. Such work would be organized by self-managed associations that would provide services made democratically accountable to users.[25]

This scenario appears as if it expresses a sphere of activities liberated from the exploitative and oppressive relations of market and state. However, the market, the state and civil society do not exist as independent spheres with different logics

---

22   See Harman, C. (2002) 'The Workers of the World', *International Socialism* 96 pp. 3–45; Mandel, E. (1986) 'Marx, The Present Crisis and the Future of Labour', in R. Miliband et al *op cit.*

23   Dauvé, G. & Nesic, K. (2002) 'Whither the World'?, *troploin newsletter* No. 2 February.

24   For an outline of the concept of 'dole autonomy' see Aufheben (undated) *Dole Autonomy Versus the Re-Imposition of Work: Analysis of the current tendency to workfare in the UK* self-published document.

25   Lipietz, A. (1992) *Towards a New Economic Order: Postfordism, Ecology and Democracy* (Cambridge: Polity) pp. 99–106.

of operation. They are actually institutional forms of the social relation of capital and therefore exist as separate but unified. The logic of capital is not restricted to the market, but governs all of society. Therefore, the Third Sector would appear to offer the promise of liberating the worker from the exploitative wage relation and oppressive work discipline through its range of self-managed and fulfilling activities. However, the reality would not challenge the impersonal subordination to wage-labour, let alone the exploitative content of work. The outcome of demanding the construction of an autonomous civil society would be to institutionalize social aspirations within a sphere that is marginal to the centres of capitalist power.

A fifth and final criticism of Gorz's analysis is that he privileged the transnational level of resistance. This was linked to the idea that a transnational body such as the EU could itself be reformed and thereby reclaimed as the institutional vehicle for a new transnational social settlement. This thinking is addressed in relation to the work of Castells and Habermas.

Castells

In the second edition of the 'Power of Identity',[26] Castells added the 'anti-globalization movement' (AGM) (p. 145) to his examples of the social movements that have emerged to contest the new global order. He did not focus explicitly on the European dimension to this movement, but he did mention how resistance to capitalist restructuring, especially amongst the labour and farmer's movements, has produced a movement to contest 'one-sided globalization … identified with the policies of the European Union' (p. 166). He therefore included the mobilization in Nice and later ones at EU summits in Gothenburg, Barcelona, and Seville as significant events in the development of the AGM/GJM.

For Castells, this movement has identified its adversary as 'global corporate capitalism and the undemocratic institutions of global governance' (p. 161). In other words, the movement has opposed 'the agents and institutions of a new global, capitalist order' (p. 161). It has also identified, according to Castells, its alternative political project which has been based around 'global democracy' (p. 163).

Castells characterized the AGM as a 'global networked social movement' (p. 147) and, in this sense, it has been brought into being by the emergence of the new era of a globally networked capitalist society. It has existed, therefore, as the mirror image of what it has opposed and to be successful has had to adopt the global character and networking logic of the new informational and capitalist society. For Castells, the AGM has been effective precisely because of its form as a 'network of networks' (p. 154) composed of the diversity of forces engaged in resisting capitalist globalization and because of its use of the internet as a tool of democratic communication between this multiplicity of actors.

Castells recognized the diverse and often contradictory values and goals existing within the AGM, but highlighted this disunity as a source of its strength. In the absence of any centralized structure of authority, those 'nodes' that hindered the

---

26   Castells, M. (2004) *The Power of Identity* (Second Edition) (Oxford: Blackwell).

development of the movement could be 'switched off' thereby enabling its 'relentless expansion' (p. 156). Indeed, no element could become hegemonic as it could only exist as a collective actor in this form of a networked movement. However, Castells did identify significant differences between those demanding the 'possible' goal of 'institutional reform' and those seeking 'another' goal which 'challenges capitalism outright' (p. 153). Nevertheless, these elements were bonded by a shared critique of the lack of democracy and by the common project of a democratic system of governance.

Castells made a distinction, but also an interconnection, between the young, middle class and mobile participants at the protests centred on the summit meetings and the social basis of the AGM in the 'plurality of social struggles' (p. 151) rooted in its diverse localities. Moreover, while the movement had developed very unevenly across the globe, it was a truly global movement that was 'challenging globalization on behalf of the whole of humankind' (p. 160). Therefore, the whole movement was greater than the sum of its constituent parts and its added value lay in its capacity to embrace its differences to project its message of an alternative set of democratic values commensurate with the establishment of a future cosmopolitan democracy.

From this perspective, the transnational mobilizations possessed a strongly symbolic quality and function due, according to Castells, to the centrality of the control of information as a source of domination. This struggle over peoples' minds translated into the mobilization of media friendly events which encapsulated the 'image of goodness' of the 'alternative project' of the movement (p. 158). The resulting changing public mood was regarded as a sufficient pressure on global governance institutions to result in an eventual change in their foundational social values and their democratic functioning. However, thus far, all that could be detected was a change in policy discourse not substantive policy and willingness by institutions to engage in dialogue with the 'respectable' (p. 159) wing of the movement.

Castells argued that the global character of the AGM marked a 'qualitative transformation' of resistance in that each of its specific elements existed for the first time 'globally together in real time' (p. 147). This suggested its emergence as a credible agency of democratization operating above and beyond the nation state which has been bypassed by the power of global flows. In the European context, I would argue that this analysis suggested an identification of the European character of the protests as evidence of the formation of a European social movement which could democratize the transnational institutions of the EU as a locus from which to civilize the new global capitalism. Such an analysis, however, would misrepresent the institutional power of the EU and therefore would tend to underplay the national dimension of the mobilizations which is still of absolutely fundamental importance.

There has not been a fundamental contradiction between the national and the transnational in either the operation of the EU or in the movement that has emerged to oppose it. The development of the EU has not meant the replacement of the nation state, but the extension and consolidation of its neoliberal form. Globalization does not mean replacing the rule of the state by the rule of markets. It rather means extending the existence of rule through the liberal form of the state exercised through the impersonal mechanisms of money and law. This restatement of the liberal state has been occurring across nation states in Europe, but is also a process in which the EU, operating as an inter-governmental body, has played an important role. From this perspective, the added value of the EU to nation states has been to act as an accelerating factor on their processes of internal restructuring to introduce policies such as EMU which has acted as a 'supranational anchor' (p. 134) against the adoption of expansionary policies in order to accommodate the demands of their populations.[27]

The corollary of this argument is that a focus on the transnational character of the mobilizations at the expense of their national foundations would be to gain access to the EU as the level at which change must be institutionalized. Without also waging a struggle in and against its constituent nation states, to target the EU would be to have influence over a hollow institutional shell. This analysis suggests that the task is neither to defend the apparently democratic nation state against an undemocratic EU, nor to democratize the EU. It is rather an argument for linking across borders the episodes of resistance to neoliberal restructuring occurring within nation states so as to compound them into an effective opposition to the constitutional power of the EU. In this sense, the added value of the European Marches lay in its capacity for developing learning across borders and in the extra legitimacy it conveyed to each nationally based movement by its international form and internationalist character.

Castells' analysis was also limited due to its celebration of the AGM as an 'informational movement' which through its 'theatrical tactics' (p. 156) gained media attention and thereby enabled it to influence the 'public mind' (p. 157) and pressure institutions to change policy course. This analysis led to an overstatement of the effectiveness of media focused protests which, although symbolically strong, were not successful in achieving even mild policy reforms. While Castells was correct in identifying the importance of an ideological dimension to struggle, he was incorrect to privilege this dimension as this would tend towards the substitution of media friendly action for mass mobilization. The public was conceived of as a passive force whose mind was to be changed through the spectacular actions of an active group of militants rather than through its own activities.

His analysis also tended to obscure the requirement to mobilize in particular the social force with the material power necessary to deliver social change: organized labour. The AGM (and the European Marches) were successful in making the social consequences of economic and state restructuring actually visible and in expanding the public debate beyond the modernization discourse to encompass alternatives which were also expressed symbolically in the forms of action developed. However, while neoliberalism was exposed as an ideological form commensurate with capitalist restructuring and new space was opened up for the development of alternative ideas, the AGM (and the European Marches) lacked the material power to impose their will on powerful institutions. Therefore, the international mobilizations expressed simultaneously both symbolic strength and material weakness. The symbolic strength was as a 'representational formation' (p. 31) which demonstrated a potential

---

27   For a more detailed analysis of this role played by the EU in the process of capitalist restructuring, see Bonefeld, W. (2002) 'European integration, the market, the political and class', *Capital & Class*, 77 pp. 117–142.

capacity for mass mobilization and disruption.[28] In this sense, they were a 'metaphor for collective strength', but also served to 'dramatise the power they still lack' (p. 755).[29] In particular, the European Marches challenged the dominant representation of labour as a social partner of capital and suggested an alternative representation as an inclusive and autonomous social movement with the capacity for disrupting the reproduction of capital. However, while the roots of the international mobilizations were in locally based resistance, as Castells suggested, in Europe this has been at a limited scale and has displayed a relatively undeveloped capacity to achieve the disruption of material production and distribution. Therefore, in order to become capable of delivering a 'social Europe', the emerging movement would have to go beyond Castells' idea of symbolic politics aimed at mobilizing informational power, and develop an expanded basis in the material power of organized labour.

Castells also overstated the use of the internet as a means of democratic participation. While anyone (with a computer and skills) could participate in debates, this missed the central role played by organizations and critical networks existing within them. The AGM (and European Marches) did not amount to new forms of democratic informational politics beyond the 'old' civil society organizations. They expressed rather the crisis and fracture of these organizations and the development of more grass roots participation that contrasted not only with their bureaucratic form, but also with that of the relatively newly established NGOs. In addition, Castells presented 'networking' through the internet as a 'new political culture' (p. 156) which expressed the new democratic logic of social movements in the information age. This logic allowed the AGM to avoid 'antagonistic meetings' and 'sharp confrontations' (p. 155) and suggested decision-making by consensus. This glossed over the real disputes that have occurred in the AGM (and European Marches) and obscured the operation of power within social movements generally by an overstatement of the democratic character of networking.

Castells misrepresented the networked form of all social movements as something new. Social movements are accurately depicted as SPINs (segmented, polycephalous, integrated networks).[30] They are also fields of contention in which the various component individuals and organizations collaborate while competing for influence and it is through this internal process (as well as in relation to opponents) that they develop, and a hegemonic political perspective may be adopted. Castells' analysis appeared to preclude such a development by limiting internal debate and celebrating disunity. He thereby condemned the AGM to continue to exist as a social movement with various contradictory alternative projects. In the initial phase of development such a situation may lead to expansion, but when no coherent alternative is adopted it is likely to lead to defeat and division.

---

28   Fantasia, R. & Voss, K. (2004) *Hard Work: Remaking the American Labor Movement* Berkeley, Los Angeles & London: University of California Press.

29   Berger, J. (1968) 'The Nature of Mass Demonstrations', *New Society* 23 May pp. 754–755.

30   Gerlach, L.P. & Hine, V.H. (1970) *People, Power, Change. Movements of Social Transformation* (Indianapolis and New York: The Bobbs-Merrill Company).

The various claims for hegemony in the AGM (and European Marches) cannot be ignored. Indeed, Castells outlook was also a political claim for unity around the lowest common denominator of 'democracy' the content of which was 'new forms of social control over new forms of capitalism' (p. 167). Although Castells did not formulate his own proposals for a 'social Europe', his perspective placed him firmly in the camp of the 'new reformism'. Moreover, while this perspective remained in the ascendancy in the AGM (and European Marches), the more revolutionary perspective could be switched off and its proponents condemned as violent or ultra-radical and left isolated in the face of state repression. Here we can see the effect of Castells' fixation on the democratic character of networking in that it failed to demonstrate the workings of power in the AGM (and European Marches) and thereby conferred a false hegemony on those ideas with which Castells was himself sympathetic.

Habermas

In the 'Postnational Constellation',[31] Habermas argued that globalization has placed the existence of welfare states in fundamental question. While the proponents of neoliberalism took advantage of this new situation to advance a project of welfare state dismantling, Habermas sought for possibilities for the development of a new social democratic project expressed through institutions existing beyond the nation state. In particular, he alighted on the EU as the most promising site for the development of a 'postnational democracy' (p. 89) and to this end he became a strong advocate for the adoption of a European Constitution.[32]

Habermas identified several ways in which globalization has disempowered the nation state including its inability to raise sufficient tax revenues and generate the economic growth required to enable redistributive policies. Therefore, the nation state's decreased capacity to deliver basic social rights and social justice resulting in growing unemployment and social polarization has increasingly brought its democratic legitimacy into question. This tendency has been reinforced by the way that globalization has resulted in the fragmentation of the collective identities on which nation states have been based.[33]

Faced with this situation, Habermas rejected outright both the neoliberal embrace, and the protectionist rejection, of globalization. He was also highly critical of the 'defensive' version of the 'Third Way' which he seemed to regard as an unnecessary conditional surrender to globalization. Habermas was not willing to sacrifice the social democratic goals of equality and social protection to global market supremacy. He rather argued for an 'offensive variant of the Third Way' (p. 54) which re-established these goals through reasserting the primacy of democratic politics, but institutionalized at a higher transnational level.[34] For Habermas, this meant further

31   Habermas, J. (2001b) *The Postnational Constellation* (Cambridge: Polity).
32   Habermas (2001a) *op cit.*
33   Habermas (2001b) *op cit.*
34   Habermas, J. (1999) 'The European Nation-State and the Pressures of Globalization' *New Left Review* 235 pp. 46–59.

and deeper European integration to produce a democratically legitimate federation of European states with the capacity to apply the market-correcting policies and the redistributive measures necessary to achieve a 'social Europe' (p. 112).[35]

Habermas stated that this new European social democratic project accepted the 'end of the labor-based society' (p. 89) thesis and its underpinnings of a knowledge and information based society.[36] As a consequence, the target of full employment would be replaced by a radical redistribution of employment and a guaranteed minimum income: measures requiring supranational coordination. The development of the EU must be redirected towards 'positive integration' (p. 97) resulting in the harmonization of social, labour and tax policies thereby countering inter-state competition.[37] This would be an expression of the development of a transnational actor with the competency to govern and thereby tame the market.

However, for Habermas, the development of this new institutional capacity to redistribute wealth and income would also require the legitimacy conferred on it by the formation of democracy at the European level. This, Habermas asserted, could be developed by the formulation of the European Constitution which would have a 'catalytic effect' (p. 16) and provoke and promote the European public sphere and civil society that would legitimize it.[38] The European Constitution would also shift the focus of politics away from the various capitals of member states towards Brussels. This would trigger the development of social movement mobilization at the European level leading ultimately to 'a properly European party system' (p. 17).[39] This was a clear demonstration of how, for Habermas, the project for a 'social Europe' was inextricably linked to that for a 'democratic Europe' whose ultimate achievement could only mean the unification of European nation states.

Although Habermas also propounded the fallacy of the end of work as support for his proposals, he did mount a much more robust defence of the 'old' goals of social democracy than most of the other proponents of the 'new reformism'. However, his argument that the EU could be recaptured from its neoliberal hijackers and made once again a vehicle for the advancement of the social democratic project did not mark a significant departure from the elite driven character of European integration which has characterized this process from its inception. Habermas recognized that in order to deliver redistributive policies, the EU would have to mobilize sufficient political resources to impose the general democratic will on unwilling market participants. To this end, he spoke of stirring mass support for a new Europe by the development of a new design for it. However, the proposals for a European Constitution did not spark the desired response in the public imagination and rather gave rise to renewed opposition to integration especially when its link to further marketization was made apparent.

The elite driven project of European integration has not produced democratic institutions or anything but the mildest social measures and therefore has failed

35   Habermas (2001b) *op cit.*
36   *Ibid.*
37   *Ibid.*
38   Habermas (2001a) *op cit.*
39   *Ibid.*

spectacularly in gaining popular legitimacy. This has been the case even when it has been supported by prominent figures on the political and intellectual left such as Habermas. The public (working class) in Europe has proven unwilling to place trust in political elites to deliver a social and democratic Europe and have therefore remained opposed to deeper European integration. In this context, although Habermas did mount a more robust defence of traditional social democratic policies than some of his counterparts, his analysis lacked a credible agency to advance them. This limitation of his thinking was addressed by Bourdieu who argued for a similar project, but backed by the renewed power of the labour movement.

Bourdieu

In 'Acts of Resistance',[40] Bourdieu rejected the idea that globalization was an inevitable process that necessitated the restructuring of the welfare state. In fact, it was a myth that served to obscure and justify the neoliberal project of rolling back the gains of previous social struggles. This project was fast becoming a 'reality of unlimited exploitation' (pp. 94–105) through the adoption of a political programme which promoted private interest and thereby undermined institutions such as trade unions that embodied collective solidarity and in particular attacked the role of the state as the guardian of the public interest.

Bourdieu argued that the state has been kidnapped by the technocratic elite that was located in the 'right hand' (p. 2) of the state and withdrew political and financial support for the social provision organized by the 'left hand' (p. 2) of the state. Moreover, the neoliberal project has developed economic policies which have actually promoted capital mobility and which have amounted to 'insecurity-inducing strategies' (p. 84). Job insecurity, which has affected most workers, and the scarcity of employment have increased the competition for jobs and have placed 'employees at the mercy of employers' (p. 84). Bourdieu's response to neoliberalism was to call for a 'new internationalism' (pp. 60–9) which required the international mobilization of the people and the formation of a transnational 'European social state' (p. 67) which would institutionalize international solidarity in a new harmonized social regime.

These themes were developed in 'Firing Back'[41] in which Bourdieu reaffirmed his view that globalization was not the product of inevitable economic processes, but of a political will to separate the economic field from political control. Therefore, far from being the unwilling victims of economic globalization, nation states (often governed by social democratic governments) have played a central role 'in the service of the politics that weakens them' (p. 49). The task, therefore, was not only to reclaim democratic control over the economy, but also to reestablish democracy within social democratic organizations.

To this end, Bourdieu argued for a 'renewed trade unionism' (pp. 44–6) which challenged the sectionalism of union organizations and the control of officials by

---

40   Bourdieu (1998) *op cit.*
41   Bourdieu (2003) *op cit.*

the rotation of positions and by uniting union and associations into a general social movement. Moreover, unions needed to mobilize new constituencies of women, migrants and insecure workers and advance a broader social agenda. They also needed to break with the ideology and practice of 'conciliation' and overcome nationalist thinking to develop 'internationalist dispositions' and an 'internationalist spirit' (pp. 58–60).

This renewed trade unionism could become the 'engine of a social Europe' (p. 57) working alongside the other social movements already mobilizing throughout Europe to form a European social movement. This would act as a 'credible counter-power' (p. 52) to the neoliberal EU and democratize it by replacing the European Commission with an executive accountable to the European Parliament. This movement could also advance a project for a real 'social Europe' which was a 'rational utopia' (p. 62) consisting of international taxation on capital movements, major public sector programmes in the social fields and the harmonization of wages, working hours, training and social provision.

While Bourdieu, like Habermas, proposed a more offensive strategy and a more progressive project in the face of neoliberal globalization, this was also based on an economic and social analysis which did not differ markedly from the other writers from the 'new reformism'. He did suggest that the rise in precariousness was the planned outcome of neoliberal policy as opposed to the inevitable outcome of economic and social change. However, there was some blurring in his work between insecurity as a subjective sense produced by labour market deregulation and as a generalized objective state arising from a economic and political regime which amounted to a new 'mode of production' and 'mode of domination' (p. 29). The latter analysis placed him closer to the proponents of the 'new reformism' and this was compounded by his description of a 'new' economy producing 'weightless objects such as information and cultural products' (p. 33). This was accompanied by a further similarity in that he depicted a workforce divided into a 'sub-proletariat' and a 'privileged minority of secure workers' (p. 31).

A further similarity with the 'new reformism' was found in Bourdieu's assertion that the fact that symbolic power played a central role in the new 'complex and refined mode of domination' (p. 36) meant that contemporary social movements were heavily reliant on media focused forms of action. Therefore, for Bourdieu, the political impact of protest now lay more in its visibility to the media than in the numbers of people it mobilized. Moreover, contemporary social movements have also been animated by a new set of leaders who have been skilled in the new art of politics which has required protest to be dramatic and to symbolize the goals in exemplary actions.

Another drawback of Bourdieu's work was that achieving a new social settlement at the transnational level and thereby civilizing the 'new' capitalism has not been a straightforward matter of mobilizing a transnational social movement to democratize transnational institutions. Despite its more grass roots focus, Bourdieu's project shared some similarities with that of Habermas, not least a confidence in the state as an expression of the democratic will of the people. He demanded the release of the state from the technocrats into the democratic hands of the people; reconstituted at the supranational level.

From this perspective it appeared as if social aspirations could be realized by making the state respond to the democratic will of the people; albeit reformed at the level of the EU rather than the nation state. However, this perspective severely underestimated the limits on state action. The state is limited in the extent to which it can respond to democratic demands for citizenship rights by its capitalist form. Indeed, the limitations of the forms in which citizenship rights are granted become the objects of future struggle.[42] Therefore, the social state does not 'safeguard the interests of the dominated' (pp. 34–5) as Bourdieu suggested,[43] it rather reproduces forms of domination. It was these forms of domination that produced demands in the European Marches for unconditional rights and for their democratic administration and fuelled the idea that these should enable the development of liberated spheres of activity. This is apparent in the work of Gorz which I set out above. While Bourdieu's analysis focused attention on the substantive content of the welfare state which did amount to a substantial gain for the working class, Gorz's analysis focused attention on attempts to escape the bureaucratic forms through which welfare was administered. What was remarkable about the demands of the European Marches was that they amounted to a defence of the progressive content of the KWS, while posing a challenge to its undemocratic forms. This suggested a reconnection between the struggle over immediate material interests and for social and political change which had been severed in the bureaucratized social democratic forms of trade unionism. Like Bourdieu, Gorz also argued for a renewed trade unionism mobilizing around a new agenda,[44] but this argument too was compatible with the overall analysis of the 'new reformism'.

A 'New' Trade Unionism

Waterman

Most of the writers from the 'New social democratic Left' appeared to confirm their earlier analysis that rendered the organized working class at worst a reactionary actor and at best a marginal force for social change. However, their analysis has also been utilized in support of an argument for the renewal of labour as a social movement. Waterman stated that his argument for a renewed labour movement as an element of the 'new' global solidarity was based on a synthesis of the work of Beck, Giddens, and Melucci and was reinforced by the then recently published work by Castells.[45] He argued therefore that there has been a radical break from the 'old' modernity of nationally based industrial capitalism to a new 'high or radical modernity ... of a complex, high-risk globalized information capitalism' (p. 203).

---

42   Clarke (1991) *op cit.*

43   Bourdieu (2003) *op cit.*

44   Gorz, A. (1999) 'A New Task for the Unions: The Liberation of Time from Work', in R. Munck & P. Waterman (eds) *Labour Worldwide in the Era of Globalization* (Basingstoke: Macmillan).

45   Waterman, P. (1998) *Globalization, Social Movements, & The New Internationalisms* (London and Washington: Mansell).

For Waterman, informational capitalism has been somehow less 'economically determined' (p. 76) than industrial capitalism and has promoted a politics based less on necessity and more on ethical choice. The terrain on which informational politics has been waged has been more inherently democratic and thereby more favourable to the 'alternative social movements' (ASMs) (p. 117) that have produced and communicated new ideas and values and have operated according to a networking logic. In addition, Waterman accepted the centrality of knowledge to the new economy and argued that the application of information technology to the labour process has resulted in a reduced demand for labour and to the polarization of the workforce. The resulting strategy for labour therefore must be to seek new forms of self-management at work and to promote the liberation from work along the lines proposed by Gorz. Moreover, Waterman's understanding of the ASMs was based very much on Giddens' model of a radical engagement with risk in a multidimensional high modernity. In this model, there has been no 'prioritized contradiction' (p. 205) and therefore labour has become just one of a multiplicity of ASMs.

For labour this new predicament has required a transformation from its 'old' institutional forms, which were characterized as 'the steam trains of the age of national, industrial and imperial capitalism' (p.139), to produce a 'new' networked movement through which alternative ethical values could be communicated and thereby a new global solidarity formed.[46] The 'old', and apparently frightening, internationalist 'rhetorical slogan' of 'workers of the world unite' has been rendered no longer appropriate in the contemporary complex global order and has had to be replaced by a 'new' and apparently inspiring 'revolutionary slogan' of 'think globally, act locally; think locally, act globally … think dialectically: act self-reflexively' (p. 240). The new complex global solidarity has been formed through dialogue with other ASMs in 'global civil society' to form alliances around 'post-modern … global alternatives' (p. 210). Waterman suggested global civil society could be the new 'privileged space for the civilising and surpassing' (p. 227) of global capitalism This has been achievable through a dual process of developing alternative autonomous projects in civil society and by engaging with the state and capital to institutionalize them.

Waterman's analysis was based on a theoretical eclecticism which was problematic in the sense that the ideas of the writers utilizing a 'post industrial' argument were not straightforwardly compatible with those arguing on the basis of the 'crisis and reformation of modernity'. This problem was compounded by his argument that the 'new' order somehow overlaid the 'old' which was only comprehensible in the sense that capitalist society has been in a transitional phase. This theoretical confusion was also present in his analysis of the multidimensionality of modernity and globalization and its implications for social movements. He argued against the idea of a central contradiction which gave rise to labour as the primary social movement. However, he asserted that capital and state have 'priority' (p. 205), but that this did not have

---

46   Waterman did acknowledge that it was strategically necessary to work both inside and outside of the old international union institutions. However, there is a clear indication in his work that the 'new' networked forms are superior due to the 'new' character of global, informational capitalism.

repercussions for the strategic centrality of the related movements. This was argued while asserting his belief in the centrality of wage labour to a world he continued to characterize as capitalist.

Waterman seemed to accept the separation of the economy from politics and other spheres of social life as a given which are over-determined by the cultural which is itself a result of the new informational mode of production. The repercussion of this analysis was to reduce exploitation to a labour issue and to make connections between labour and other social movements at the level of discourse. However, while such separations are real, they are the products and objects of struggle. Capital is not reducible to an economic relation, but is a total social relation. Production is the central element of capitalism and therefore the class relations which arise from it are of central importance. However, labour is not therefore inevitably a narrowly economistic movement, but rather there is a struggle to overcome this reduction and make practical connections to form a broader social movement which focuses on all the manifestations of capitalist exploitation and the related oppressive social relations.

Waterman admitted that his analysis was based on the weakness of the labour movement. In line with the thinking of the 'new reformism', he elevated this weakness into an epochal state due to changed structural conditions. These conditions produced new forms of social movement with which labour was compelled to make alliances. However, this analysis overstated the weakness of labour and compounded it. As I argued in chapter 2, labour weakness has been conjunctural and has also been the product of strategic failures such as the refusal to make common cause with the NSMs. This is not to argue that nothing has changed, but rather to base strategies for labour renewal on firmer theoretical footing which does not render labour inevitably weakened due to socio-structural changes.[47]

A 'New' Social Democratic Politics

This idea of socio-structural change has also been a central element of the arguments of influential writers on the crisis of 'old' style social democracy and its transformation into a 'new' social democratic politics. Although he maintained the importance of factors internal to social democracy for its successful transformation, Kitschelt[48] argued that 'traditional social democratic policies *ought no longer* be pursued, because they *cannot* be successfully implemented in the socioeconomic and cultural environment of advanced capitalism' (p. 7). He therefore shared the perspective that changes in the external environment have been influencing the transformation of European social democracy.

These changes have almost compelled social democratic parties to break the link with unions and to move away from its electoral base in the 'shrinking traditional industrial working class' (p. 301) towards a new constituency of technicians and

---

47   Such a strategy for the renewal of labour as a social movement has been set out in Moody, K. (1997) *Workers in a Lean World* (London & New York: Verso).

48   Kitschelt, H. (1994) *The Transformation of European Social Democracy* (Cambridge: Cambridge University Press).

engineers, white-collar workers and middle managers and welfare professionals. This constituency has been attracted to the new libertarian politics associated with the NSMs and its demands for the extension of citizenship rights and therefore these issues, rather than the question of redistribution, have formed the 'new' political terrain for the transformed social democracy.

Moschonas has shown how social democracy has been undergoing a 'recasting' (p. 6) in Europe.[49] From this perspective, the new social democracy has accelerated and reinforced the marginalization of the working class from politics. However, this has been a longer-term process which was the outcome of the way that the working class has been 'undermined, circumvented, outflanked, and finally weakened in its potential for collective mobilization by a profound sociological transformation in the structure of the wage-earning class and working conditions' (p. 323). This analysis led Moschonas to rather pessimistic conclusions about the future of social democracy, although he did highlight its current vulnerability in relation to its inability to respond to the social question which has remained the central question by which social democracy is measured. Its acceptance of mass unemployment and the minimalist character of its answer to the social question have led to significant deterioration in the 'bond of representation' between the new social democracy and the disadvantaged 'popular strata' who have been facing 'social insecurity' (p. 322).

It has been the 'new' social question, and the related matter of the represented basis of social democracy, that some of the authors of the 'new reformism' seem to have been addressing. They have tended to do so in a way which has inverted the argument that the changing economic and social conditions of the post-war period and generalized affluence gave rise to the instrumentality of the 'new' working class alongside the expressive concerns of the' new' middle classes. The 'new reformism' has appeared to highlight fundamental economic and social change and generalized insecurity as the conditions in which a new set of individualistic, but progressive values have been formed and around which a new consensus could be produced. According to this perspective, these values, therefore, could provide the new foundations for a new social contract.

However, as Goldthorpe et al[50] commented, the notion that a political strategy for labour of winning the middle ground was 'made *necessary* by the changing nature of economic and social conditions' was 'inspired by ideology more than by sociology' (pp. 190-1). Similarly in the current conjuncture, the argument that apparently 'new' socio-structural conditions have impelled an abandonment of class politics and an embrace of new values, new projects, and new electoral alliances remains one that has little or no valid sociological basis. It is an argument that has justified the politics of the 'new reformism' which has argued for the displacement of the working class as the central focus of progressive politics as well as the abandonment of the defence of the KWS. Moreover, even those writers who have been critical of the extent of

49   Moschonas, G. (2002) *In the Name of Social Democracy. The Great Transformation:1945 to the Present.* (London: Verso).

50   Goldthorpe, J.H., Lockwood, D., Bechhofer, F. & Platt, J. (1969) *The Affluent Worker in the Class Structure* (Cambridge: Cambridge University Press).

the retreat of social democracy, and especially of the 'Third Way', also seem to have accepted the sociological ideas on which this retreat has been based.

Although social democracy has been in retreat in the face of neoliberalism,[51] it has remained the primary intellectual current on the Left and its primary political practice. Therefore, as Panitch's[52] argument suggested, it has remained vital not only to demonstrate the limits that contemporary social democratic thinking and practice has placed on progressive politics (which I have attempted to do in this chapter so far), but also to identify the possibilities that its retreat has opened up for the development of more radical political alternatives. In relation to the European Marches and the broader social movement, two main strands can be identified: 'autonomist anti-capitalism' (pp. 80–3) and 'socialist anti-capitalism' (pp. 83–5).[53] The first of these radical alternatives has been typified by the writing of Tony Negri.

Negri

In 'Empire',[54] Negri (and Hardt) argued that the 'irresistible and 'irreversible' (p. xi) forces of economic and cultural globalization have fatally undermined the sovereignty of the nation state. However, a new decentred and deterritoralized networked form of political rule (Empire) has arisen to provide a new global order for capital accumulation. This has now become an informational accumulation due to the postmodernization of the economy which has given rise to new immaterial forms of labour. 'Empire', understood as a structure of imperial command, has given rise to resistance and in particular in the form of the 'multitude' (pp. 60–6) which through self-organization could form itself into a counter-power or 'posse' (pp. 407–11) which would be capable of self-government on a global scale.

The 'postmodernization' or 'informatization' of production (pp. 280–303) has been absolutely fundamental to the emergence of the new epoch over which 'Empire' rules. Informatization has amounted to a third economic revolution which has not only resulted in a fundamental quantitative shift of employment towards the service sector, but has also produced a qualitative transformation of all sectors of production. Therefore, this process has resulted in the replacement of Fordism by Toyotism which is a flexible system of production which is more responsive to markets as a result of the rapid communication of market data.

Informatization has not simply been a matter of the introduction of new technology into production, but has also entailed a transformation in the character and quality of labour which has driven it. Negri referred to this as 'immaterial labour' defined as 'labour that produces an immaterial good, such as a service, a cultural product, knowledge, or communication' (p. 290). Immaterial labour has developed two faces. The first has involved interaction with new technology and has entailed the creation

---

51   I have taken the idea that social democracy has been in retreat in the face of the advance of neoliberalism from Aufheben (1998) 'Retreat of social democracy' available at <*http://www.geocities.com/aufheben2/auf_7_socdem.html*> accessed on 23/01/2000.

52   Panitch (1986) *op cit.*

53   Callinicos, A. (2003) *An Anti-Capitalist Manifesto* (Cambridge: Polity).

54   Hardt, M. & Negri, A. (2000) *Empire* (London: Harvard University Press).

and manipulation of information and symbols to produce knowledge. The second has involved human interaction and has entailed the creation and manipulation of affect to produce feelings such as 'ease, well-being, satisfaction, excitement, or passion' (p. 293).

Immaterial labour is fundamentally new and different in that the co-operative element has not been imposed upon labour by capital, but has been 'completely immanent' (p. 294) to it and therefore this form of labour has developed the capacity to self-valorize. In other words, the nature of immaterial labour provides the workers with an intrinsic autonomy from capital and thereby provides the basis for 'a kind of spontaneous and elementary communism' (p. 294).

For Negri, globalization has amounted to a rupture with previous forms of capitalist production and state power. The new globally networked production systems and transnational corporations have undermined the power of the nation state which has also been overwhelmed by the global flows of money, technology, people, and goods. However, the regulatory functions of the state and its constitutional powers have been transferred to a higher supranational level. Power in the new global epoch is structured as a pyramid with three tiers. These layers of power have become mechanisms of 'imperial command' over world politics exercised through 'the bomb' (p. 345), over the world market exercised through 'money' (p. 346), and over world culture exercised through the 'ether' of networks of communication (p. 347). Empire is inherently unstable and uncontrollable. The political task has become not to take over and wield these mechanisms of power, but rather to destroy them as instruments of domination.

Negri rejected the 'Leftist' strategies of localism and nationalism in favour of developing the alternative to 'Empire' at the same global level at which it has been constituted. For Negri, the opposition to 'Empire' was developing through the various economic and social struggles that, although apparently 'incommunicable', possessed a 'new quality of social movements' (p. 56). These struggles were based locally, but targeted the global centres of power. They also overcame a narrow economic focus to become immediately political struggles whose demands amounted to a new political programme around which a new political subject was forming. This subject was forming out of a new social actor which Negri characterized as the 'multitude' which he defined as 'the set of all the exploited and the subjugated' (p. 393). This figure was also described through the image of the 'poor' (pp. 156–9) which subsumed the new proletariat itself understood broadly as all categories of exploited workers whether directly or indirectly productive. The 'multitude' asserted its power through forms of resistance understood as desertion from exploitation and subjugation and constituted itself more positively through its circulation which expressed its desire for liberation.

The central political task was to overcome the 'segmentations' (p. 399) of the multitude to form a new political programme composed of three main elements. 'Global citizenship' (p. 400) asserted the demand for freedom of movement and residence, the 'social wage and a guaranteed income' (p. 403) validated the productivity of all forms of labour, and the 'right to reappropriation' (p. 403) enabled access to, and control over, the new means of immaterial production: knowledge, information, communication, and affect. This programme was not recuperable as a set of rights within the new constitution of 'Empire', but was immediately revolutionary as through these rights the 'multitude' constituted itself as an independent global citizenry.

Negri's work has been subjected to substantial positive and negative criticism some of which has accused him rather unfairly of hostility towards employed workers and the welfare state.[55] It is striking, however, to note that Negri's work shared the main assumptions of some of the writers from the 'New social democratic Left' thereby producing a radicalized version of the 'new reformism'. Negri shared the assumption that there has been a radical rupture in socio-structural conditions which has produced a new terrain on which social movements mobilize. His work has been accused of integrating many of the most modish bourgeois theories of economic and social change,[56] and in particular it resembled the informational mode of production described by Castells and the post-Fordist production methods outlined by Gorz.[57] While his analysis is therefore subject to the same criticism of technological determinism, more significant are its ramifications for the identification of the social actors capable of animating a social movement actually able to deliver progressive social change.

For Negri, the industrial working class 'has not disappeared or declined in numbers', but due to the new immaterial forms of production it has lost its 'hegemonic position' (p. 256). Not only has the industrial working class been rendered an anachronistic force, but the new dispersed forms of power have also resulted in the replacement of the 'old' central conflict in the factory with a host of micro-conflicts in the wider society. While Negri did identify a new proletariat of all exploited workers and suggested its new strategic core of knowledge or service workers,[58] the new proletariat has become only one of many actors amidst the broader multitude.

The 'multitude' appeared to express a broad social movement against the 'new' capitalism composed of the exploited and oppressed. However, while Negri utilized the language of Marxism, his analysis was akin to post-Marxism which suggests that the nature of this movement was as a popular bloc, not a class-centred alliance. The term 'social labour power' (p. 209)[59] is useful if it refers to the 'second process of production' (p. 51)[60] which reproduces the working class in a form that is compatible with capital valorization. This would suggest a broadening of class struggle to include the other side of working class existence and its components of the social wage such as health, education, transport and welfare.

For Negri, however, the social factory did not mean a second front in the class war, but the displacement of it from the factory to society, from production to reproduction. The latter was represented as a terrain of production, but this was only

---

55   Callinicos, A. (2001) 'Tony Negri in perspective' *International Socialism* 2 (92) pp. 33–61; Thompson, P. (2005) 'Foundation and Empire:A critique of Hardt and Negri', *Capital & Class* 86 pp. 73–98.

56   Aufheben (2006) 'Keep on smiling: Questions on immaterial labour', *Aufheben* 14 pp. 23–44.

57   Thompson (2005) *op cit.*

58   *ibid*

59   Negri (1988) *op cit.*

60   Lebowitz (1992) *op cit.*

achieved by presenting all activity as productive labour which served to obscure real class distinctions and their social basis.[61] As a consequence, capital has disappeared as a social actor and the 'multitude hardly speaks of class or the hidden abode of production' (p. 87).[62] The 'factory' appeared as a realm of immaterial production in which immaterial labour has been developing an immanent autonomy, whereas the reality has been greater control and deskilling which has intensified material exploitation. By bidding farewell to the capitalist class, Negri rendered the 'multitude' little more than an undifferentiated grouping. This placed him alongside the other writers from the 'New social democratic Left' who deny the strategic and political centrality of the working class to anti-capitalist movements. Therefore, Negri did not so much display hostility towards waged workers, but was rather indifferent to the political potential of any workers other than those with high levels of knowledge and highly developed affective and communication skills.

Negri's analysis also tended to present the defeat of previous struggles as victories and this has been related to his tendency not to oppose the trajectory of capitalist development and therefore to discount and side step important strategic questions or even to suggest the wrong strategic course. In this sense, his perspective was akin to the deterministic idea that treated 'capitalist civilisation as if it were a one-way street to revolution ... the more capitalism we have, the nearer we get to communism' (p. 34/38).[63] This was evident in the way that his echo of the 'hyperglobalization' thesis,[64] led him to disregard the nation state as a significant locus of resistance to capital. While I agree with Negri with respect to the undesirable consequences of defending the nation state, it would be misleading to discount this as a possible, and indeed perhaps credible, anti-neoliberal (pro-social democratic) strategy.

Negri's analysis also suggested that post-Fordism was paradigmatic whereas it appears to have been a largely unsuccessful accumulation strategy. Moreover, it has been stated that Negri proposed a vote in favour of the European Constitution.[65] These arguments are only sustainable when these economic and political forms are regarded as new structures which provide a new terrain on which oppositional politics is now waged. However, as my analysis in chapter two made apparent, struggle does not occur merely over the forms as constituted, but rather more profoundly over the constitution of these forms. Negri's analysis was similar to that of the Regulation School, discussed in chapter two, in that it attributed a 'but also' (p. 5) role for class struggle.[66] The outcome of this analysis was to offer short cuts to liberation which would turn out to be cul-de-sacs for anti-capitalist politics. This becomes more apparent when considering his political programme for the 'multitude'.

Negri's argument that there now exists a 'new' era of capitalist production would mean that his call for the 'right to reappropriation' of information would amount to

---

61   Aufheben (2006) *op cit.*

62   Thompson (2005) *op cit.*

63   Dauvé (undated) *op cit.*

64   Callinicos (2001) *op cit.*; Thompson (2005) *op cit.*

65   Aufheben (2006) *op cit.*

66   Bonefeld & Holloway (1991) *op cit.*

nothing more than the 'self-management of the present production' (p. 42).[67] The rights to citizenship and to a citizenship income are also highly problematic if they are considered as the foundational basis of an alternative political constitution to the capitalist state. This analysis would lead to a political strategy which attempts to bypass or side-step the state which is regarded as an external force. Negri presented 'Empire' and 'counter-Empire' as two opposed forces standing in external relation and therefore the increased power of the latter would reduce the power of the former. However, this cannot account satisfactorily for how the capitalist state could grant citizenship rights and thereby bolster its legitimacy. The state only appears as an external force, but actually expresses the contradictory relation of capital in a political form. Therefore, it can respond to demands to fulfil working class needs, but only within the limits of its form and to the extent to which it does not undermine the basis of its own foundations in profitable capital accumulation.[68] This means that the demand for substantive citizenship rights which express general needs actually poses the problem of state power rather than resolves it.

Negri's analysis suggested a strategy of developing the institutions of an alternative society alongside the institutions of capitalist society. In this sense, his was a strategy of radical disengagement. However, the call for substantive rights, as part of a broader programme of demands, could also be regarded as requiring a radical engagement with the state and thereby direct the opposition to neoliberal globalization along the path to the socialist transformation of society.

A Socialist Alternative?

Brie

The argument for a democratic socialist version of a 'social Europe' has been set out clearly by André Brie MEP who, as well as representing the PDS, is also a political scientist. He argued that in the face of the neoliberal challenge to the KWS, the Left has vascillated between its adaptation to the new conditions of globalization and its outright defence. He outlined, therefore, a set of theses which suggested a different path seeking the maintenance of the welfare state and its renewal. His starting point was the recognition that the KWS settlement was, in a sense, an illusion in that it 'only modified the basic asymmetrical distribution of power between capital and labour … not structurally dissolved it' (p. 89).[69]

Consequently, a fundamental shift in power and a resolution of the social consequences of capitalist globalization would require the formation of a social state with a socialist character due to its foundations in the 'democratic socialisation of the means of production' (p. 89). The corollary of this basic idea for the maintenance

---

67   Aufheben (2006) *op cit.*.

68   Clarke, S. (1991) 'State, Class Struggle, and the Reproduction of Capital', in Clarke (ed) *op cit.*.

69   Brie, A. (2004) 'The Future of the Social State in Europe: Eight Theses', in R. Blackburn, A. Brie, K. Coates, C. Beatty & S. Fothergill *The Social Europe We Need* (Nottingham: Spokesman).

and renewal of the welfare state was to look beyond the immediate concern with achieving social justice to consider matters of political economy. In other words, tackling mass unemployment and the other social consequences of neoliberalism would require different economic and financial policies as well as different employment and social policies.

For Brie, the socialist alternative to neoliberal globalization amounted to a 'qualitative Keynesianism' (p. 95) institutionalized at the level of the EU. This translated into investment in cutting edge technology so as to develop ecologically friendly forms of production. This would be accompanied by a social reorientation of production resulting in the expansion of social and cultural services and therefore the creation of socially useful work leading to a new kind of full employment. This would be regulated at the level of the EU which has become a large enough and closed enough economy to function effectively outside of global competition. The EU would develop an institutional capacity to steer the economy through co-ordinating financial and economic policies as well as setting mandatory social goals for member states.

The renewed welfare state would guarantee social rights to citizens through 'universal and unconditional services in the framework of a public all-encompassing insurance' (p. 96) for which contributions and claims would be on the basis of residence not employment status. Gender equality would be a foundational principle achieved through 'egalitarian patterns of gainful employment' (p. 97) alongside the provision of services whose focus would no longer be the married couple, but 'households with children' (p. 98). Although full employment would be a central matter of state policy, the unemployed would be guaranteed an unconditional right to a high level of benefit as well as a free choice of employment and a right to training. Social security would be based on the principle of 'participative justice' (p. 98) and this would be guaranteed at the European level by setting benefit levels at '60% of the national average income of the member state, in which a person chooses to reside' (p. 100).

It was not least this final element which placed Brie's outline of a 'social Europe' in tune with that the demands advanced by the European Marches and its supporting organizations in the wider social movement. Indeed, Brie identified the minority critical tendencies in the unions alongside the associations involved in the ESF as the social forces which could advance this project. These social forces, and the associated political forces, could be regarded as a 'radically alternative hegemonic bloc' (p. 217).[70] This coalition has been advancing its project for a 'social Europe' in competition not only with the dominant project of 'embedded neoliberalism' (p. 216), but also with those of rival emergent hegemonic blocs. Such an analysis is consistent with the ideas expressed earlier in the chapter that the social movement from below has been engaged in a contest with the social movement from above which has been advancing the neoliberal project. Moreover, this movement itself has been a field of contention in which alternative projects have been developing.

---

70   Bieler, A. & Morton, A.D. (eds) (2001) *Social Forces in the Making of the New Europe* (Basingstoke: Palgrave).

Unlike the writers from the 'New social democratic Left', Brie identified an important role for organized labour as an agent of the project for a 'social Europe'. Moreover, he also raised the central question of the political economy of the welfare state largely neglected by most writers from the 'New social democratic Left'. For some, this neglect masked their acceptance of the neoliberal argument for austerity and flexibility as the basis for the renewal of the welfare state. For others, arguing for the development of an autonomous sphere of production, it directed attention away from the crucial matters of social ownership and political power. While raising the crucial question of the political economy of the welfare state, it was by no means clear that Brie provided a clear and satisfactory answer.

His project did amount to a robust defence of the progressive elements of the KWS such as the de-commodification and collectivization of basic human needs while addressing its exclusionary limits with respect to marginalized groups. It also suggested its underpinning in the development of ecologically and socially progressive forms of production. However, it was unclear whether, and how, this project actually posed a fundamental challenge to capitalist forms of ownership and power. Would, and should, a 'social Europe' have a stabilizing effect and thereby amount to a 'new' form of regulation for a 'new' era of capital accumulation? Or would it have a destabilizing effect and thereby produce a deepening politicization of the economic and social crisis unfolding in the current conjuncture? If the latter, then what political strategy should be adopted to address this situation?

The above analysis of Negri suggested that elements of the radical dimension of the GJM (and European Marches) were not quite as revolutionary as they might have seemed. However, another element of the radical wing existed which also focused on, and promoted, the demands for a 'social Europe', but in a rather critical fashion. This socialist perspective supported the idea of mobilizing around demands for reforms. But not in order to usher in a new period of stable accumulation, but rather to pose the question of the legitimacy of capitalist state-like institutions and thereby reset the course of the movement in the direction of revolutionary transformation. This revolutionary socialist perspective has been associated mainly, although by no means exclusively, with the ideology of Trotskyism. Trotskyist organizations were particularly influential in the European Marches, but less so in the broader movement. However, despite its limited influence, this mode of thinking is significant. It has suggested a clear and credible alternative trajectory of political development for the social movement against neoliberal globalization to that offered by the proponents of the reforming 'New social democratic Left' as well as the other radical reformers. It is therefore worthwhile to outline the relevant work of two key theorists writing from this perspective: Ernest Mandel and Alex Callinicos.

Mandel

Twenty years ago, Ernest Mandel[71] argued directly against the ideas of André Gorz and others that economic transformations were rendering the working class

---

71   Mandel (1986) *op cit.*

obsolete as an agent of social transformation. He highlighted the technological determinism inherent in such thinking and asserted that the crisis, (and its symptoms of mass unemployment and social polarization), was not comprehensible in terms of fundamental structural transformations, but as a conjunctural capitalist crisis of overaccumulation. At the heart of this crisis lay a contradiction between massive overproduction and mass unemployment which was being tackled by a capitalist strategy of developing the 'dual society' (p. 445).

This new divide *within* the working class was an attempt to undermine the class solidarity developed through previous struggles which was institutionalized in the welfare state which covered 'the reproduction costs of the proletariat *in its totality*' (p. 444). The successful outcome of this restructuring process would be to reduce the overall costs of reproduction and pave the way for increasing the rate of exploitation and thereby profitability levels. In these terms, the responses of the 'new reformism' actually went with the grain of capitalist restructuring by accepting this division within the working class and can be regarded therefore as a strategy based on an acceptance of the partial victory of capital in the struggle over the future of the welfare state.

In contrast, Mandel argued for an alternative strategy grounded in an objective definition of the working class as a class of wage labourers which was expanding not contracting, both inside and outside of Western Europe. This strategy was also based on a recognition that labour was engaged in a protracted struggle with capital over the resolution of the crisis. Mandel rejected any idea that the labour movement should accept a defence of 'national competitiveness' (p. 439) as the solution to mass unemployment and instead promoted international solidarity around the demand for a 35 hour week without loss of pay and compulsory hiring. This strategy was aimed at recomposing the working class around 'an anti-capitalist programme of action starting from the real existing concerns and needs of the real existing wage labourers, in all their varieties, the necessity to unite this mighty force into a battering ram to shake the fortresses of capital, the necessity to organise for the overthrow of capitalism' (p. 442).

The value of Mandel's work in relation to the writers of the 'New social democratic Left' lies in his analysis of capitalist development which provides a basis for the renewal of class politics. Rather than seek new forms of politics and new projects which seek to civilize a new stable era of capital accumulation, his work suggests that the current crisis is an ongoing one and that it is still far from resolved in favour of capital. Although labour is undoubtedly on the back foot, it is far from routed. However, the dominant strategic identity within European trade unionism has been as a social partner willing to accept welfare state 'modernization' so as to restore the competitiveness of European capital in the world market. Nevertheless, the recent round of resistance has demonstrated a determined defence of previous social gains and has led to mobilization on new fronts and alongside new forces so as to suggest the formation of a new strategic identity for labour at the heart of an anti-capitalist social movement. Mandel's work suggests how this radical potential of the resistance to neoliberal globalization could be realized by making a link between the immediate conditions of life and an alternative society and thereby bringing about social and political change by way of a transitional process involving making demands upon the state.

Callinicos

In 'An Anti-Capitalist Manifesto',[72] Callinicos outlined a set of measures which he argued combined 'immediate remedies' to the consequences of neoliberal policies with a 'different social logic' (p. 132). These demands included those prominent in the European Marches such as the Tobin Tax, the universal basic income, the reduced working week, the defence of public services, and the redistribution of wealth and income. It also included those arising from the broader movement like the abolition of immigration controls and third world debt, the defence of civil liberties, and measures to ensure environmental protection (pp. 132–9).

For Callinicos, these demands arose from contemporary grass roots movements and were to be placed upon both nation states and international state-like institutions as these were vulnerable to the international mobilization of political pressure by citizens. These demands also possessed an anti-capitalist logic and dynamic and were transitional in the sense that they were 'reforms that emerge from the realities of existing struggles but whose implementation in the current context would challenge capitalist economic relations' (p. 140). This challenge to capitalism lay in the implementation of this programme which would inevitably generate resistance by capital. Therefore, the social movement would be faced with a choice between reform and revolution. The former path would lead to retreat in the face of capital and compromise over its programmatic demands and the latter path would require further advance to seize power to enable democratic control over the economy required to satisfy the needs contained in the demands.

A similar perspective is also offered by Robert Went who identified issues such as the regulation of the financial sector, sustainable development, and the redistribution of work and income (pp. 123–5) which express a 'different economic and social logic' (p. 122) to that driving neoliberal globalization. These issues were being placed on the agenda by the counter-offensive waged by trade unions and social movements which have started to develop 'new forms of practical internationalism' (p. 127).[73]

This strategy is subject to specific criticisms such as that some of these demands were not based sufficiently in mass struggles and therefore there was an element of artificiality to them. From this perspective, the formation and development of the European Marches and broader social movement did not offer a substantial challenge to the new social democratic politics. This was because they were tied up too closely with opposition arising internally to existing social democratic organizations as opposed to arising from independent working class organization. While this criticism does highlight the necessity of reconstructing a working class counter-culture, it

---

72   Callinicos (2003) *op cit.*

73   Went, R. (2000) Globalization: Neoliberal Challenge, Radical Responses (London: Pluto Press).

does not negate the need to relate politically to resistance to neoliberal globalization so as to extend and intensify it.

The 'impasse of working class politics' (p. 50).[74] lies partially in the real disorganizing effects produced by neoliberal restructuring which can only be tackled effectively at the levels of everyday working class life and through the reconstruction of the grass roots basis of working class organizations. However, there is also a need to act at the broader political level which also structures working class consciousness and organization.

Moschonas[75] argued that in contrast to the past, the new social democracy has exerted a negative formative influence on the development of a working class identity. This, he asserted, marked the final exhaustion of the socialist project to develop autonomous working class political representation due to the social trends which occurred towards the end of the twentieth century. However, far from marking the end of an epoch, this has marked a conjunctural failure of social democracy to provide a credible political answer to the current capitalist offensive. In relation to the 'New social democratic Left', this has been due largely to its acceptance of the demobilization of the working class and, moreover, its rejection of it as the primary agent of social change.

Any credible alternative to neoliberalism must be centred on a reassertion of the centrality of the working class and on a political practice which seeks to reconstruct a powerful working class counter-culture. However, advancing a coherent set of demands which addresses the various social and environmental consequences of neoliberal globalization in an uncompromising fashion could also pose a political challenge to the hegemony of social democracy over the working class and its organizations and could assist in the formation of a new socialist consciousness and organization.

Moschonas emphasized how unemployment and job insecurity have produced a 'heterogeneous set of situations, not a more or less 'compact' self-confident force' (p. 308) and how this fragmentation has militated against the formation of a coherent working class political identity. The networks formed to link the diversity of economic and social struggles on which this book has focused have made some progress in overcoming this fragmentation, but so far have not been able to develop any significant measure of political coherence. Those writers wishing to maintain the political autonomy of the social movement have celebrated this ideological diversity. However, while its ideological diversity is a fact, its celebration has obscured the actual substantial influence of the 'new reformism' within the movement which has served to limit its political development. Indeed, writers like Touraine have stressed the need to guard against any political influence from the 'ultra left' so as to claim it for the 'social left' (pp. 74–88).[76] Faced with such a situation, it is incumbent on socialists to take up the ideological and political challenges posed to the social movement against neoliberal globalization by the 'new reformism'.

---

74   Panitch (1986) *op cit.*
75   Moschonas (2002) *op cit.*
76   Touraine (2001) *op cit.*

What kind of Social Movement?

Castells utilized Touraine's analytical framework for understanding the formation of a coherent social movement to conclude that, despite its ideological divisions, the AGM/GJM has already become a coherent social movement.[77] The corollary of this analysis has been to limit its political development to within the framework of the 'new' social democratic politics which has sought to manage the 'new' capitalism. However, applying this framework does produce some key issues whose clarification could lead to an alternative trajectory for the development of the resistance to neoliberal globalization in Europe leading towards a fundamental break with capitalism.

The idea that the identity of the social movement has been based on European citizens may actually dissolve a distinct working class identity and divert it away from its antagonistic character. However, the identity of citizens may represent an advance over the idea of the working class defined as a category of nationally and instrumentally oriented workers opposed implacably to the demands of other social movements. This social democratic conception of the working class is, and must be, challenged by developing a 'politics of social need' (p. 16).[78] This kind of politics produces a broader representation of the working class in terms of the identification of common needs across sectors and borders and how these needs are being denied by capital (and capitalists). This is in line with the argument that I presented in chapter two that economic and social struggles are comprehensible as class struggles over opposed needs: a struggle within, and through, which classes are constantly in the process of formation.

In this sense, there will be an ongoing struggle over the meaning of the demand for rights such as that for a guaranteed income. This demand could be translated into a minimum income which facilitates labour market flexibilization and acts as a basic safety net. This would suggest a role for the state as the guarantor of 'new' rights which would serve to humanize and stabilize the 'new' global capitalism. In contrast, this demand might be maximalized and thereby disrupt the functioning of flexible labour markets and become linked to rights of access to services thereby decommodifying human needs. The mobilization of a social movement around these demands would pose a challenge to the legitimacy of the state and thereby open up the possibility for social and political transformation.

Identifying the movement's opponent solely in terms of neoliberal globalization suggests a limited set of options for an alternative political project. It reduces the political choice to one between ... 'regulation by the market' (neoliberalism) and 'regulation of the market' (p. 189) (social democracy). While the reality of social democracy in the current conjuncture has increasingly been an attempt to synthesize the latter with the former,[79] this has placed socialist planning off the agenda. However, both neoliberalism and social democracy are the ideological manifestations of

---

77   Castells (2004) *op cit.*

78   Kennedy, P. (1997) 'Reflections on Social Movements & the Politics of Need: Locating the Dialectic Between Identity & Difference', *Common Sense* 20 pp, 5–19.

79   Moschonas (2002) *op cit.*

forms of capitalist rule. Therefore, an identification of the opponent not merely as neoliberalism understood as the ideology of the market, but more completely as capitalism as a social system based on production for the market would highlight the fundamental political choice to be made. This is a choice between an acceptance of the capitalist market and an attempt to civilize it or its complete elimination through democratic socialist planning.

Moreover, the idea of globalization has connoted a process resulting in the formation of new transnational interests above and beyond those existing in and between nation states. This analysis has suggested the formation of an alternative 'Europeanism' formed in a European civil society which should engage with transnational institutions to form a European civilization. However, globalization has become a code word for a new phase of imperialism. From this perspective, the formation of transnational institutions has been tied inextricably with the interests of capital within, and across, particular nation states. Therefore, the institutionalization of a 'social Europe' is problematic in that as an expression of a new transnational social settlement it would, in all likelihood, tie the working class in Europe into the broader project of European integration which is, arguably, increasingly producing a new inter-imperialist rivalry between competing regional blocs.[80] The challenge for socialists is consequently to advance a 'new internationalism'[81] which is rooted in the economic, social, and political struggles within nation states, but seeks to connect them across borders both within the boundaries of the EU and beyond. This project stands in stark contrast to the promotion of a bogus internationalism based on democratizing transnational institutions and to an equally spurious progressive nationalism tied to supposedly democratic institutions within nation states. The EU and other transnational institutions do not provide unproblematic 'new' opportunities to regulate the 'new' global capitalism. They do, however, provide a new terrain of struggle on which the organized working class can mobilize and form itself into an international and internationalist force. In this sense, June 14 1997 may indeed prove to be a significant date in the development of the labour movement in Europe.

---

80   There is a significant debate over the nature of the 'new' imperialism with interesting contributions including: Panitch, L. & Leys, C. (2003) *Socialist Register 2004: The New Imperial Challenge* (London: Merlin Press); Bromley, S. (2003) 'Reflections on Empire, Imperialism and United States Hegemony', *Historical Materialism* 11 (3): 17–68; Wood, E.M. (2002) 'Infinite War', *Historical Materialism* 10 (1): pp. 7–27; Callinicos, A. (2005) 'Imperialism and global political economy', *International Socialism* 108 pp. 109–127.

81   There are two main positions on the nature of the 'new' internationalism. The first position is that internationalism today remains mainly a 'national-internationalism' (p. 11) Gindin, S. (2002) 'Social Justice and Globalization: Are They Compatible?' *Monthly Review* 54 (2) pp. 1–11. The other position is that in contrast to the 'old internationalism', the 'new internationalism' no longer has an instrumental and subordinate relationship to nationally based struggles. De Angelis, M. (2000) 'Globalization, New Internationalism and the Zapatistas' *Capital & Class* 70 pp. 9–35.

Postscript

Keep on Struggling for a Social Europe!

We want to overcome the crisis of this European construction that has the market as its idol and secret negotiations as its liturgy so as to found a social, democratic, peaceful, feminist and ecological Europe of solidarity between the peoples.

Together, we want to involve a broad citizen's movement on a European scale to develop, from the local to the European level, in solidarity with all the peoples of the world, political and social dynamics in favour of Another Europe.[1]

Employment and Social Policy Developments after Nice ...

As I suggested in chapter one, in the period since the IGC that culminated at the summit in Nice in December 2000, the institutions of the EU have been continuing to promote policies that, in the name of the modernization of the 'European Social Model', have actually been producing an 'Unsocial Europe'.[2] The Belgian Presidency in 2001 was marked by a slightly more socially oriented agenda with an emphasis on the quality as well as the quantity of employment generated by the European Employment Strategy and a focus on the reduction of poverty and social exclusion. However, this soon gave way in 2002 to a more liberalization focused agenda advanced by the Spanish Presidency which was a reflection of the formation of a new alliance between the governments of Spain, Italy and the UK epitomized by the joint declaration between Blair and Berlusconi.[3]

The Barcelona European Council emphasized three areas to promote economic recovery: the Lisbon strategy for full employment, the deregulation of the public sector and the improvement of education and training. It also affirmed that social exclusion should be tackled by promoting employment through developing an active welfare state and that pension systems should be reformed so as to encourage increased labour market activity amongst older people.[4] The reform of pension systems was advanced through the Open Method of Co-ordination (OMC) which was regarded as a 'big step forward' (p. 371) for a matter usually regarded as a

---

1   'Declaration of the European Conference. A new era can open up for Europe', available at *<http://www.euromarches.org/english/05/non05.htm>* accessed on 15/09/2006.

2   Gray (2004) *op cit.*

3   Barbier, C., de la Porte, C. & Pochet, P. (2002a) 'Digest', *Journal of European Social Policy* 12 (2) pp. 159–169.

4   Barbier, C., de la Porte, C. & Pochet, P. (2002b) 'Digest', *Journal of European Social Policy* 12 (3) pp. 241–248.

national prerogative. Despite an apparent consensus around the three main pillars of financial sustainability, increased employment rates amongst older workers and reducing early retirement, there remained considerable controversy over this issue.[5]

The OMC has come to be regarded as a particularly useful policymaking method in controversial fields and therefore the Commission also suggested its application to the issue of illegal immigration.[6] The Commission also proposed common management of EU borders including, in the longer-term, the formation of a 'European Corps of Border Guards' so as to assist in the goal of a 'clamp down on terrorism and illegal immigration' (p. 243).[7] Illegal immigration became a priority issue at the summit in Seville in June 2002. Proposed measures to impose economic sanctions on countries regarded as not co-operating sufficiently in dealing with illegal immigration were rejected by the Swedish and French governments. The summit focused eventually on immediate measures to speed up deportations and on developing a common policy on repatriation.[8]

Resistance after Nice ...

In the period since the summit in Nice at the end of 2000, there have continued to be mobilizations of the unemployed against the new social protection measures introduced by member states in line with the guideline for employability. However, these have tended to be at a lower level than those described in chapter four.[9] It is possible that this was due to a number of factors including a rise in employment levels due to the proliferation of low paid insecure jobs denounced by the European Marches as well as some government success in mobilizing the unemployed into these jobs. Indeed the main point of reducing social protection has been to ease the transition between unemployment and insecure work. Nevertheless, the growth in insecure employment has also been accompanied by a rise in struggles amongst insecurely employed workers.

Once again the epicentre of these struggles has been in France where since 2000 there have been strikes notable for their radicalism and length and for the determination of the strikers in such diverse sectors as fast food restaurants,

---

5   Barbier, C., de la Porte, C., Peña Casas, R. & Pochet, P. (2001a) 'Digest', *Journal of European Social Policy* 11 (4) pp. 363–373.

6   Barbier at al (2002a) *op cit.*

7   Barbier at al (2002b) *op cit.*

8   Barbier, C., de la Porte, C., Baeten, R.& Ghailani, D. (2002c) 'Digest' *Journal of European Social Policy* 12 (4) pp. 347–357.

9   A significant exception to this process of demobilization was seen in Germany in 2004 where tens of thousands of people mobilized against the 'Hartz IV' law which reformed unemployment benefit so as to cut its level to that of social assistance.

See Eironline (2004) 'Major protests against cuts in unemployment assistance' available at   *<http://www.eiro.eurofound.eu.int/2004/09/inbrief/de0409204n.htm>l*   accessed   on 19/09/2006.

commerce, cleaning, government schemes for young people, and entertainment.[10] Particularly significant strikes have occurred at MacDonalds in Paris where workers struck for four months and then for a year over union rights and at Pizza Hut with two month long strikes over pay. Another highly significant struggle occurred in the Accor hotel chain during which thirty women cleaners of African origin went on strike for a year over discriminatory terms and conditions of work.

These struggles received backing from unions such as the CGT and SUD, but also gave rise to inter-union committees and networks which organized high profile media focused actions such as blockades and occupations of shops as well as weekly 'pic-nics' in the hotels.[11]

Despite the relatively high profile and success of these struggles of insecurely employed workers, they have remained on a relatively small scale. However, the period since Nice has also witnessed large scale mobilizations, including general strikes, organized by trade unions in defence of social protection legislation. In 2001, trade unions in Greece organized two one-day general strikes over social security and, in particular, pension reforms which received 'unprecedented levels of support'(p.1).[12]

In 2002, Spanish trade unions organized a one-day general strike in protest against government reforms of the unemployment benefit system. The aim of these reforms was 'to mobilise the supply side of the labour market, in line with the European employment strategy' (p. 1).[13] The measures taken were aimed at promoting individual responsibility and imposing an obligation on the unemployed to become active jobseekers. These included withdrawal of benefit for not taking up offers of employment within thirty kilometres of residence as well as the complete elimination of benefit entitlement for seasonally employed workers. Unions regarded these and other measures as changing the benefit system from a right's based legal system into an adjunct of labour market policy.[14]

The general strike was held on the day prior to the opening of the EU summit in Seville. The government claimed that the strike was supported by only 17% of workers whereas the unions maintained they held 84% backing. Electricity consumption was the same as for public holidays which commentators regarded as evidence of widespread support for the strike. The unions refused to return to negotiations without substantial changes to the reforms which were introduced by the government through royal decree.[15] The unions continued to mobilize after

---

10   Perrin, E. (2005) 'Les Jeunes Précaires, leur vecu, leurs luttes' in C. Pozzo di Borgo (ed) *Vues de l'Europe d'en Bas* (Paris: L'Harmattan).

11   *ibid.*

12   Eironline (2001) 'Government and unions still at odds over social security system', available at *<http://www.eiro.eurofound.eu.int/2001/06/inbrief/gr0106111n.html>* accessed on 19/09/2006.

13   Eironline (2002) 'Controversy over government's unemployment benefit reform', available at *<http://www.eiro.eurofound.eu.int/2002/06/feature/es0206210f.html>* accessed on 19/06/2006.

14   *ibid.*

15   Eironline (2002) 'General strike held on 20 June', available at *<http://www.eiro. eurofound.eu.int/2002/07/inbrief/es0207201n.html>* accessed on 19/09/2006.

the general strike and this campaign was eventually successful as the government repealed most of the reforms in October 2002.[16]

In July 2002, two of the three main union confederations signed a 'Pact for Italy' whose objectives were based on those agreed at the EU summits in Lisbon and Barcelona. The section of the Pact on 'welfare to work' brought in the new idea of 'active protection' which translated into measures to ensure increased monitoring of unemployment benefit recipients and compulsory training programmes. The Pact also included mechanisms for circumventing Article 18 of the Worker's Statute which ensured legally the reinstatement of workers dismissed unfairly. An earlier attempt to amend this article had been met with a one-day general strike in April 2002.[17] The CGIL regarded the 'Pact for Italy' as detrimental to workers' interests and condemned the 'American recipe' (p. 1) of introducing measures to promote flexible labour markets. Amongst other factors, this contributed to its call for further one-day general strikes in October 2002 and February 2003.[18] The Pact also recognized the importance of concertation[19] as a fundamentally important method for achieving the objectives set at EU summits. The application of this method for pension reform in France actually served to disconcert and divide the unions and despite widespread mobilization this contributed to their ultimate defeat on this issue.[20]

These impressive mobilizations of organized labour within member states posed a considerable challenge to the reform agenda championed by EU institutions which certainly slowed down its implementation. They also made manifest the growing polarization within organized labour between the moderate and radical critics of neoliberal globalization. This polarization also became increasingly evident at the European level.

The ETUC offered a more moderate criticism of the lack of progress towards a 'social Europe' while the militant unions outside of its fold, as well as its internal critics, related more to the radical criticisms developed through the GJM. The ETUC called its own demonstrations prior to several of the EU summits while the radical tendency participated in the European Social Forums and the broader protests that coincided with the EU summits which continued to grow in size and scope. With this expansion of the emerging European social movement, its significant early risers, such as the European Marches tended to take a lower profile. However, it continued

---

16   Eironline (2002) 'Government repeals most of its unemployment reform', available at   *<http://www.eiro.eurofound.eu.int/2002/12/inbrief/es0212201n.html>*   accessed   on 19/09/2006.

17   Eironline (2002) 'Government and social partners sign Pact for Italy', available at *<http:www.eiro.eurofound.eu.int/2002/07/feature/it0207104f.html>* accessed on 19/09/2006.

18   Eironline (2003) 'Cgil calls general strike', available at *<http://www.eiro.eurofound. eu.int/2003/02/inbrief/it0302103n.html>* accessed on 19/09/2006.

19   Concertation has been defined by the EU as a 'method of managing labour, social and economic issues by means of consultation and social concertation between the public authorities and bodies representing employees and employers' (p. 126) European Commission (2002) *Industrial Relations in Europe: Industrial Relations and Industrial Change* (Luxembourg: Office for Official Publications of the European Communities).

20   Gordon, A. & Mathers, A. (2004) 'State restructuring and trade union realignment', *Capital & Class* 83 pp. 9–18.

to play a significant role by highlighting the new struggles waged by insecurely employed workers, by promoting cross-border exchanges, and by continuing to promote links between the networks forming around the various issues so as to form a recognizable European social movement.

The mobilizations in Gothenburg in June 2001 were notable for a new level of repressive policing of the protests which produced 539 arrests, 77 injuries and even 3 shootings of protestors by the police. Journalists suggested that the rising levels of violent protest and policing was a new departure at EU summits and highlighted the issue of 'the growing divide between politicians and the voters they purport to represent' (p. 4).[21] This divide was even greater in Genoa later in the month where the violent repression and criminalization of the protests at the G8 reached an even higher level with the fatal shooting of Carlo Giuliani and the raid on the media centre. However, this resulted in an even higher level of mobilization with up to 300,000 people joining the demonstrations.[22] This figure was exceeded for the demonstration 'Against the Europe of Capital' held in Barcelona at the EU summit in March 2002 which was also subjected to intense media and police pressure. However, the sheer size of the demonstration (with estimations varying from 250,000 according to the police and 500,000 according to the organizers) seemed to militate against any widespread violent confrontations.[23]

This demonstration was preceded a couple of days earlier by a now comparatively modest 100,000 strong mobilization called by the ETUC. This followed three earlier demonstrations it had organized in 2001 during the Belgian Presidency. The demonstration in Liège focused on such matters as promoting full employment through stimulating economic growth.[24] Those in Ghent and Brussels were called under the slogans of 'For a social Europe' and 'Europe that's us' respectively the latter of which was also the slogan for its mobilization in Barcelona.[25]

The European Marches also mobilized for these demonstrations, but focused mainly on continuing its own initiatives such as the second 'European Assembly of the Unemployed and the Insecurely Employed in Struggle' which took place

21   Castle, S., Goodchild, S. & Carrell, S. (2001) 'Rioters plan to stalk the summits from city to city; Gothenburg protests: Swedish police panicked and used firearms to control crowds because they had no access to tear gas', *Independent on Sunday* 17 June.

22   Vidal, J. (2001) 'Genoa summit: police hit hard at core of dissent', *The Guardian*, 23 July; Notes from Nowhere (eds) (2003) *We are everywhere: the irresistible rise of anticapitalism* (London: Verso).

23   Spadoni, P. (2002) 'Entre 3 et 400 000 personnes contre 'l'Europe du Capital'!' available at *<http://www.euromarches.org/francais/02/barc6.htm>* accessed on 15/09/2006; Aguiton, C. (2002) 'La plus grande manifestation jamais organisée contre la mondialisation libérale', available at *<http://www.euromarches.org/francais/02/barc4.htm>* accessed on 15/09/2006.

24   Eironline (2001) 'Euro-demonstration held in Liège', available at *<http://www.eiro. eurofound.eu.int/2001/10/iinbrief/eu0110205n.html>* accessed on 19/09/2006.

25   'Euro-demonstration – Ghent – 19/10/2001', available at *<http://www.etuc.org/ a/2702>* accessed on 25/09/2006; 'Euro-demonstration – Brussels – 13/12/2001', available at *<http://www.etuc.org/a/2718>* accessed on 25/09/2006; 'Euro-demonstration – Barcelone – 13/12/2001', available at *http://www.etuc.org/a/2619* accessed on 25/09/2006.

in Brussels on 11 and 12 December 2001. This event included commissions on the themes of income, employment, insecurity and alternative economics which continued the work of specifying more precisely the demands and the ideas on which they were based.[26] It also concluded with a declaration which called for a global day for income on 30 October 2002 which eventually translated into mobilizations in towns and cities in France, Germany, Belgium and Holland.[27] Brussels was also the symbolic departure point for the 'International March of Social Resistance' which culminated at the EU summit in Seville in June 2002. The marchers carried train drivers' torches so as to demonstrate their link with the strikers in France in 1995 which they argued was the dawn of the social movement.[28]

This march actually began on 8 June with approximately twenty people preparing to depart from Clermont-Ferrand in France. This venue was chosen as it was the residence of Valéry Giscard d'Estaing, the Chair of the Convention on the Future of Europe. About a hundred demonstrators converged on his *château* to protest about his lack of focus on the problems of unemployment, job insecurity and poverty. He refused to enter into dialogue with the protestors who were prevented from entering his premises by the police. Later the same evening, about fifty people joined a debate on the Constitutional Treaty. The following day saw an occupation of the local office of the French National Employment Agency (ANPE) in Millau to highlight its offers of insecurely employed jobs. There was also an hour long occupation in Montepelier of an office of the electricity provider so as to demonstrate opposition to utility disconnections. In Millau, the marchers had also participated in a debate on the criminalization of social movements alongside members of *la Confederation Paysanne* [Confederation of Small Farmers].

Crossing the border into Spain, the marchers' vehicles were thoroughly searched by the police and a banner and magazines were seized. The marchers received practical and political support from the Spanish CGT and aimed not only to highlight the conditions of workers in the agricultural and tourism industries, but also their environmental consequences. The marchers were joined in Spain by a small group of feminists from Morocco and by a larger group of Swedish syndicalists which swelled the size of the march to sixty. This encouraged the marchers to hold a street demonstration in Malaga and also to participate in a picket of the railway station in support of a strike as well as to take part in a meeting on 'Women and Insecurity' at the university. The marchers added an international flavour to the street demonstrations mobilized in support of the general strike which managed to delay the start of the EU summit by two hours. However, a small group managed to travel

26   'Assemblée des chômeurs et chômeuses le 11–12 décembre 01 à Bruxelle', available at *<http://www.euromarches.org/francais/ass.htm#01>* accessed on 13/05/2002.

27   'En Euro C'est Combien ta Misere', available at *<http://www.euromarches. org/francais/01/assdecl.htm>* accessed on 15/09/2006; 'Journée d'action européene ++ Aktionstag ++ European action day 30/10/2002 12H Pour le Droit au Revenu, Für das Recht auf Einkommen, For the right to an income' available at *<http://www.euromarches. org/021030a.htm>* accessed on 11/12/2003.

28   'DÉPART DE LA MARCHE INTERNATIONALE DES RÉSISTANCES SOCIALES' available at *<http://www.euromarches.org/francais/01/mouvem2.htm#ma>* accessed on 25/09/2006.

to Tarifa to draw attention to the plight of migrants seeking to enter Europe from Africa. The march arrived finally in Seville on 21 June where they participated in a long demonstration which set the scene for the subsequent demonstrations which marked the whole weekend of the summit meeting.[29]

The mobilizations at the summits held during the Spanish Presidency highlighted and reinforced the separation seen in Nice. This was between the mobilizations called by the ETUC as the official representative of organized labour within the EU and those organized by the unions and associations forming part of the European dimension of the GJM. However, the first ESF held in Florence in November 2002 was regarded as notable by commentators as the first time that the major unions in Europe, and the ETUC in particular, had entered into a direct dialogue with the activists and organizations of the GJM.[30] Yet more notable was how most participants at this ESF made the link 'between the hegemony of neoliberal restructuring and its ultimate extra-economic enforcement through military power' (p. 320) and so joined the 500,000 strong demonstration against the invasion of Iraq.[31] Nevertheless, there were wide-ranging debates over such issues as the welfare state and social rights; the Charter and the Convention; immigration and enlargement of the EU; and the privatization of public services.[32] These debates did enable some clarification of points of agreement and disagreement within European trade unions as well as between unions and the other SMOs engaged in contesting neoliberal globalization in Europe.[33]

There seemed to be less engagement from the ETUC at the next ESF held in Paris/St.Denis in November 2003.[34] Indeed the ETUC held its own forum just before this ESF and there was a very uneven participation in the ESF amongst, for example, French unions. Moreover, there was both competition and co-operation amongst the European unions participating in this ESF.[35] The ESF process has contributed

---

29   'Mouvement des <sans>', available at <*http://www.euromarches.org/francais/02/sev10.htm*> accessed on 19/09/2006; 'Giscard refuse d'entendre les chômeurs et précaires ...', available at <*http://www.euromarches.org/francais/02/sev09.htm*> accessed on 25/09/2006; 'Marches Européenes – en route vers Séville' available at <*http://www.euromarches.org*> accessed on 15/09/2006.

30   Eironline (2002) 'European Social Forum discusses labour issues', available at <*http://www.eiro.eurofound.eu.int/2002/12/feature/it0212312f.html*> accessed on 19/09/2006.

31   Bieler, A. & Morton, A.D. (2004) 'Another Europe is Possible'? Labour and Social Movements at the European Social Forum', *Globalizations* 1 (2): pp. 305–327.

32   Eironline (2002) 'European Social Forum discusses labour issues', available at <*http://www.eiro.eurofound.eu.int/2002/12/feature/it0212312f.html*> accessed on 19/09/2006.

33   Bieler & Morton (2004) *op. cit.*

34   For an account and analysis of the social question at the second ESF which also deals with other issues see Agrikoliansky, E. & Sommier, I. (eds) (2005) *Radiographie du Mouvement Alternondialiste: Le Second Forum Social Européen* (Paris: La Dispute/SNEDIT).

35   Giraud, B. & Yon, K. (2006) 'Do Unions think global? The No-Global movement as a field for building union strategies in Europe', Paper delivered at the IREC Conference available at <*http://guests.fdv.uni-lj.si/irec/conf_programme.htm*> accessed on 19/09/2006.

to the recognition of common issues around which broader common campaigning and mobilizations have become possible an example of which has been opposition to the so-called 'Bolkestein Directive'.[36] However, the ESF has also made even more clearly apparent the specific criticisms that the participants in the GJM have developed of the ETUC and its affiliates such as their 'unconditional endorsement' of the development of the Constitutional Treaty.[37]

This demonstrates the existence of a fundamental difference which has distinguished the ETUC and its allies amongst the Social NGOs from those unions, associations and networks associated with the GJM. Whatever criticisms the former have developed of the way that European integration has failed to deliver a 'social Europe', these have been stifled by its overall support for yet further integration whatever the social and political consequences. In contrast, the latter have opposed any further integration whose social consequences have been regressive. This difference was extremely stark over the issue of the formulation and ratification of the Constitutional Treaty.

The European Council held in Laeken in 2001 made a 'Declaration on the Future of the Union' which made provision for the formation of a Convention of 105 members which deliberated in 26 plenary sessions to formulate a draft treaty in 2003 for a Constitution for Europe.[38] This project was welcomed enthusiastically by the President of the European Commission, Romano Prodi, who declared that 'the time has come to launch a great political project that our fellow citizens of Europe can identify with. ... Such a project must take up the great challenge of laying the foundations for a supranational democracy' (p. 350).[39] The Convention

---

36   The so-called 'Bolkestein Directive' is otherwise known as the Directive on Services of General Interest whose aim is to create a single market in services. It has been highly controversial due to the country of origin principle which enables service providers to deliver services in one of more countries without being subject to the rules of these countries. This has raised fears of wage and social dumping which has given rise to opposition not only from the trade union movement, but also from the European Parliament and European Council resulting in heavy pressure on the European Commission to exclude health care from the Directive. See Barbier, C., de la Porte, C., Ghailani, D. & Pochet, P. (2005a)'Digest', *Journal of European Social Policy* 15 (2): pp. 173–188; Barbier, C., Ghailani, D., Baeten, R. & Pochet, P. (2005b) 'Digest', *Journal of European Social Policy* 15 (4): pp. 381–394. The ETUC General Secretary, John Monks, has called the Bolkestein Directive the 'Frankenstein of a Services Directive' and has called mobilizations against it which have been supported across the whole of the trade union movement in Europe. See Eironline (2005) 'Trade unionists demonstrate in support of employment and social rights' available at <*http://www.eiro.eurofound. eu.int/2005/03/inbrief/eu0503201n.html*> accessed on 19/09/2006; 'Euro-Manifestation 19 March 2005', available at *http://www.etuc.org/a/975* accessed on 25/09/2006; 'Non à la directive Bolkestein!', available at <*http://www.euromarches.org/francais/06/bolke03.htm*> accessed on 15/09/2006.

37   Eironline (2002) 'European Social Forum discusses labour issues', available at   <*http://www.eiro.eurofound.eu.int/2002/12/feature/it0212312f.html*>   accessed   on 19/09/2006.

38   Barbier et al (2002a) *op cit.*; Barbier, C., de la Porte, C., Ghailani, D. & Baeten, R. (2003a) 'Digest', *Journal of European Social Policy* 13 (4): pp. 388–401.

39   Barbier at al (2002c) *op cit.*

was therefore to be made open to citizens of the EU through a Forum which involved civil society organizations. This translated into those organizations already recognized as legitimate institutional actors such as the ETUC which itself launched a 'Campaign on the Future of Europe'.[40] This campaign called for an authentic constitution incorporating the Charter of Fundamental Rights.[41] The ETUC therefore expressed mixed feelings about the draft treaty which did include the Charter in Part II, but failed to include the goal of full employment or pay due attention to gender equality in Part III. This final part was considered as insufficient to ensure the 'European social model' and therefore the ETUC organized a demonstration in Rome in October 2003 which mobilized 200, 000 citizens in support of its call for a strong social dimension for the Constitution.[42]

The mobilization capacity of the organizations and networks which formed the European dimension of the GJM was focused more on the ESFs and on the opposition to the invasion of Iraq. However, the ESFs also provided an opportunity for advancing European level collaboration against the draft treaty and for an Alternative Constitution. This initiative was supported by the European Marches, that also held further 'European Assemblies of the Unemployed and Insecurely Employed' at the ESFs in Florence and Paris. The European Marches made a 'Proposal to the European Social Movements' assembling in Florence that the Convention was engaged in an illegitimate process that would result in 'the non-recognition of the social rights'. Therefore mobilization was required to ensure recognition of an array of social rights at the head of which was 'the right to an individual guaranteed income, enabling anyone to live decently'.[43]

This initiative was taken up by unions and associations from eight countries which met in Brussels in March 2003 to form the 'European Network for a Charter of Social Rights'. This network criticized the weakness of the consideration of social rights by the Convention while asserting its support for a European Citizenship based on residence and the indivisibility and effectiveness of rights. This network, along with others, also supported a seminar titled 'For a Europe of Democracy and Social Rights' which was held in June 2003 in Thessalonika immediately prior to the EU summit.[44]

The ESF held in Paris/St. Denis included seminars that debated the Charter and the Convention as well as on an alternative 'Charter of Rights'.[45] The final 'Assembly of Social Movements and Activists' declared that the draft treaty did not meet its aspirations. This was reiterated by the same assembly, held at the 2004 ESF in

---

40   'Campaign on the Future of Europe – 2001' available at <*http://www.etuc.org/a/2713*> accessed on 25/09/2006.

41   Barbier, C., Baeten, R., Peña Casas, R. & Pochet, P. (2002d) 'Digest', *Journal of European Social Policy* 12 (1): pp. 67–74.

42   Eironline (2003) 'ETUC organises demonstration in Rome', available at <*http://www.eiro.eurofound.eu.int/2003/11/inbrief/it0311101n.html*> accessed on 19/09/2006.

43   'Proposal to the European Social Movements: Call of Florence for a Europe of Social Rights' printed document.

44   'La bataille pour les droits sociaux: RESEAU EUROPEEN POUR LES DROITS SOCIAUX', *Marches Européenes/News* Avril/Mai/Juin 2003 No. 25.

45   *Programme du 2ème FORUM SOCIAL EUROPEEN 2003* Printed Document.

London, which also declared that the 'constitution treaty consecrates neoliberalism as the official doctrine of the EU' and that it 'puts the market first by marginalising the social sphere, and hence accelerating the destruction of public services'.[46] Some of the opponents of the draft treaty, such as the 'European Network for Social Rights in Europe' formed in November 2003, began to develop a call for a 'true charter of rights' as part of a 'real constitution'. Its content would include measures to ensure gender equality, rights to work, income and services as key elements of a 'social Europe', and the right to freedom of movement and settlement with citizenship rights based on residency. It also called for the formation of 'Assemblies for another Europe' to enable the democratic construction of an alternative to the present course of European integration.[47]

In March 2004, an assembly of approximately a hundred people was held in Brussels to consider the question of 'Social Rights in the Enlarged Europe'.[48] The draft treaty was singled out for particularly harsh criticism. Speaking on behalf of the G10 unions, Annick Coupé argued for its rejection as it 'ratifies liberalism, competition and markets as the foundations of Europe' (p. 58). Sonia Mitralias of the WWM condemned the Constitution on the grounds that it identified gender equality only amongst its objectives and not amongst its fundamental values. The report back from the Working Group on 'Social Rights, Citizenship and Constitutional Issues' found that 'some organizations think that it is 'better than nothing', others think that nothing is better than this unacceptable text' (p. 79). However, despite this difference there appeared to be a consensus that the Constitutional Treaty should not be ratified without proper citizen consultation through referenda.

The text for the Constitutional Treaty was signed in Rome in October 2004 which was the first step in the ratification process.[49] This was followed by a series of votes in favour by parliamentary chambers in Lithuania, Hungary, Italy, Greece, Belgium, Austria, Slovakia and Germany. Where a referendum was held in Spain, three-quarters of citizens voted 'yes', but less than half of the citizens voted.[50] Further referenda in France and then in the Netherlands resulted in 'no' votes which effectively scuppered the launch of the Treaty and triggered a period of reflection amongst EU institutions and member state governments.[51]

In an attempt to relaunch the Constitution, the Commission introduced its Plan D to promote democracy, dialogue and debate with citizens so as to develop a new consensus around the agenda for European integration which did include social

---

46   'The Call of the Assembly of Social Movements' available at <*http://www.ukesf. net/en/esf.shtml?x=2234&als[SSECTION]=Home*> accessed on 25/09/2006.

47   'Declaration proposed to the European Network for Social Rights in Europe (RED)', available at *http://www.euromarches.org/english/04/0319_8.htm* accessed on 19/09/2006.

48   Dufour, J-G. (ed) (2004) *Social Rights in the Enlarged Europe* (Paris: Editions Syllepse).

49   Barbier, C., de la Porte, C., Ghailani, D., Baeten, R. & Pochet, P. (2005c) 'Digest', *Journal of European Social Policy* 15 (1): pp. 81–93.

50   Barbier et al (2005a) *op cit.* 15 (2); Barbier, C., de la Porte, C., Ghailani, D. & Pochet, P. (2005d) 'Digest', *Journal of European Social Policy* 15 (3): pp. 269–279.

51   Barbier et al (2005b) *op cit.*

as well as economic development.[52] However, its communication to the European Council in June 2006 entitled 'A Citizens' Agenda for Europe' did not mark any departure from its existing agenda for 'modernisation' (p. 2) through the application of the Lisbon Strategy for promoting more employment through growth and active labour market policies.[53]

The vote in the referendum in France was not split along the lines of the Left voting 'yes' and the Right voting 'no' as would have been expected if the issue had been debated in the simplistic terms often presented by the media. As Bourdieu suggested, this representation characterized those for Europe as 'progressive, open, modern, liberal' and those against it as 'archaic, outdated, reactionary, and nationalist' and thereby failed to recognize any other 'legitimate option but the unconditional endorsement of Europe *as it is*' (p. 53).[54] The debate in France escaped from this dichotomy to consider the social consequences of the Constitution which also became entwined with the question of the 'Bolkestein Directive'.

Unions such as SUD had been supporters of the European Marches and had participated in the broader GJM and therefore could claim that their opposition to the Constitution was not a matter of nationalist defensiveness, but rather an internationalist defence of social rights. Indeed, during the referendum campaign, an 'Appeal of 200 European citizens' was launched in solidarity with the 'No' campaign of the French Left. This appeal made clear that the opposition to the Treaty was due to its inadequacy in relation to the development of a social and democratic Europe and concluded by stating its aspiration 'That another Europe may become possible'.[55] This added an extra legitimacy to the left wing element of the 'No' campaign which assisted in boosting the 'No' vote amongst unions and parties associated broadly with the 'Left'. *Le Parti Socialiste* was split with more than half of its supporters voting against the Constitution and *Les Verts* achieved only a slightly lower 'Yes' vote. Amongst the unions, more than three-quarters of the adherents of the CGT and SUD voted 'No'.[56]

The ETUC expressed its regret about the 'no' vote which it attributed to the fear of a neo-liberal Europe and to the EU not listening enough to 'the voice of Social Europe'. However, while recognizing that the EU faced a crisis, it maintained that the Constitution was not neo-liberal after all and therefore required ratification.[57] This kind of double-think was indicative of how the ETUC was tied into supporting further integration almost regardless of its social consequences. The European Marches, meanwhile, rejoiced at the referendum results in France and Holland

---

52   Barbier, C., Ghailani, D. & Pochet, P. (2006) 'Digest', *Journal of European Social Policy* 16 (1): pp. 81–93.

53   European Commission (2006) Communication *A Citizens' Agenda – Delivering Results for Europe* COM (2006) 211 of 10 May.

54   Bourdieu (2003) *op cit.*

55   'An Appeal by 200 Europeans', available at *<http://www.euromarches.org/english/05/non01.htm>* accessed on 19/09/2006.

56   Grunberg, G. (2005) 'Le Référendum Français e Ratification du Traité Constitutionnel Européen du 29 Mai 2005', *French Politics, Culture & Society*, 23 (3): pp. 128–144.

57   'The Constitution, which is not neo-liberal, has become a casualty of Member States ignoring Social Europe', available at *<http://www.etuc.org/a/1328>* accessed on 25/09/2006.

which were regarded as a rejection of a neoliberal Constitution which would have become 'another source of unemployment and misery'. It also demonstrated the need for a 'radical reorientation' of European employment policies away from the Lisbon strategy which was resulting in growing insecurity and towards measures that redistributed wealth so that a universal right to a decent income could be achieved.[58]

The support given to the 'no' campaign of the Left in France and the Netherlands was an example of the kind of 'national-internationalism'(p. 11)[59] which has thus far been paramount for the defence of existing social rights in the face of the neoliberal attacks occurring through the institutions of the EU. However, the crisis of legitimacy of EU institutions, which has deepened as a result of the rejection of the Constitutional Treaty, has opened up yet more space for a debate over the development of an alternative to a neoliberal Europe.

As I have shown, the transnational mobilizations have been largely a mechanism for intervening into this debate to highlight the failings of neoliberal Europe and to present different versions of a 'social Europe'. The development of transnational organization and mobilization around the question of a 'social Europe' has been relatively limited and participation has been very uneven across nation states. However, through outlining the birth and infancy of a nascent European social movement, I have identified the development of two models of organization and mobilization. The first is a top-down model linked to the strategy of social partnership advanced by the ETUC whose aim is to modernize the 'European Social Model' through institutional action within the EU.[60] The second is a bottom-up model linked to the strategy of mobilizing a social movement autonomous of EU institutions which has been advanced by the European Marches and the other organizations and networks which have participated in the GJM in Europe. The project emanating from this strategy is less clear cut, but has focused rather on the promotion of key demands which have arisen from the grass roots opposition within nation states to neoliberal globalization. Rather than suggesting that organized labour has been superseded as an agent of social change, the existence of two alternative models of organization and mobilization suggest that the struggle for a 'social Europe' will involve a struggle within organized labour as its central social agent.

---

58   'A No of hope for the unemployed women, the unemployed men, the precarious workers and the excluded of all of Europe', available at <*http://www.euromarches.org/english/05/non04.htm* >accessed on 15/09/2006.

59   Gindin (2002) *op cit.*

60   The ETUC reasserted its belief in the existence of a 'European Social Model' in the lead up to the Social Affairs Summit in October 2005. It also expressed its wish to formulate with business organizations a 'Pact to modernise the European economy' (p. 92) Barbier et al (2006) *op cit.*

Appendix

Abbreviations of Organizations

AC!	*Agir Ensemble Contre Le Chômage!* (Act Together Against Unemployment!)
ADC	*Association de défense des chômeurs* (Association for the Defence of the Unemployed)
ALSO	*Arbeitslosenselbsthilfe Oldenburg* (Unemployed Self-Help Oldenburg)
APEIS	*Association pour l'emploi, l'information et la solidarité* (Association for Employment, Information and Solidarity)
ATTAC	Action for a Tobin Tax for the Assistance of Citizens
BABC	Brighton Against Benefit Cuts
BAG-E	*Bundesarbeitsgruppen der Initiativen gegen Arbeitslosigkeit and Armut (BAG-Erwerbslose)* (National Working Group of Initiatives Against Unemployment and Poverty)
BAG-SHI	*Bundesarbeitsgemeinschaft der Sozialhilfeininitiativen* (National Working Association of Income Support Initiatives)
BBAG	Bristol Benefits Action Group
CC.OO	*Confederación Sindical de Comisiones Obreras* (Union Confederation of Workers Committees)
CFDT	*Confédération Française Démocratique du Travail* (French Democratic Confederation of Workers)
CGIL:	*Confederazione Generale Italiana del Lavoro* (Italian General Confederation of Workers)
CGT (Spain)	*Confederación General del Trabajo* (General Confederation of Workers)
CGT (France)	*Confédération Generale des Travaillers* (General Confederation of Workers)
CGTP	*Confederação Geral dos Trabalhadores Portugueses* (Portuguese General Confederation of Workers)
CNT (France)	*Confédération Nationale du Travail* (National Confederation of Workers)
CNT (Spain)	*Confederación Nacional del Trabajo* (National Confederation of Workers)
COBAS	*Comitati di Base* (Rank and File Committees)
DAL	*Droits au Logement* (Rights to Housing)
DD	*Droits Devant!* (Rights Ahead!)
DGB	*Deutsche Gewerkschaftsbund* (German Trade Union Congress)
EAPN	European Anti-Poverty Network
ENU	European Network of the Unemployed

Struggling for a Social Europe

EU	European Union
ETUC	European Trade Union Confederation
EZLN	*Ejército Zapatista de Liberación* (Zapatista Army for National Liberation)
FeLS	*Für eine linke Strömung* (For a Left Wing Current)
FERPA	*Fédération Européene des Retraités et des Personnes Âgées* (European Federation of Pensioners and Older People)
FGTB	*Fédération Générale du Travail de Belgique* (Belgian General Federation of Workers)
FO	*Force Ouvrière* (Workers Power)
FSU	*Fédération Syndicale Unitaire* (United Federation of Unions)
FTAA	Free Trade Agreement of the Americas
G8	Group of Eight Leading Industrialised Nations
G 10	*Groupe de Dix* (Group of Ten)
GUE/NGL	Confederal Group of the European United Left/Nordic Green Left
ILO	International Labour Organisation
IMF	International Monetary Fund
INOU	Irish National Organisation of the Unemployed
KOS	*Koordinierungsstelle gewerkschaftlicher Arbeitslosengruppen* (Coordination of Trade Union Unemployed Groups)
LCR	*Ligue Communiste Révolutionaire* (Revolutionary Communist League)
MNCP	*Mouvement National des Chômeurs et Précaires* (National Movement of Unemployed and Insecurely Employed)
NATO	North Atlantic Treaty Organisation
NGG	*Gewerkschaft Nahrung, Genuss und Gaststätten* (Union of Food, Catering and Restaurant Workers)
ÖTV	*Gewerkschaft Öffentliche Dienste, Transport und Verkehr* (Union of Public Service, Transport and Traffic Workers)
PCF	*Parti communiste français* (French Communist Party)
PDS	*Partei des Demokratischen Sozialismus* (Party of Democratic Socialism)
PES	Party of European Socialists
PGA	Peoples Global Action
RC	*Refondazione Comunista* (Communist Refoundation)
SoZ	*Sozialistische Zeitung* (Socialist News)
SPD	*Sozialdemokratische Partei Deutschlands* (German Social Democratic Party)
SUD	*Solidaires, Unitaires, Démocratiques* (Solidarity, United, Democratic)
TUC	Trade Union Congress
TUCs	Trade Union Councils
UAG	Unemployed Action Group
UNICE	Union of Industrial and Employers' Confederations of Europe

Ver-di	*Vereinte Dienstleistungsgewerkschaft* (United Service Workers Union)
WAC	Workers Advice Centre
WEF	World Economic Forum
WTO	World Trade Organisation

Author's Participation in Demonstrations, Assemblies, Meetings and Press Conferences

12/06/1998 – 14/06/1998: **Assembly**: 'Reclaim Europe! Counter Summit' held at the University of Cardiff Student Union organized by Reclaim Europe!

13/06/1998: **Demonstration**: 'No to Big Business Europe – Yes to Jobs, Public Services and Democracy', held in Cardiff on the occasion of the EU summit and called by the Cardiff Summit Demonstration Committee.

05/09/1998: **Meeting**: European Marches UK Steering Committee held at the Leeds Trade Union Council Centre.

07/11/1998: **Meeting**: European Marches UK Steering Committee held at the Leeds Trade Union Council Centre.

23/01/1999 – 24/01/1999: **Assembly**: 'Cologne meeting against unemployment, job insecurity, social exclusion and racism' (Cologne Conference) held at the University of Cologne.

27/02/1999: **Meeting**: European Marches UK Steering Committee held at the Leeds Trade Union Council Centre.

28/05/1999 – 02/06/1999: **Assembly**: 'EU-Alternative Summit' held at the 'Alte Feuerwache' in Cologne and organised by the 'Cologne counter-summit collective'.

29/05/1999: **Demonstration**: 'European demonstration against Unemployment, Job Insecurity, Exclusion and Racism. For a Europe and a World of Solidarity and Liberty' held in Cologne on the occasion of the EU summit.

30/05/1999 – 01/06/1999: **Assembly**: 'European Parliament of the Unemployed and those in Insecure Jobs in the Struggle' (the 'Parliament') held at the 'Alte Feuerwache' in Cologne.

02/06/1999: **Press Conference**: called by the European Marches Network and the 'Cologne counter-summit collective' and held at the Antoniker Church in Cologne.

16/06/1999 – 18/06/1999: **Assembly**: 'Alternative Economic Summit' held at the 'Volkshochschule' in Cologne.

19/06/1999: **Demonstration**: 'Drop the Debt' held in Cologne on the occasion of the G8 summit.

20/06/1999: **Meeting**: German European Marches Network Co-ordinating Committee held in Cologne.

02/10/1999: **Meeting**: European Marches UK Liaison Committee held at the Leeds Trade Union Council Centre.

10/12/2000: **Demonstration**: Picket against the New Deal held at the Nelson Street Job Centre called by BBAG.

29/01/2000: **Meeting**: Annual General Meeting of the UAG held at the Trades Club, Birmingham.

06/06/2000: **Press Conference**: called by the Belgian European Marches Network, ATTAC and the 'Collective against UNICE' held at the 'Nova' rue d'Arenberg, Brussels.

08/06/2000: **Meeting**: 'Dissonant Voices-UNICE summit' held at Salle 'Helder Camara', rue Pletinckx, Brussels.

10/06/2000: **Meeting**: *International Colloque* 'A social minimum in Europe for all' held at the 'Madaleine' rue Duquesnoy, Brussels.

10/06/2000: **Demonstration** 'United Against UNICE' held in Brussels and called by the 'Collective against UNICE'.

02/12/2000 – 04/12/2000: **Assembly**: 'European Assembly of the Unemployed and Insecurely Employed in the Struggle' (the 'Assembly') held in Paris at the 'Bourse du Travail' and the 'Maisons des Syndicats'.

05/12/2000: **Action**: 'A free train to Nice' held at the Gare de Lyon in Paris.

06/12/2000: **Demonstration**: 'Euro-Demonstration' held in Nice, called by the ETUC followed by the alternative demonstration called by the 'Collective for Another Charter'.

06/12/2000: **Meeting**: 'Meeting of European Civil Society' held in Nice at Cinema Pathe Massena, Avenue Jean Médicin and organised by the Permanent Forum of Civil Society, the European Movement and the European Commission.

07/12/2000: **Demonstration**: 'Make our voice heard'. Blockade of the EU summit held in Nice and called by the 'Collective for Another Charter'.

06/11/2002 – 10/11/2000: Various events held as part of the European Social Forum in Florence

12/11/2003 – 15/11/2003: Various events held as part of the European Social Forum held in Paris, St. Denis & Ivry-sur-Seine.

15/10/2004 – 17/10/2004: Various events held as part of the European Social Forum held in London

List of Interviews In Chronological Order

Date: Participant: Organizational Affiliations: Location: Language of Interview

03/06/1999: **Willi Lubkes**: ALSO, Green Party: Oldenburg, Germany: German

03/06/1999: **Uwe Durchbach**: ALSO: Oldenburg, Germany: German

04/06/1999: **Andi Dallmann**: ALSO: Oldenburg, Germany: German

11/06/1999: **Gitti Götz**: PDS: Munich, Germany: German

11/06/1999: **Anonymous activist:** no affiliation: Munich, Germany: English

16/06/1999: **Barbara Trowe**: ÖTV: Dortmund, Germany: German

21/06/1999: **Angela Klein**: SoZ: Cologne, Germany: German

23/06/1999: **Gerhard Klas**: SoZ: Cologne, Germany: German

25/06/1999: **Joachim Glund**: Euromarsch Duisburg: Duisburg, Germany: German

27/06/1999: **Kai Pust**: none: Essen, Germany: German

17/08/1999: **Ailko van der Veen**: 'Solidarity': Amsterdam, Holland: English

7/08/1999: **Piet van der Lende**: Platform for Another Europe, Amsterdam, Holland: English

13/09/1999: **Michel Rousseau**: SUD: Paris, France: French

14/09/1999: **Patrice Spadoni**: AC!: Paris, France: French

15/09/1999: **Laurent Guilloteau**: AC!: Paris, France: French

16/09/1999: **Irène Bonnaud**: AC!: Paris, France: German

16/09/1999: **Yvonne Rocomaure**: AC!: Paris, France: English

17/09/1999: **Nassera Abbed**: AC!: Paris, France: French and English

12/11/1999: **Ken Coates**: ex-PES: Nottingham, UK: English

16/11/1999: **Denise Wood**: Hinckley Pensioners Action Group: Hinckley, UK: English

09/12/1999: **Activist 1**: BABC: Bristol, UK: English

11/12/1999: **Activist 2**: BABC: Bristol, UK: English

29/01/2000: **Andy Robertson**: UAG: Birmingham, UK: English

29/01/2000: **Assaf Asif**: WAC: Birmingham, UK: English

29/01/2000: **Wehbe Badameh**: WAC: Birmingham, UK: English

05/06/2000: **Erryl McNally**: PES: Brussels, Belgium: English

05/06/2000: **Herman Schmid**: NGL/GUL: Brussels, Belgium: English

06/06/2000: **Vincent Forrest**: EAPN: Brussels, Belgium: English

06/06/2000: **Anne van Lancker**: PES: Brussels, Belgium: English

07/06/2000: **Ilke Schröder**: NGL/GUL: Brussels, Belgium: English

08/06/2000: **Simon Wilson**: European Platform of Social NGOs: Brussels,
      Belgium: English

08/06/2000: **Ute Müller**: PES: Brussels, Belgium: German

08/06/2000: **Corinne Barella**: *Chômeurs pas Chiens*: Brussels, Belgium: English

09/06/2000: **Marie-Paule Connan**: European Marches Belgium: Brussels,
      Belgium: French

19/07/2000: **Peter Coldrick**: ETUC: telephone interview: English

03/12/2000: **Antonino Campenni**: Confederazione Cobas: Paris, France: English

03/12/2000: **Paolo Iafrete**: S.in Cobas: Paris, France: English

Selected Bibliography

Agrikoliansky, E. & Sommier, I. (eds) (2005) *Radiographie du Mouvement Alternondialiste: Le Second Forum Social Européen* (Paris: La Dispute/ SNEDIT).

Bachet, D. & Durand, J-P. (2001) 'Social-Liberalism in France', *Capital & Class*, 75 pp. 135–148.

Balme, R., Chabanet, D. & Wright, V. (eds) (2002) *L'action collective en Europe* (Paris: Presses de Science Po).

Bandy, J. & Smith, J. (eds) *Coalitions Across Borders* (Lanham, Maryland: Rowman & Littlefield).

Barker, C. & Dale, G. (1998) 'Protest Waves in Western Europe: A Critique of 'New Social Movement' Theory, *Critical Sociology,* 24 (1–2) pp. 65–104.

Beck, U. (1992) *Risk Society: Towards a New Modernity* (London: Sage).

Beck, U. (2000) *The Brave New World of Work* (Cambridge: Polity).

Bédoyan, I. , Van Aelst, P. & Walgrave, S. (2004) 'Limitations and Possibilities of Transnational Mobilization: The Case of EU Summit Protestors in Brussels, 2001', *Mobilization*, 9 (1) pp. 39–54.

Behan, T. (1999) 'The return of Italian Communism?' *International Socialism* 2 (84) pp. 101–8.

Berger, J. (1968) 'The Nature of Mass Demonstrations', *New Society* 23 May pp. 754–755.

Bieler, A. & Morton, A.D. (eds) (2001) *Social Forces in the Making of the New Europe* (Basingstoke: Palgrave).

Bieler, A. & Morton, A.D. (2004) 'Another Europe is Possible'? Labour and Social Movements at the European Social Forum', *Globalizations* 1 (2): pp. 305–327.

Bircham, E. & Charlton, J. (eds) (2001) *Anti-Capitalism: a guide to the movement* (London: Bookmarks).

Blackburn, R. et al (2004) *The Social Europe We Need* (Nottingham: Spokesman).

Bonefeld, W. (ed) (2001) *The Politics of Europe: Monetary Union and Class* (Basingstoke: Palgrave).

Bonefeld, W. (2002) 'European integration, the market, the political and class', *Capital & Class*, 77 pp. 117–142.

Bonefeld, W. & Holloway, J. (eds) (1991) *Post-Fordism & Social Form: A Marxist Debate on the Post-Fordist State* (Basingstoke: Macmillan).

Bonefeld, W., Gunn, R. & Psychopedis, K. (eds) (1992) *Dialectics and History: Open Marxism Volume One* (London: Pluto).

Bonefeld, W., Gunn, R., Holloway, J. & Psychopedis, K. (eds) (1995) *Emancipating Marx: Open Marxism Volume Three* (London: Pluto Press).

Bourdieu, P. (1998) *Acts of Resistance*, (Cambridge: Polity Press).

Bourdieu, P. (2003) *Firing Back* (Cambridge: Polity Press).

Bourdieu, P. Debons, C., Hensche, D. & Lutz, B. u.a. (1997) *Perspektiven des Protests* (Hamburg: VSA-Verlag).

Bromley, S. (2003) 'Reflections on *Empire,* Imperialism and United States Hegemony', *Historical Materialism* 11 (3): 17–68.

Burawoy, M. (1998) 'The extended case method' *Sociological Theory* 16 (1) pp. 4–33.

Burgess, R. (1994) *In the Field: an introduction to field research* (London: Allen & Unwin).

Callinicos, A. (1983) *The Revolutionary Ideas of Karl Marx* (London: Bookmarks).

Callinicos, A. (1999) 'Social Theory put to the Test of Politics: Pierre Bourdieu and Anthony Giddens' *New Left Review* 236 pp. 77–102.

Callinicos, A. (2001) 'Tony Negri in perspective' *International Socialism* 2 (92) pp. 33–61.

Callinicos, A. (2001) *Against the Third Way* (Cambridge: Polity).

Callinicos, A. (2003) *An Anti-Capitalist Manifesto* (Cambridge: Polity).

Callinicos, A. (2005) 'Imperialism and global political economy', *International Socialism* 108 pp. 109–127.

Carvell, T. (1975) *Karl Marx Texts on Method* (Oxford: Basil Blackwell).

Castells, M. (1983) *The City and the Grassroots* (London: Edward Arnold).

Castells, M. (1996) *The Rise of the Network Society* (Oxford: Blackwell).

Castells, M. (1997) *The Power of Identity* (Oxford: Blackwell).

Castells, M. (1998) *End of Millennium* (Oxford: Blackwell).

Castells, M. (2004) *The Power of Identity* (Second Edition) (Oxford: Blackwell).

Clarke, S. (ed) (1991) *The State Debate* (Basingstoke: Macmillan).

Cohen, J. (1985) 'Strategy or Identity: New Theoretical Paradigms and Contemporary Social Movements', *Social Research*, 52 (4) pp. 663–716.

Cohen, S. (1991) 'Us and Them: business unionism in America and some implications for the UK' *Capital & Class* 45 pp. 95–127.

Cohn-Bendit, G. & Cohn-Bendit, D. (1969) *Obsolete Communism the Left-Wing Alternative* (London: Penguin Books).

Conference of Socialist Economists State Apparatus and Expenditure Group (CSE-SAEG) (1979) *Struggle Over The State: Cuts and Restructuring in Contemporary Britain* (London: CSE Books).

Crouch, C. & A. Pizzorno (eds) *The Resurgence of Class Conflict in Western Europe since 1968* (Basingstoke: Macmillan).

Dalton, R.J. & Kuechler, M. (eds) *Challenging the Political Order* (Cambridge: Polity).

De Angelis, M. (2000) 'Globalization, New Internationalism and the Zapatistas' *Capital & Class* 70 pp. 9–35.

Della Porta, D. & Diani, M. (2006) *Social Movements: An Introduction* (Second Edition) (Oxford: Blackwell).

Denzin, N.K. & Lincoln, Y.S. (eds) (1994) *Handbook of Qualitative Research* (London: Sage)

Fajertag, G.& Pochet, P. (eds) (1997) *Social Pacts in Europe,* (Brussels:ETUI).

Falkner, G. (1998) *EU Social Policy in the 1990s. Towards a corporatist policy community*, (London:Routledge).

Fantasia, R. & Voss, K. (2004) *Hard Work: Remaking the American Labor Movement* (Berkeley, Los Angeles & London: University of California Press).

Fisher, D. R., Stanley, K., Berman, D. & Neff, G. (2005) 'How do Organizations Matter? Mobilization and Support for Participants at Five Globalization Protests', *Social Problems*, 52 (1) pp. 102–121.

Gabaglio, E. & Hoffman, R. (eds) (2000) *European Trade Union Yearbook 1999*, (Brussels:ETUI).

Gall, G. (1995) 'The emergence of a rank and file movement: the Comitati di Base in the Italian worker's movement *Capital & Class* 55 pp. 9–20.

Gerlach, L.P. & Hine, V.H. (1970) *People, Power, Change. Movements of Social Transformation* (Indianapolis and New York: The Bobbs-Merrill Company).

Giddens, A. (1990a) *The Consequences of Modernity* (Cambridge: Polity Press).

Giddens, A. (1990b) 'Modernity and utopia', *New Statesman* 2 November.

Giddens, A. (1991) *Modernity and Self-identity* (Cambridge: Polity Press).

Giddens, A. (1994) *Beyond Left and Right: The Future of Radical Politics* (Cambridge: Polity Press).

Giddens (1998) *The Third Way: The Renewal of Social Democracy* (Cambridge: Polity Press).

Giddens, A. (2000) *The Third Way and its Critics* (Cambridge: Polity).

Gindin, S. (2002) 'Social Justice and Globalization: Are They Compatible?' *Monthly Review* 54 (2) pp. 1–11.

Goetschy, J. (1999) 'The European Employment Strategy: Genesis and Development', *European Journal of Industrial Relations*, 5(2) pp. 117–137.

Goetschy, J. & Pochet, P. (1997) 'The Treaty of Amsterdam: a new approach to employment and social affairs?' *Transfer*, 3(3) pp. 607–620.

Goldthorpe, J.H., Lockwood, D., Bechhofer, F. & Platt, J. (1969) *The Affluent Worker in the Class Structure* (Cambridge: Cambridge University Press).

Gordon, A. & Mathers, A. (2004) 'State restructuring and trade union realignment', *Capital & Class* 83 pp. 9–18.

Gorz, A. (1967) *Strategy for Labour: A Radical Proposal* (Boston: Beacon Press).

Gorz, A. (1982) *Farewell to the Working Class: an Essay on Post-Industrial Socialism* (London: Pluto Press).

Gorz, A. (1985) *Paths to Paradise: On the Liberation from Work* (London: Pluto Press).

Gorz, A. (1989) *Critique of Economic Reason* (London: Verso).

Gorz, A. (1990) 'The New Agenda', *New Left Review*, 184 pp. 37–46.

Gorz, A. (1999) *Reclaiming Work: Beyond the Wage-Based Society* (Cambridge: Polity Press).

Gray, A. (2004) *Unsocial Europe* (London: Pluto Press).

Grunberg, G. (2005) 'Le Référendum Français e Ratification du Traité Constitutionnel Européen du 29 Mai 2005', *French Politics, Culture & Society*, 23 (3): pp. 128–144.

Habermas, J. (1981) 'New Social Movements', *Telos*, 49 pp. 33–37.

Habermas, J. (1987) *The Theory of Communicative Action. Volume Two: Lifeworld and System: A Critique of Functionalist Reason* (Cambridge: Polity).

Habermas, J. (1998) 'There Are Alternatives', *New Left Review* 231 pp. 3–12.

Habermas, J. (1999) 'The European Nation-State and the Pressures of Globalization' *New Left Review* 235 pp. 46–59.

Habermas, J. (2001a) 'A Constitution for Europe?', *New Left Review* 11 pp. 5–26.

Habermas, J. (2001b) *The Postnational Constellation* (Cambridge: Polity).

Hammersley, M. & Atkinson, P. (1995) *Ethnography: Principles in Practice* (London: Routledge).

Harding, S. (ed) (1987) *Feminism and Methodology* Milton Keynes: (Open University Press).

Hardt, M. & Negri, A. (2000) *Empire* (London: Harvard University Press).

Harman, C. (2002) 'The Workers of the World', *International Socialism* 96 pp. 3–45.

Harvey, L. (1990) *Critical Social Research* (London: Unwin Hyman).

Hertz, R. (ed) (1997) *Reflexivity and Voice* (Thousand Oaks, CA: Sage).

Holloway, J. (2002) *Change the World Without Taking Power* (London: Pluto).

Imig, D. & Tarrow, S. (eds) *Contentious Europeans* (Lanham, Maryland: Rowman & Littlefield).

Inglehart, R. (1977) *The Silent Revolution: Changing Values and Political Styles among Western Publics* (Princeton: Princeton University Press).

Jeffreys, S. (1996) 'France 1995: the backward march of labour halted? *Capital & Class* 59 pp. 7–21.

Johnston, J. & Goodman, J. (2006) 'Hope and Activism in the Ivory Tower: Freirean Lessons for Critical Globalization Research', *Globalizations*, 3 (1) pp. 9–30.

Jorgensen, D.L. (1989) *Participant Observation: A Methodology for the Human Sciences* (London: Sage).

Keck, M. E. & Sikkink, K. (1998) *Activists beyond Borders: Advocacy Networks in International Politics* (Ithaca & London: Cornell University Press).

Kennedy, P. (1997) 'Reflections on Social Movements & the Politics of Need: Locating the Dialectic Between Identity & Difference', *Common Sense* 20 pp, 5–19.

Kitschelt, H. (1994) *The Transformation of European Social Democracy* (Cambridge: Cambridge University Press).

Kuper, B-O. (1994) 'The Green and White Papers of the European Union: the apparent goal of reduced social benefits', *Journal of European Social Policy*, 4 (2) pp. 129–137.

Kvale, S. (1996) *Interviews: An Introduction to Qualitative Research* (Thousands Oaks, CA: Sage).

Laclau, E. & Mouffe, C. (1985) *Hegemony & Socialist Strategy: Towards a Radical Democratic Politics* (London & New York: Verso).

Lahusen, C. (2004) 'Joining the Cocktail Circuit: Social Movement Organizations at the European Union', *Mobilization*, 9 (1) pp. 55–71.

Larana, E., Johnston, H. & Gusfield, J.R. (eds) *New Social Movements: From Ideology to Identity,* (Philadelphia: Temple University Press).

Lebowitz, M. A. (1992) *Beyond Capital: Marx's Political Economy of the Working Class* (Basingstoke Macmillan).

Lipietz, A. (1992) *Towards a New Economic Order: Postfordism, Ecology and Democracy* (Cambridge: Polity).

London to Edinburgh Weekend Return Group (LEWRG) (1979) *In and Against the State* (London: Pluto Press).

MacGregor, S. (1999) Welfare, Neo-Liberalism and New Paternalism: Three Ways for Social Policy in Late Capitalist Societies', *Capital & Class* 67 pp.91–118.

Marx, K. (1976) *Capital Volume 1* (Harmondsworth: Penguin).

Mathers, A. (1999) 'Euromarch – The Struggle for a Social Europe' *Capital & Class* 68 pp.15–20.

Mathers, A. & Novelli, M. (2007) 'Researching Resistance to Neoliberal Globalization: Engaged Ethnography as Solidarity and Praxis', *Globalizations*, 4(2).

Mazey, S. & Richardson, J. (1997) 'Policy Framing: Interest Groups and the lead up to 1996 Inter-Governmental Conference', *West European Politics*, 20 (3) pp. 111–133.

Melucci, A. (1985) 'The Symbolic Challenge of Contemporary Movements', *Social Research,* 52 (4) pp. 789–816.

Melucci, A. (1989) *Nomads of the Present* (London: Hutchinson Radius).

Melucci, A. (1996) *Challenging Codes: collective action in the information age* (Cambridge:Cambridge University Press).

Miliband, R., Saville, J., Liebman, M. & Panitch, L. (eds) (1986) *Social Democracy and After: Socialist Register 1985/6* London: Merlin Press.

Moody, K. (1997) *Workers in a Lean World* (London & New York: Verso).

Moschonas, G. (2002) *In the Name of Social Democracy. The Great Transformation:1945 to the Present.* (London: Verso).

Mullard, M. & Lee, S. (eds) (1997) *The Politics of Social Policy in Europe*, Cheltenham: Edward Elgar.

Munck, R. & Waterman, P. (eds) (1999) *Labour Worldwide in the Era of Globalization* (Basingstoke: Macmillan).

Murray, C. (1990) *The Emerging British Underclass* (London: IEA).

Murray, C. (1994) *Underclass the Crisis Deepens* (London. IEA).

Neary, M. (1997) *Youth, training and the training state* (Basingstoke: Macmillan).

Negri, A. (1988) *Revolution Retrieved* (London: Red Notes).

Negri, A. (1991) *Marx Beyond Marx: Lessons on the Grundrisse* (New York: Autonomedia).

Notes from Nowhere (eds) (2003) *We are everywhere: the irresistible rise of anticapitalism* (London: Verso).

Offe, C. (1984) *Contradictions of the Welfare State* (London: Hutchinson).

Offe, C. (1985) 'New Social Movements: Challenging the Boundaries of Institutional Politics', *Social Research*, 52 (4) pp. 817–869.

Offe, C. (1996) *Modernity and the State: East and West* (Cambridge: Polity).

Offe, C. (2000) 'The German Welfare State: Principles, Performance And Prospects After Unification' *Thesis Eleven* 63 pp. 11–37.

Offe, C. (2003) 'The European Model of 'Social' Capitalism: Can It Survive European Integration?', *The Journal of Political Philosophy* 11 (4) pp. 437–69.

Panitch, L. & Leys, C. (2003) *Socialist Register 2004: The New Imperial Challenge* (London: Merlin Press)

Pozzo di Borgo, C. (ed) (2005) *Vues de l'europe d'en bas* (Paris, L'Harmattan).

Red Notes (1979) *Working Class Autonomy and the Crisis* (London: Red Notes).

Regini, M. (ed) (1992) *The Future of Labour Movements* (London: Sage).

Rein, H. (1997) 'Wir kämpfen um das, was wir brauchen', *Forschungsjournal NSB* 10 (2) pp. 70–5.

Roney, A. (1998) *EC/EU Fact Book* (London:Kogan Page).

Routledge. P. (1996) 'The Third Space as Critical Engagement', *Antipode*, 28 (4) pp. 399–419.

Sauvageot, J., Geismar, A., Cohn-Bendit, D. & Duteuil, J-P. (1968) *La Révolte Etudiante* (Paris: Editions du Seuil).

Schmitt, B. & Spadoni, P. (eds) (2000) *Les sentiers de la colère* (Paris: L'esprit frappeur).

Scott, A. (1990) *Ideology and the New Social Movements* (London: Unwin Hyman).

Sen, A. (1997) 'Inequality, unemployment and contemporary Europe', *International Labour Review*, 136 (2) pp. 155–172.

St Clair, J. (1999) 'Seattle Diary: It's a Gas, Gas, Gas', *New Left Review* 238 pp. 81–96.

Tarrow, S. (1997) 'Protest in France: La crise à la française', *French Politics & Society*, 15 (2) pp. 30–33.

Tarrow, S. (1998) *Power in Movement* (Second Edition) (Cambridge: Cambridge University Press).

Taylor, G. & Mathers, A. (2002) 'The politics of European integration: a European labour movement in the making?' *Capital & Class* 78 pp. 39–60.

Teague, P. (1998) 'Monetary Union and Social Europe', *Journal of European Social Policy*, 8(2) pp. 117–137.

Thompson, E.P. (1966) *The making of the English working class* (New York: Vintage).

Thompson, E.P. (1978) *The Poverty of Theory* (London: Merlin Press).

Thompson, P. (2005) 'Foundation and Empire:A critique of Hardt and Negri', *Capital & Class* 86 pp. 73–98.

Touraine, A. (1974) *Post-Industrial Society* (London: Wildwood House).

Touraine, A. (1981) *The Voice and the Eye. An Analysis of Social Movements* (Cambridge: Cambridge University Press).

Touraine, A. (1983) *Anti-nuclear protest: the opposition to nuclear energy in France* (Cambridge: Cambridge University Press).

Touraine, A. (1985) 'An Introduction to the Study of Social Movements', *Social Research,* 52 (4) pp. 749–88.

Touraine, A. (1991) 'Face à l'exclusion', *Esprit*, February pp. 7–13.

Touraine, A. (2001) *Beyond Neoliberalism* (Cambridge: Polity Press).

Touraine, A., Wieviorka, M. & Dubet, F. (1984) *Le Mouvement Ouvrier*, (Paris: Fayard).

Touraine, A., Dubet, F., Lapeyronnie, D., Khosrokhavar, F. & Wievorka, M. *Le Grand Refus: Réflexions sur la grève de décembre 1995* (Paris: Fayard).

Tucker, K.H. (1991) 'How New are the New Social Movements?' *Theory, Culture & Society,* 8 pp. 75–98.

Waterman, P. (1998) *Globalization, Social Movements, & The New Internationalisms* (London and Washington: Mansell).

Williams, R. (1983) *Towards 2000* (London: Chatto & Windus/The Hogarth Press).

Wolfreys, J. (1999) 'Class struggles in France' *International Socialism* 2 (84) pp. 31–68.

Went, R. (2000) *Globalization: Neoliberal Challenge, Radical Responses* London: Pluto Press.

Wood, E. M. (1995) *Democracy Against Capitalism: Renewing Historical Materialism* (Cambridge: Cambridge University Press).

Wood, E.M. (1996) 'Modernity, Postmodernity or Capitalism?', *Monthly Review,* 48 (3) pp. 21–39.

Wood, E.M. (2002) 'Infinite War', *Historical Materialism* 10 (1): pp. 7–27.

Index